D1082024

We Hold These Truths

We Hold These Truths

Catholic Reflections on the American Proposition

John Courtney Murray, S.J.

Foreword by Walter Burghardt, S.J.
Critical Introduction by Peter Lawler

A SHEED & WARD BOOK

ROWMAN & LITTLEFIELD PUBLISHERS, INC.
Lanham • Boulder • New York • Toronto • Oxford

A SHEED & WARD BOOK

ROWMAN & LITTLEFIELD PUBLISHERS, INC.

Published in the United States of America
by Rowman & Littlefield Publishers, Inc.
A wholly owned subsidary of The Rowman & Littlefield Publishing Group, Inc.
4501 Forbes Boulevard, Suite 200, Lanham, Maryland 20706
www.rowmanlittlefield.com

PO Box 317
Oxford
OX2 9RU, UK

British Library Cataloguing in Publication Information Available

This book was previously catalogued by the Library of Congress
Library of Congress Catalog Card Number 60-12876

Cloth 0-7425-4900-3
Paper 0-7425-4901-1

Printed in the United States of America

♾™ The paper used in this publication meets the minimum requirements of American
National Standard for Information Sciences—Permanence of Paper for Printed Library
Materials, ANSI/NISO Z39.48-1992.

Contents

~

Foreword

Time Magazine's issue of December 12, 1960, had for cover story "U.S. Catholics & the State." Against a background that reproduced a title page of St. Robert Bellarmine's *Controversies*, artist Boris Chaliapin had drawn the distinguished features of Jesuit John Courtney Murray. The writer, Douglas Auchincloss, author of 16 other such pieces, called this "the most relentless intellectual cover story I've ever done." The occasion? The appearance of Murray's book *We Hold These Truths: Catholic Reflections on the American Proposition*, with a Catholic President about to direct the course of American public life. "In the months to come," Auchincloss predicted, "serious Americans of all sorts and conditions—in pin-stripes and laboratory gowns, space suits and housecoats—will be discussing [Murray's] hopes and fears for American democracy" (p. 64).

The unifying thread of these 13 essays, fashioned over the previous decade, was Murray's effort to explore, on a high level of reason and rhetoric, America's public philosophy, the civic consensus whereby a people acquires its identity and sense of purpose. With the Founding Fathers, Murray held that there exists an ensemble of substantive truths that "command the structure and the courses of the political-economic system of the United States" (*We Hold These Truths*, p. 106), truths that can be known by reason—not indeed self-evident but reached by "careful inquiries" of "the wise and honest" (p. 118). Reduced to its skeleton, the consensus affirmed a free people under a limited government, guided by law and ultimately resting on the sovereignty of God.

Does the consensus still exist? Not really, Murray argued. Especially if you combine the consensus with its basis in natural law. "By one cause or another it has been eroded" (p. 86). Influenced by modern rationalism and philosophy, "the American university long since bade a quiet good-bye to the whole notion of an American consensus, as implying that there are truths that we hold in common, and a natural law that makes known to all of us the structure of the moral universe in such wise that all of us are bound by it in a common obedience" (p. 40). For its part, Protestant theology has never been happy with the thesis of a human reason so sheltered from original sin that it can know God unaided by grace. Perhaps the people are wiser than their philosophers and pastors, but such a hope Murray found too "cheerful" for his intellectual comfort. As for Roman Catholics, traditionally their "participation in the American consensus has been full and free, unreserved and unembarrassed, because the contents of this consensus—the ethical and political principles drawn from the tradition of natural law—approve themselves to the Catholic intelligence and conscience" (p. 41). Regrettably, within our philosophically and religiously pluralist society we do not have a common universe of discourse: we do not know what the other is talking about.

Do we need the consensus? Yes indeed, Murray trumpeted. And we need it on the basis of reason, of natural law. But not a natural law misunderstood. Its adversaries "seem forever to be at work . . . burying the wrong corpse" (p. 298). Murray stressed the new validity of natural law in a new age, "its secure anchorage in the order of reality" (p. 320). He rejected not only the old Liberal individualism, not only the Marxist concept of human rights based solely on economic productivity, but also "the new rationalism," because it is unreasonable and is destructive of sound political philosophy. In contrast to those options, "the doctrine of natural law offers a more profound metaphysic, a more integral humanism, a fuller rationality, a more complete philosophy of man in his nature and history." Over and above all that, "it furnishes the basis for a firmer faith and a more tranquil, because more reasoned, hope in the future" (p. 335).

A quarter century ago, Auchincloss called John Courtney Murray "unquestionably the bellwether of [the] new Catholic and American frontier" (*Time*, Dec. 12, 1960, p. 70). Despite his sudden death at 63 in 1967, this architect of Vatican II's Declaration on Religious Freedom has been increasingly recognized as primarily responsible for bringing the Catholic tradition on Church, state, and society into civilized conversation with the "American proposition" of pluralist democracy. *We Hold These Truths* is the most comprehensive and cogent expression of his positions and arguments in this area, and for that reason alone it is gratifying to have the volume once again available for purchase. But an added reason lends the book a timely significance. *We Hold These Truths* lies at the heart of a crucial discussion in contemporary political/social philosophy: Will the Church contribute more responsibly and more persuasively to public and ethical discourse in America if, in Murray's steps, it formulates its positions in the categories of philosophical reason, or would it be wiser to express them in the symbols of religious belief?

The problem has been highlighted in an article appropriately titled "Theology and Philosophy in Public: A Symposium on John Courtney Murray's Unfinished Agenda" (*Theological Studies* 40 [1979] 700–715). In this symposium, John A. Coleman, S.J., of the Jesuit School of Theology at Berkeley, and Robin Lovin of the University of Chicago Divinity School suggested that Murray's efforts to renew the American public philosophy can and should be supplemented by a public discourse that explicitly appeals to Christian religious symbolism. J. Bryan Hehir of the U.S. Catholic Conference called for a reappropriation of Murray's method as indispensable in today's situation and stressed the need for a renewed public philosophy if both America and the American Church are to move intelligently toward greater justice in a world marked by deep pluralism of ultimate beliefs. David Hollenbach, S.J., of the Weston School of Theology, concluded that neither an exclusively particularist public theology nor an exclusively universalist public philosophy will serve the needs of the Church at this historical moment. The task of fundamental political theology, he claimed, is to discover the relationship between these two spheres of meaning. American Catholic theologians are beginning to address this task, but, in Hollenbach's reading of the literature,

> the most recent efforts in this area have not addressed the critical relationship between Christian tradition and prevailing forms of *American* political and social discourse in a serious way. Though Murray's suppositions about the compatibility of these two traditions may be too simple, he took

the American secular political position much more seriously than have most contemporary American theologians. Creative development of American Catholic social thought will occur when Murray's lead is followed in this regard.

John Courtney Murray hoped only to limit the warfare of conflicting philosophies and to enlarge the dialogue. His death and the intervening two decades have increased our awareness that a flaming torch has been passed on to us (Murray would have smiled engagingly and called it a hot potato). To refuse it would be to risk incomparable harm to both the Church universal and society American style. Not to read *We Hold These Truths* is to miss the cutting edge of the "conversation" in its original Latin sense: living together and talking together.

Walter J. Burghardt, S.J.
Georgetown University

Preface

It is classic American doctrine, immortally asserted by Abraham Lincoln, that the new nation which our Fathers brought forth on this continent was dedicated to a "proposition."

I take it that Lincoln used the word with conceptual propriety. In philosophy a proposition is the statement of a truth to be demonstrated. In mathematics a proposition is at times the statement of an operation to be performed. Our Fathers dedicated the nation to a proposition in both of these senses. The American Proposition is at once doctrinal and practical, a theorem and a problem. It is an affirmation and also an intention. It presents itself as a coherent structure of thought that lays claim to intellectual assent; it also presents itself as an organized political project that aims at historical success. Our Fathers asserted it and most ably argued it; they also undertook to "work it out," and they signally succeeded.

Neither as a doctrine nor as a project is the American Proposition a finished thing. Its demonstration is never done once for all; and the Proposition itself requires development on penalty of decadence. Its historical success is never to be taken for granted, nor can it come to some absolute term; and any given measure of success demands enlargement on penalty of instant decline. In a moment of national crisis Lincoln asserted the imperilled part of the theorem and gave impetus to the impeded part of the project in the noble utterance, at once declaratory and imperative: "All men are created equal." Today, when civil war has become the basic fact of world society, there is no element of the theorem that is not menaced by active negation, and no thrust of the project that does not meet powerful opposition. Today therefore thoughtful men among us are saying that America must be more clearly conscious of what it proposes, more articulate in proposing, more purposeful in the realization of the project proposed.

This is my excuse, if excuse be needed, for editing and collecting in this volume a series of essays that were done over the past decade. Their thread of unity is an effort to explore the content, the foundations, the mode of formation, the validity, etc., of the American Proposition, or as it is otherwise called, with nuances of meaning, the public consensus or the public philosophy of America. There is some argument in these pages about the Proposition—in its uniqueness, in its continuity with, and progress over, the longer civilizational tradition of the West, in certain of its applications, and in some of its problematic aspects. In particular, I have felt obliged, as others have, to raise the question, whether and to what extent this nation, now no longer new, still remains dedicated to the conception of itself that first constituted us a people organized for action in history.

One idea, rooted in the American tradition, has seemed to me to be central, and therefore it has been recurrent. Every proposition, if it is to be argued, supposes an epistemology of some sort. The epistemology of the American Proposition was, I think, made clear by the Declaration of Independence in the famous phrase: "We hold these truths to be self-evident. . . ." Today, when the serene, and often naive, certainties of the eighteenth century have crumbled, the self-evidence of the truths may legitimately be questioned. What ought not to be questioned, however, is that the American Proposition rests on the forthright assertion of a realist epistemology. The sense of the famous phrase is simply this: "There are truths, and we hold them, and we here lay them down as the basis and inspiration of the American project, this constitutional commonwealth."

To our Fathers the political and social life of man did not rest upon such tentative empirical hypotheses as the positivist might cast up. The dynamism of society was not furnished, as in Marxist theory, by certain ideological projections of economic facts or interests. The structure of the state was not ultimately defined in terms of a pragmatic calculus. The rules of politics were not a set of operational tools wherewith to further at any given juncture the dialectic process of history. On the contrary, they thought, the life of man in society under government is founded on truths, on a certain body of objective truth, universal in its import, accessible to the reason of man, definable, defensible. If this assertion is denied, the American Proposition is, I think, eviscerated at one stroke. It is indeed in many respects a pragmatic proposition; but its philosophy is not pragmatism. For the pragmatist there are, properly speaking, no truths; there are only results. But the American Proposition rests on the more traditional conviction that there are truths; that they can be known; that they must be held; for, if they are not held, assented to, consented to, worked into the texture of institutions, there can be no hope of founding a true City, in which men may dwell in dignity, peace, unity, justice, well-being, freedom.

The essays that follow make no pretense of completeness in the treatment of their central theme. Originally they were "occasional" papers; here they are entitled "reflections." They are the reflections of a citizen who considers it his duty to be able to answer the fundamental civil question: "What are the truths we hold?" They are also the reflections of a Catholic who, in seeking his answer to the civil question, knows that the principles of Catholic faith and morality stand superior to, and in control of, the whole order of civil life. The question is sometimes raised, whether Catholicism is compatible with American democracy. The question is invalid as well as impertinent; for the manner of its position inverts the order of values. It must, of course, be turned round to read, whether American democracy is compatible with Catholicism. The question, thus turned, is part of the civil question, as put to me. An affirmative answer to it, given under something better than curbstone definition of "democracy," is one of the truths I hold.

The American Proposition makes a particular claim upon the reflective attention of the Catholic in so far as it contains a doctrine and a project in the matter of the "pluralist society," as we seem to have agreed to call it. The term might have many meanings. By pluralism here I mean the coexistence within the one political community of groups who hold divergent and incompatible views with regard to religious questions—those ultimate questions that concern the nature and destiny of man within a universe that stands under the reign of God. Pluralism therefore implies disagreement and dissension within the community. But it also implies a community within which there must be agreement and consensus. There is no small political problem here. If society is to be at all a rational process, some set of principles must motivate the general participation of all religious groups, despite their dissensions, in the oneness of the community. On the other hand, these common principles must not hinder the maintenance by each group of its own different identity. The problem of pluralism is, of course, practical; as a project, its "working out" is an exercise in civic virtue. But the problem is also theoretical; its solution is an exercise in political intelligence that will lay down, as the basis for the "working out," some sort of doctrine.

As it found place in America the problem of pluralism was unique in the modern world, chiefly because pluralism was the native condition of American society. It was not, as in Europe and in England, the result of the disruption and decay of a previously existent religious unity. This fact made possible a new project; but the new project required, as its basis, a new doctrine. This requirement was met by the First Amendment to the Constitution, in itself and in its relation to the whole theory of limited government that the Constitution incorporates.

On any showing the First Amendment was a great act of political intelligence. However, as in the case of all such acts, precisely because they are great, the question arises, how this act is to be understood. Concretely, what is the doctrine of the First Amendment? How do you define the project that it launched? On what grounds does the First Amendment command the common assent and consent of the whole citizenry? And how is it that this common assent and consent do not infringe upon the "freedom of religion," that is, the freedom of consciences to retain the full integrity of their own convictions, and the freedom of the churches to maintain their own different identities, as defined by themselves. I take it that every church claims this freedom to define itself, and claims too the consequent right to reject definition at the hands of any secular authority. To resign this freedom or to abdicate this right would be at once the betrayal of religion and the corruption of politics.

These questions, I presume, are put to every citizen, when he undertakes to articulate for himself the fundamental civil question, what are the truths we hold. They are put with special sharpness to the Catholic intelligence. Not that the questions themselves are embarrassing, but that the inner exigencies of the Catholic intelligence are high. The Catholic may not, as others do, merge his religious and his patriotic faith, or submerge one in the other. The simplist solution is not for him. He must reckon with his own tradition of thought, which is wider and deeper than any that America has elaborated. He must also reckon with his own history, which is longer than the brief centuries that America has lived. At the same time, he must recognize that a new problem has been put to the universal Church by the American doctrine and project in the matter of pluralism, as stated in the First Amendment. The conceptual equipment for dealing with the problem is by no means lacking to the Catholic intelligence. But there is the obligation of some nicety in its use, lest the new problem be distorted or the ancient faith deformed. I hope I have displayed the needed nicety.

One hardly knows, after a while, how much of one's own thought is derivative. Hence I shall make no effort here to acknowledge my intellectual debts. There is, however, an editorial debt that may not be overlooked. It is owed to Mr. Frank Sheed and to Sheed and Ward's gifted editor, Mr. Philip Scharper. The existence of this book, and therefore any usefulness it may have, are due to them—not only to their interest but also to their talent for tactful harassment. The author's need of *vires a tergo* measures his gratitude, which is therefore great.

John Courtney Murray, S.J.

~

Acknowledgments

I wish to thank the editors of *Religious Education*, *America*, *Social Order*, *Modern Age*, *The Critic*, and *Theological Studies* for their kind permission to reprint essays which have appeared in their pages. Thanks are also due to The Fund for the Republic, the College of New Rochelle, and Marquette University, sponsors of seminars at which some of the papers printed in this book were originally delivered. Grateful acknowledgment is made to The Institute for Religious and Social Studies for permission to reprint an essay which originally formed a chapter in *Great Expressions of Human Rights* (edited by R. M. MacIver; distributed by Harper & Brothers, New York, 1950; reprinted by permission of the copyright holders) and to Meridian Books, publishers of *Religion in America* (edited by John Cogley; copyright 1958 by The Fund for the Republic) in which one of the essays reprinted in this book was first printed.

Critical Introduction

Peter Lawler

The Jesuit John Courtney Murray (1904–1967) was, in his time, probably the best known and most widely respected American Catholic writer on the relationship between Catholic philosophy and theology and his country's political life. The high point of his influence on his own country was the publication of *We Hold These Truths* in the same year as the election of our country's first Catholic president. Those two events were celebrated by a *Time* cover story (December 12, 1960) on Murray's work and influence. The story's author, Protestant Douglas Auchincloss, reported that it was "the most relentlessly intellectual cover story I've done." His amazingly wide-ranging and dense—if not altogether accurate—account of Murray's thought was crowned with a smart and pointed conclusion: "If anyone can help U.S. Catholics and their non-Catholic countrymen toward the disagreement that precedes understanding—John Courtney Murray can." My limited purpose here is to defend that conclusion through an introduction—and only an introduction—to the unfashionable but always timely argument of this still underrated book. Murray's work, of course, is treated with great respect and has had considerable influence, but now it's time to begin to think of him as one of America's very few genuine political philosophers.

Murray's *We Hold These Truths* is one of two astute and comprehensive books written by American Catholic citizens about their country. Murray's disarmingly lucid and accessible prose has caused his book to be widely

1

cited and celebrated, but it still is not well understood. It is both praised and blamed for reconciling Catholic faith with the fundamental premises of American political life. It is praised by liberals for paving the way for Vatican II's embrace of the American idea of religious liberty, and it is blamed by conservatives and traditionalists for obscuring the real conflicts between Catholicism and "Americanism." Both the liberal praise and the conservative blame are somewhat misguided. The last thing Murray wanted to do is bring the church up to date with the latest currents in American thought. He wanted to show how distinctively Catholic thought could illuminate the authentic American idea of liberty.

The truth is that Murray wrote as a Catholic to transform his country politically and evangelize it religiously. He wrote as an orthodox proponent of the Catholic natural-law tradition that began with St. Thomas Aquinas. He thought that this medieval and Christian view of philosophy and theology is not only our Catholic inheritance but still quite reasonable and true. He also thought that only the Catholic community in thought could illuminate what was true and good about what our founders accomplished. Because they built better than they knew, they themselves could not be relied on to give an adequate account of what they had done. In order to defend our Constitution effectively today, our duty as citizens is to give it a better theoretical foundation than its framers did.

The other great Catholic book on America written by an American Catholic is Orestes Brownson's *The American Republic* (1866; page references to the ISI edition, 2003). Murray never expressed any debt to Brownson, and it's very unlikely that Brownson had any significant direct influence on his writing. Despite enormous differences in style—Murray's writing is rather pithy and dry while Brownson's is redundant and passionate—the similarities in both the character of their Catholicism and their analysis of America are quite striking. Those similarities are worth emphasizing to save Murray from both his friends and his enemies who make him much more of an innovator than he was.

We can say that there is sort of a tradition in American Catholic thought that begins with Brownson and ends (so far) with Murray. Because it is based in the truth about reason or human nature and revelation, it is a tradition that always might be revived. The last two chapters of *We Hold These Truths* proclaim the death and the eternal rebirth of the doctrine of natural law—the realistic view that the human mind is fitted to know the truth about human purposes and that what we know through revelation completes—not contradicts—what we know through reason. The fact that in our time this doctrine is taught almost nowhere in American colleges and universities—in Murray's day it was taught in Catholic colleges and universities—and almost universally disparaged by our intellectual elites should not make us unduly pessimistic.

The modern and postmodern crises in self-understanding can only be overcome through natural law's revival, and that revival is always possible because the doctrine of natural law never becomes obsolete. It always expresses what we really know about ourselves and our openness to God. From Murray's view, what we usually call postmodernism is really hypermodernism, an openly anti-rational exaggeration of the modern insight that the purpose of human freedom is the imposition of our wills upon a nature indifferent to our existence. Genuine postmodernism—a real reflection on the failure of the modern project—would be a recovery of the idea that the lives of free and rational beings are really directed by purposes given us by nature and God.

Murray's Ambitious, Innovating Traditionalism

Brownson's *The American Republic* is ambitiously comprehensive in intention; it means to transform our nation's self-understanding through an extensively detailed account of American political life in light of the true structure of all reality. Its very ambition is one reason for its neglect. It carries too much rather peculiar philosophical and theological baggage to be convincing to most Americans or even most Catholic Americans. *We Hold These Truths* seems, by contrast, to be a modest collection of essays written for a variety of occasions and purposes, and even Murray's friends usually call his writing unsystematic. But in his preface, Murray alerts us that these essays are to be read with a "thread of unity" in mind. Each is an exploration of the "American Proposition" or what is "otherwise called . . . the public consensus or public philosophy of America" (xii).

The word *proposition*, of course, comes not from our Constitution but from Lincoln's Gettysburg Address, where our most ambitious and philosophic president affirmed and transformed the work of "our Fathers." Lincoln meant to articulate our common purpose better than they did in light of the crisis that was the Civil War. Murray views his transformative task as more urgent and ambitious than even Lincoln's. His book, like Brownson's, means to define American public or political philosophy— and not just for Catholics—for his time. Murray's appeal to Lincoln is meant to locate his book securely in the mainstream American tradition of reverent constitutional reform.

Murray's most urgent question is "whether and to what extent this nation, now no longer new, still remains dedicated to the conception of itself that first constituted us as a people organized for action in history" (xii). The question is that of an American citizen. Are his people still a people properly speaking? Do they still have any common purpose that is the foundation for effective action? Does being an American citizen now mean anything at all? Especially for those who believe that Murray was simply adjusting his church to contemporary American realities, it is important to see that Murray answers all those citizen's questions negatively. He shows, as Lincoln did, both that our dedication to what our Fathers (both spiritual and political) have given us has declined over time, and that part of this decadence can be attributed to the fact that we never were constituted fully and properly. He also follows Lincoln in muting his criticism of our founding to draw upon the gratitude people naturally and rightly have for the sources of their being.

Murray's political piety is not really feigned; he does distance himself from most of his fellow citizens by examining carefully and systematically the intentions of our founders. And he certainly holds that their thought was better—more informed by the truth—than the dominant strains in American thought today. Murray's "Catholic reflections on the American proposition" are finally not from the perspective of an American citizen, but they show that the citizen's perspective is only deepened—not alienated—by the older and more comprehensive Catholic tradition in thought. If veneration for the true accomplishment of our political Fathers is the standard of citizenship, those within the Catholic natural-law community of thought are the least alienated of Americans today.

Murray's project for revitalizing our constitutional principles is not just a reconstitution. His very first assertion is that "it is classic American doctrine, immortally asserted by Abraham Lincoln, that the new nation which our Fathers brought forth on this continent was dedicated to a 'proposition'" (xi). This close paraphrase of Lincoln's greatest speech subtly calls attention to how the president attempted to understand anew what we were given by our Fathers. The word *proposition* is Lincoln's, not theirs; it is found neither in their Declaration of Independence nor in their Constitution. It made more definite and central a particular nation's dedication. The men Lincoln called our Fathers would not want that title to be confused with the Patriarchs of the Bible or even God the Father. They, for the most part, thought of themselves as too rationalistic, too liberated, to base good government on sacred tradition. Lincoln's veneration for our political Fathers is, in part, a criticism of their own illusions about their own and American liberation.

Lincoln blurs the distinction between the words of our Fathers and those of the Bible because the Fathers' rather abstract and secular rationalism is an inadequate foundation for human dedication. The selfish individualism of their Lockean theory (explained below) is an inadequate foundation for either the eradication of slavery or an extremely bloody war in defense of both the nation they created and their principle of equality. Lincoln's careful, measured, and rhetorically astute criticism of our founding thought has become, Murray observes, "classic American doctrine." He became the authoritative interpreter of our political inheritance; he established for us an improved but nonetheless more sacred tradition.

Neither the theoretical nor the practical demonstration of the proposition's truth is ever finished. We never become wise, and history never comes to an end or perfects itself through our efforts. The proposition demands, Murray contends, "development on penalty of decadence." It is not given to us imperfect thinkers and actors to be able to rest content with what our Fathers gave us. Genuine devotion to our Fathers' affirmation and intention requires their "enlargement." The necessity and opportunity for such enlargement occur most readily at "a moment of national crisis," such as the Civil War. Then Lincoln "asserted the imperilled part of the theorem and gave impetus to the impeded part of the project in the noble utterance, at once declaratory and imperative: 'All men are created equal'" (xi–xii). People in their pride came to doubt that we all are equal, and Father Abraham renewed our dedication with less a proof than a project. That crisis could be solved through willful resolution or dedication because it was so partial and particular. The remaining truths we hold in common were not in doubt, and the crisis was contained to a particular country.

Murray both learned from and is ultimately critical of Lincoln's tendency to attribute ultimate or religious significance to the merely political project of a particular country. He takes from Lincoln the phrase "ancient faith," and he too repeatedly refers to "our Fathers." All political principles are held, in part, as "patrimony" or "prejudice," and to be effective they must be rooted in the soil or traditional way of life a people share (28, 61). All political reform, Murray learned from Lincoln, is best understood as renewal of a nation's dedication to its original, constituting self-conception, and he uses Lincoln's rhetoric of innovating traditionalism to his advantage. But for him, our ancient faith finds its most complete expression not in our political Fathers, but in the Fathers of the Church. He appeals to the prejudice—that happens in this case to be full of truth—that the more ancient the Father, the more wise he is. For Murray, our political foundation always points beyond itself to our philosophical and theological foundation. What is most true in what Thomas Jefferson said was better said and understood by Thomas Aquinas.

Our spiritual Fathers' doctrine of natural law points us away from Lincoln's political assertiveness and even the "voluntarism" of our political Fathers' doctrine of individual rights and toward the rational creature's dutiful subordination of a moral order discoverable through reason and which exists independently of our own making. It points beyond political piety toward gratitude for the deepest sources of our being. "Our decisions," Murray asserts, "cannot be purely political." They must be "much more profound" than our Founding Fathers'. We must make "a metaphysical decision" about "the nature of man" (288). Our choice or decision—our enlargement of our proposition—must be in accord with what is really true about the dignity of free, rational, and social creatures. We Americans must make a metaphysical decision—embrace what is for us a theoretical innovation—to defend our free political life.

The crisis of Murray's time was to rescue the "central" idea of the American proposition—the "realist epistemology" asserted by "We hold these truths"—by showing both its reasonableness and its indispensability. Our crisis concerns not our devotion to this or that self-evident truth but the very idea that we can know the real truth about our real situation. Gone seems to be our Fathers' "conviction" that good or just government "is founded . . . on a certain body of objective truth . . . accessible to the reason of man, definable, defensible" (xiii). Our crisis is our excessive pluralism and relativism; we've lost confidence in the possibility that there are truths we social and rational beings can hold together as the foundation of our political life.

To defend the truth of the American Proposition, Brownson (who, unlike Murray or Lincoln, saw the crisis of his time—the Civil War—as one concerning our truthful self-understanding) and Murray employ Catholic natural-law thinking as good American citizens in three key ways. First, they expose the merely destructive and implicitly nihilistic character of the thought of John Locke and, second, they criticize our Constitution's framers insofar as they employed that thought. Third, they explain that our Constitution, quite providentially, is nonetheless not fundamentally Lockean. Our Constitution, instead, places Americans "under God."

Locke's Political Atheism

The core of our crisis is that we seem to have every reason today to question the self-evidence of what our Fathers held to be true. Their theoretical guide, Murray holds, was the English philosopher John Locke, who, as the old and true joke goes, is the key to America, at least in theory. Every schoolboy and schoolgirl now seems to know that his views of God, nature, and truth became "the serene, and often naive, certainties of the eighteenth century," which "have crumbled" (xii). Those certainties were based, for the Fathers, on Locke's individualistic law of nature, which depends on certain premises about the individual's natural, asocial existence in the "state of nature" and the contractual origin of government. Murray held that the "genuine and true [critical] insights" of "Darwin, Freud, and Marx" have, whatever their shortcomings, had the theoretical merit of destroying completely the Lockean idea of man (279).

The French revolutionaries, Murray adds, had the theoretical merit of understanding Locke's individualistic or asocial law of nature more consistently than he did himself. They understood that its "naked essence" was to reduce politics—really all of human life—to a question of power. The individual, as a result, lost any perspective, either theoretical or practical, by which he might oppose the power of the state. By depriving the human individual of any social, natural content, Locke leaves him or her defenseless against superior power. The result was the "monism" or politically imposed unity of the French Revolution, and that "omnipotent" or totalitarian democracy was the inspiration for the harder totalitarianism of the twentieth century. Inspired by Rousseau, the French Revolution attempted to reduce human beings to citizens and nothing more, and religion to "civil religion" and nothing more (277–278). There are no real limits to the state's power to shape human beings according to its political requirements.

The strength and weakness of Lockean individualism is that it is merely destructive. Its undeniable achievement has been "to destroy an order of political privilege and inaugurate an era of political equality" (286). But it gives no content to the liberty that we all are free to exercise equally. Lockean individualism frees the individual from all constraints for nothing in particular, thereby creating a vacuum that might be filled by anything. If human liberty has no purpose, then it is no good. That's why Murray writes that "Communism"—which claims to be the absolute negation of the Lockean individual—"is political modernity carried to its logical conclusion" (194). The collectivist tyranny of communism is the product of Locke's deepest thought; there is no real support for or any intrinsic dignity in individual or personal life. And that's why theories that deny the real existence of human liberty—such as Darwinian sociobiology (which denies any qualitative distinction between human and other forms of animal life)—are the natural consequence of Locke's emptying human liberty of its content. But neither communism nor sociobiology can eradicate the emptiness at the core of the modern individual.

Lockeanism, from that view, turns out not to be destructive enough; no modern solution can eradicate the longings given us by nature and God. We're still stuck with "a spiritual vacuum" that it seems no modern theoretical or practical effort can fill (198). Our relentless pursuit of individual happiness has made us powerful, wealthy, and free but far more anxious than happy. We long for a "definition of freedom," for liberty with "positive content," for "an order of human freedom" (286–87). We need more than ever to know the truth about the purpose of the liberty we hold in common. "Self-understanding," Murray writes, "is the necessary condition of a sense of self-identity and self-confidence. . . . If the American people can no longer base this sense on naive assumptions of self-evidence, it is imperative that they find other more reasoned grounds for their essential affirmation that they are uniquely a people" (24). We need a self-understanding less naive and more reasonable than the one our political Fathers gave us. For Murray, our postmodern moment is the result of our discovery of the emptiness at the core of modern thought, and that's why he suggests that the recovery of the realism of Thomistic natural law may turn out to be postmodernism rightly understood.

Murray's attack on our Fathers' theory insofar as it was Lockean is cast as a Lincolnian concern. It does owe to Lincoln the thought that the Constitution of 1787—with its individualistic silence on God—is pretty purely Lockean, but the Declaration of Independence is only ambiguously so. But Murray's attack really does owe more to the American Catholic natural-law tradition inaugurated by Brownson. Brownson is even more emphatic that our Fathers understood their Constitution according to destructive, individualistic theory, and he blames their theory for the national disintegration that caused the Civil War.

Brownson did not hesitate to write that "the theory held by our fathers" is "unsound and incompatible with the essential nature of government" (154). He adds that it was already true in his time that no sound statesmen held to the theory that government originated in a compact among sovereign individuals. After that theory culminated in the indiscriminate leveling of the French Revolution, no political leader—and no theorist—could take seriously either its truth or its utility. Nonetheless, Brownson admits, that theory "is the political tradition of the country" (34). The history of America is the working out of the details of a destructive theory that nobody really any longer believes is true. That observation is the beginning of the contribution that Catholic thinkers can make to restoring on a new foundation our nation's self-understanding, to making sense of the truths we hold.

Brownson is an unambiguous critic of the theory of the primary author of the Declaration of Independence. By making consent and only consent the foundation of government, Jefferson "declared law derives its force of law from the will of those it is to bind." He, in other words, declared "the purely human origins of government"; the foundation of obedience is nothing more than the enlightened self-interest of sovereign individuals. According to Brownson, "the so-called Jeffersonian democracy, in which government has no powers but such as it derives from the consent of the governed, is . . . pure individualism—philosophically considered, pure egoism, which says, 'I am God'" (222). Government needs more than the unfettered egoism of a purely atheistic philosophy to sustain dutiful citizens loyal to republican government.

On the basis of this Lockean/Jeffersonian theory—the almost universal belief of the time among those in the know—the framers of our Constitution built quite incoherently. They thought they were both "constituting a real government" and producing "a treaty, compact, or agreement among sovereigns" (153). If individuals are sovereign or autonomous in the sense nations are, then all obedience to authority is voluntary and may be withdrawn at will. Locke compared the condition of individuals in the state of nature before government's institution with relations among sovereign nations today. Sovereign nations surely have the right to break treaties when their self-interest dictates without being invaded, and so sovereign individuals surely have the right to withdraw their consent from government. In Brownson's view, it makes sense to say that the "right of secession" is the same in both cases.

The right of secession, Brownson admits, was decisively rejected by the framers of the Constitution. But that doesn't mean they gave a coherent argument against it. Under Lockean compact theory, the Confederates were right: The United States had no right to treat secession as rebellion and "to suppress it by employing all the physical forces at its command" (138). A Lockean union consists not of citizens but of confederates—individuals merely allied with each other in pursuit of their sovereign private interests. Brownson himself was the strongest of unionists, but only because he thought the theory of our framers did not really account for our Constitution. He sought to explain why what they accomplished actually deserved our loyalty.

The failure of our founders' theory to prevent the Civil War or account for the need and genuine existence of human loyalty is why Brownson contends that the United States "has more need of full knowledge of itself" (1) than ever in the wake of that war. And by giving a genuinely realistic account of the truths we hold common he aims to assist the American people in "the realization of the true idea of the state, which secures at once the authority of the public and the freedom of the individual" (3). Like Murray, he aims to show that reasonable, Catholic reflections on the truth about human nature are what his country especially *needs* to resolve a nationally destructive crisis.

For Brownson, "the right of secession" sums up what's destructive about Lockean theory generally. The sovereign individual has rights, not duties, especially the right to free himself or herself from all social ties that bind. His prediction—which Murray repeats—is that, unchecked, Lockean theory will transform all human relationships—including marriage and friendship—into mere alliances. Who can deny that Lockean individualism has transformed marriage in our time into something pretty close to just another contract to be broken at will? And even friendship is turning into networking—a convenient alliance of independent operators. The process that empties human life of social, moral, and political contents in the name of liberty we now see in the creeping libertarianism emerging as our mainstream political consensus. Lockeanism guides us more in practice now than ever before, despite our rejection of Locke's theory. Our relativism is really the Lockean view of liberty divorced from its theoretical foundation.

Our Providential Constitution

The Catholic attack on the theory of Locke, for both Murray and Brownson, is a prelude to the gratitude they want us to have for the "providential" fact that our Constitution is more, much more, than a reflection of that theory. Murray quotes a key statement of the Third Plenary Council of Baltimore (1884): "We consider the establishment of our country's independence, the shaping of its liberties and laws, as a work of special Providence, its framers 'building better than they knew,' the Almighty's hand guiding them." The American bishops rejected the theory but affirmed the result of our framers' building, attributing that miraculous disjunction to the providential hand of God. Murray himself gives a more specific explanation: "The providential aspect of the matter, and the reason for the better building, can be found in the fact that the American political community was organized in an era when the tradition of natural law and natural rights was still vigorous" (46). The reason our framers built better than they knew is that they were more influenced by a decaying but still vigorous tradition than they knew. The destructive side of their theorizing about nature exhibited itself to good effect in the Declaration of Independence, which both dissolved our bonds with Great Britain and declared illegitimate any political standard but what we know about nature through reason. But it left intact the thought that we share self-evident truths in common, and it was a somewhat traditional rather than Lockean understanding of those truths that guided the construction of our political institutions. Our framers built better than they knew, ironically, because they thought they knew less than they really did.

Murray writes more than once that the American Constitution, properly understood, was "a great providential blessing" for American

Catholics in particular. Catholic American citizens—unlike citizens of, for example, the French Third Republic—can affirm the goodness of their political institutions not out of mere expediency—or "the need to accept what one is powerless to change"—but out of "conscience and conviction." They can see "the evident coincidence of the principles which inspired the American republic with the principles that are structural to the Western Christian political tradition" (56–57). The providence is the coincidence; American Catholics are both blessed and lucky. Our Fathers—not Catholics or Thomists or even many Christians themselves of course—happened to be under the influence of the Christian natural-law tradition.

The key providential fact, for Murray, is that "the distinction between church and state, one of the central assertions of this tradition, found its way into the Constitution." They understood that separation as "the distinction between state and society," which followed the tradition in its assertion of "the existence of a whole wide area of human concerns which were remote from the competence of government." Among those concerns about which government has no competence is religion (76–77). Our framers distinguished themselves from the French successors by denying the "primacy of the political"; for them, it was not true that there is "nothing above the state" (78).

Murray explains that "here again it was a matter of the Fathers building better than they knew" (77). Although they were in thought rather anti-Catholic and even anti-ecclesiastical, they still, despite themselves, defended "the freedom of the Church." Although the Fathers did not affirm, they did not deny—and so they presupposed without really being conscious of it—the reality of the Church as an organized social community, a genuine intellectual community, an "order of culture" (50) that transcends political life and resists politicization. They knew that government cannot "presume to define the Church or in any way supervise her exercise of authority in pursuit of her own distinct ends." For us Americans, religious freedom is not merely guaranteed to the individual—including the individual Catholic—"but to the Church as an organized society with its own law and jurisdiction." The area from which our framers excluded government "coincides with the divine mission of the Church" as the Church herself understands it (80).

"The Jacobin thesis," Murray contends, "was basically philosophical"; it was a claim about all of reality and so a claim over the whole human being.

So the Church can only exist—if at all—under the terms government sets for it, and religious or intellectual freedom are given only to isolated individuals who have no effective way to resist the state's allegedly rational and comprehensive jurisdiction. Murray claims both that "the American thesis is simply political" and that its limitation of political life is "recognizably part of the Christian political tradition" (78–79). Both those claims can be true at the same time only because the American Constitution also implies a philosophy of the nature of man; "man has certain original responsibilities precisely as man, antecedent to his status as citizen" (51–52). Our Constitution roots our rights in our responsibilities, and higher than our responsibilities as citizens are our responsibilities to the Creator as creatures. "The American Bill of Rights," Murray boldly concludes, "is not a piece of eighteenth-century rationalist theory; it is far more the product of Christian history," and the person whose rights it guarantees against government had to "learn . . . his own personal dignity in the school of Christian faith." The person whose rights are protected by our Constitution "is, whether he knows it or not, the Christian man" (53). From this view, what's most providential about the Constitution is the First Amendment, which guarantees our freedom *for* the free exercise of religion. It is the part of the Constitution that most presumes the existence of the providential Creator of nature described in the Declaration as the source of our rights.

Murray's account of the providential character of our Constitution is meant for several audiences. First, he writes for good Catholics—including those at the Vatican in the 1950s and under its influence—who confused the American view of liberty with the repressive "monism" of the political liberalism originating with Jacobinism—the murderous ideology of the French Revolution. American liberalism is based on the principle that human beings are not merely material or political beings; they are social creatures open to the truth about God and the good. America recognizes the freedom the Church claims for herself, and so Catholics can affirm American principle and not merely cooperate with an alien power out of expediency. Murray also writes for all American citizens. Only a Thomistic or natural-law understanding can make sense of our framers' accomplishment. It is not enough merely to return to their self-understanding; we have to understand them better than they understood themselves. The destructive character of their theory is the main reason why we have lost contact with the purposes of their positive achievement.

Finally, Murray writes for American Catholics; it is the tradition of thought alive in the Catholic community in America that might provide what our nation most needs in response to the crisis of our time—a crisis of both truth and purpose that we sometimes call relativism. Far from wanting to adjust themselves to the dominant climate of opinion in their country today, American Catholics should lead their nation to rediscover the true foundation of the truths Americans once held in common. One reason, Murray thought, that "the Church in America has accepted this thing which is the American economy" is that "Catholic education in its present many-storied structure" would not exist without the widespread prosperity it has created (169). The Church always should understand American freedom and abundance not just as goods in themselves but above all as instruments for her distinctive, divine mission.

The Catholic view that our framers providentially built better than they knew began with Brownson. Every nation, he thought, has a providential constitution, which in the American case precedes and shapes the possibilities of the written Constitution. A providential constitution is "given by God himself, operating through historical events or natural causes" (91). The statesman who consults history and human nature discovers what God intends for his nation. Our framers, "as wise and able statesmen, who understood their age and country" (112), were guided by the providential constitution far more than by an abstract, individualistic theory. They are to be distinguished from those "mad theorists"—such as the French—who attempted to establish a wholly new government uprooted from "national traditions, the national character, or the national life" (122). Our framers were too sane or statesmanlike to reject what they had been given and could not or should not change.

Our framers gave us, Brownson observes, a republican form of government because our providential constitution included no monarchy or nobility. Because only the "commons" came to America, they saw democracy not only as choiceworthy, but as necessary for us. They were also indebted to the republicanism of Greece and Rome, as well as to Greece's science and art. They owed more than they knew to Christianity, which made republicanism compatible with rights—both the rights of citizens and the rights of man—the rights of the creature by nature open to the truth about his Creator. Our providential constitution also incorporates certain British political institutions, such as Common Law, which also, in a democratized form, keeps alive in America something of the Christian tradition.

Brownson thought that our unwritten, providential constitution is both prior to and more fundamental than our written one, and that even the ambiguities of the Declaration of Independence must be resolved in its light. Read in light of Locke, according to Brownson, our Declaration of Independence comes close to "political atheism"; read in light of our providential Constitution, it recognizes the rights of free human beings under God. We must admit that Brownson's account of the content of the unwritten or providential constitution is too idiosyncratic to have had any chance to sweep the nation, but his basic insight that our framers' accomplishments were better—because of debts they did not properly acknowledge—than their theory—which was based on an abstract or unrealistic view of human liberty—is indispensable for reconciling our Constitution with the Catholic tradition in thought, with the natural purposes of beings who are social and religious by nature.

A century before Murray, Brownson maintained that the Catholic Church has no reason to be dissatisfied with the American Constitution properly understood. Its mission of evangelization is not impeded by American government, and the Church has full freedom as an institution to wield moral and political influence through persuasion. He admits that some Catholics might be dissatisfied that "the church is not formally established as the civil law of the land." But his view is that "nor is it necessary that she should be; because there is nothing in the state that conflicts with her freedom and independence, with her dogmas or her irreformable canons" (262). So there is no reason why Catholics cannot be good or even the best American citizens. So confident was Brownson in the natural-law principle that what human beings know through revelation completes and does not contradict what they know through reason that he thought that Americans were particularly ready for Catholic instruction precisely because they were "freemen" who distrusted "blind obedience" and demanded reasons (264).

Under God

The Catholic contribution to understanding the American Proposition, Murray explains, is to show why ours is "a nation under God."

That explanation seems more necessary today than even in Murray's time. Part of the Supreme Court seems to think that saying those words unconstitutionally mixes church and state, and the other part says those words are constitutional because rote repetition has emptied them of any genuinely religious content at all. Those who find the words unconstitutional appear to have the text of the Constitution on their side. "Under God" is conspicuous by its absence in the Preamble after "We the people." Our written Constitution by itself, our intellectuals have finally figured out, can be construed to embody "political atheism."

Murray's response, following Lincoln, is to appeal to the Declaration of Independence. But his interpretation of that document is not so Jeffersonian: He contends that the key teaching of that "landmark of political theory" is that there's "a truth that lies beyond politics: it imparts to politics a fundamental human meaning. I mean the sovereignty of God over nations as well as over individual men." And according to Murray, the Declaration asserts that we can know of God's sovereignty through our natural reason. That "first article of American political faith" distinguishes "America from the Jacobin laicist tradition of Continental Europe," one that "proclaimed the autonomous reason of man to be the first and sole principle of political organization" (44). Americans, unlike those Europeans, believed at the time of our founding that human beings are not autonomous; what they think and will is limited by the truth about God.

Knowing that the Declaration and even the First Amendment are more ambiguous than he says, Murray also appeals to our political life to make the American distinction clear. "In the Jacobin tradition," he observes, "religion is at best a purely private concern, a matter of personal devotion, quite irrelevant to public affairs" (44). Those within that political tradition view government and statesmen as "by definition agnostic or atheist" (44). They have no right to accept guidance from any source higher than the sovereign people, and the people means simply, in the Jacobin tradition, the party in power.

But in "the authentic American tradition," parties and statesmen who "erect atheism into a political principle" are rejected (45). We expect American statesmen to be in some sense believers; if they don't believe, they are compelled (like Jefferson, Madison, and so forth) to keep their agnosticism or atheism secret, as Madison did in his "famous *Memorial and Remonstrance*" (75). We don't trust statesmen who don't present themselves "under God." Murray reminds us that President John Adams proclaimed that "men . . . should, as a society, make acknowledgements of dependence and obligations to Him." That thought was echoed by Lincoln in another proclamation: "it is the duty of nations as well as of men to own their dependence upon the overruling power of God." President Eisenhower (in office when Murray wrote) quoted Lincoln's words in a similar proclamation, and our Supreme Court stated in 1952 that "We are a religious people whose institutions presuppose a Supreme Being" (45–46). It's because our Constitution presupposes a Supreme Being that it had no particular need to mention Him; that's the common sense of citizens and statesmen in our authentic tradition. Murray's quoting of proclamations and opinions is certainly selective, but for a Thomist our authentic tradition must certainly be construed according to our nation at its best.

Our political history is the decisive evidence that our Constitution does not allow the people to usurp the place of God. There is also, Murray acknowledges, a secularist tradition in America, but it has basically been in dissent and far from militant. Our atheists have respected believers, and they too characteristically view themselves as bound by some reality that exists independently of their own making. The American political tradition rejects the ideas of both individual and political autonomy. The thought of both our believing statesmen and best skeptical thinkers points them together in the direction of the truth about nature they can share in common.

Part of that truth is "that only a virtuous people can be free." What that means, according to our authentic tradition, is that "political freedom is endangered in its foundations as soon as the universal moral values, upon whose shared possession the self-discipline of a free society depends, are no longer vigorous enough to restrain the passions and shatter the selfish inertia of men" (50–51). Our constitutional foundation must be "an order of reason and therefore of freedom," a "work of reason, but not of an absolutely autonomous reason." That must mean that "reason does not create its own laws, any more than man creates himself." According to Murray, once we've gone that far together a final step is suggested by reason itself: "My situation is that of a creature before God"

(294–95). The Declaration, as well as our great presidents, says something like those very words, although Murray does not claim that they understood them as well as they might have.

Brownson is even more definite about why our nation, like every other free republic, is under God. For him, the creation of the world by God is self-evident, a necessary premise of all reasoning about human nature. It is clear that "nothing in man, in nature, in the universe, is explicable without the creative act of God, for nothing exists without that act. That God 'in the beginning created the heaven and the earth' is the first principle of all science." And creation cannot have occurred once and for all but must be active and continuous. "It is as bad theology and philosophy," he explains, "to suppose that God created the universe, endowed it with certain laws of development or activity . . . and left it to go of itself. It cannot go of itself, because it does not exist of itself" (82). Something like Deism, or belief in the God described in the Declaration, who "endowed" but does not actively endow, could not possibly be true. So we must, in the name of reason, abandon all pretensions to self-sufficiency or autonomy. The Declaration's account of God is, finally, incoherent: His creative activity could not be both only past-tense and providential.

The real world and our apprehension of it are possible only because of Providence or God's gifts to us. Because of his confidence in the gift of reason, Brownson thought he could be certain that science does not and cannot conflict with the revelation of God. Thinking about that gift shows the need for revelation to complete what we know through reason. We will never know, through reason alone, why rational, finite beings came into being. Human reason, by reflecting on itself, can acknowledge the human need for revelation. "The human mind," Brownson realistically concludes, "cannot have all science, but it has real science as far as it goes" (58).

We must affirm that natural law originates with a Creator, and that we are dependent on Him and not on ourselves. It is that affirmation, the very opposite of the Lockean principle of sovereignty or self-ownership, that is the foundation of human equality or our "equal rights as men." All governments that protect rights depend on the assumption that man is not God, and all despotism originates in the "sophism," "error," or "sin" that in some sense he is. The idea that natural law somehow binds us all depends on the existence of a Creator who commands us all. "An imperative will, the will of a superior who has the right to command what reason dictates or approves," Brownson contends, "is essential to government; and that will is not developed from nature, because it has no germ in nature" (59). It is because we see that natural law has its foundation in "the eternal will or reason of God" that we can say that "all acts of state that contravene it are . . . violences rather than laws" (60).

Murray is more aware than Brownson of the problems in holding that we know through our natural powers alone that we are creatures and that there is a Creator. His thought that we need a metaphysical decision about our natures suggests that the evidence might point more than one direction. But he firmly agrees with Brownson that surely something like that idea is required to justify the American view that a human being has responsibilities—and not just rights—as a human being, and not just as a citizen. And for those responsibilities to be characteristic of human beings as human beings, they must be given to us as knowing, natural beings of a certain kind.

Murray's Relevance Today

Murray offered his interpretation of the American Proposition in opposition to an intellectual pluralism he perceived in America, one so extreme and in some ways so dogmatic that it made moral and political community impossible. He saw some—if not all—of what separated American Catholics and Protestants as based on a misunderstanding. The Protestants wrongly suspected American Catholics of being politically authoritarian, of accepting the American idea of religious liberty only expediently and temporarily. His teaching about American religious liberty was in anticipation of the time when Catholics and Protestants "under God" would ally against an increasingly more aggressive effort to secularize completely all of American life. He knew that Lockeanism or libertarianism would continue to expand in America, moving from being an economic and political doctrine (Murray saw our free economy, properly limited to its sphere, as a true human good) to a "cultural" one. All of life should be reconfigured according to the doctrine of autonomy or all human relationships should be based on contract and consent. The "mainstream" or moderate factions of both of our parties today are now both pretty libertarian—for economic freedom and "pro-choice" on the various social or cultural issues.

Murray wrote, in part, to prepare American Catholics for the "culture war" or at least the rather deep cultural division of our time. It's basically between those who are in some sense religiously orthodox and those who are not. It is, to use the most unflattering, extreme, and misleading terms available, between "fundamentalists" and "secular humanists." The largest and most devoted group on the orthodox or fundamentalist side is Christians who call themselves evangelical.

The evangelical view is that America is a great nation because it has a Christian or Biblical foundation. America, for them, is divided today into those who live by God's word—as did our Constitution's framers—and those who do not. Our libertarians respond to them that we're not going to let your arbitrary and tyrannical view of that word limit our liberty, a view which is reflected in your distorted view of what is really a basically secular Constitution. There is, of course, room for compromise between these two views, and our Republican party today is all about that compromise. But there is no real ground on which to find reasonable agreement.

From a Catholic, natural-law view, the evangelical way of conceiving our cultural conflict more or less guarantees their political defeat in America. Their view looks unreasonable—or contrary both to the true enlightenment of our framers and to our nation's idea of liberty. The evangelicals, their critics too easily say, have no right to impose their merely Biblical views on, say, abortion or same-sex marriage on those who do not share their faith. If our choice is between Biblical fundamentalism and Lockean individualism—as those on both sides of the culture war so often think it is—then the individualists—as the rationalists—will win, and win completely. But from the natural-law view, there's reason and error on both sides.

The Catholic view, as articulated by Murray, is that Lockean individualism is itself somewhat unreasonable. It doesn't correspond with what we can see with our own eyes as the truth about our natures; it, in particular, can't account for the free and responsible being open to the truth about all things, including God. We really can know that the misguided, destructive effort to reconfigure all of life according to the abstract, individualistic principles will empty human life of much of its moral contents. We really can know that what we can know through reason has its limits, and the reductionism of modern rationalism is an attack on the complex truth about human liberty.

From Murray's and Brownson's natural-law view, for example, we can know that Darwinism or evolutionism as a comprehensive explanation of being human is not only anti-Biblical but unreasonable. The point is not whether evolution in some sense happened (the previous pope said it did) or whether the earth—as some fundamentalists say—is literally a little over 6,000 years old (virtually no Catholic believes that), but whether evolutionary explanations really can account for what we know about our natures. Can they explain why we are theologians, poets, philosophers, physicists, princes, or presidents? Can they even account for the individual's liberty to conquer nature that the Lockeans cherish so much? Surely few phrases are more oxymoronic than "libertarian sociobiologist," but it describes more than ever the views of our mainstream intellectual elite.

That means, of course, that Darwin's thought has merit in undermining the vain pretenses of the creeping libertarianism or Lockeanism of our time. Murray explains that "evolutionary theory" has the merit of reminding us that "man is solidary, by all that is material in him, with all life." Sociobiological materialism is erroneous as a form of reductionistic "monism" that denies what is distinctive of human beings, and Lockeanism has the merit of reminding us of its inability to account for human liberty or individuality. But Murray adds that "purified of monistic connotations," the Darwinian principle of natural continuity "is compatible with a central thesis of Christian anthropology" that "asserts the law of solidarity for both flesh and spirit" (280). Human beings are social beings both as animals like the others and as free and rational social beings. Darwin is right on natural sociality, and Locke is right on our distinctive freedom. Natural-law properly understood brings what is true about sociobiology and libertarianism together in a complete understanding of distinctive but still natural human being.

Brownson devoted many, many pages to refuting the scientific reductionism—including the Darwin-inspired eugenic schemes—of his time; he showed that such reductionism both perniciously denied the dignity of human liberty and moral responsibility and just did not square with the facts we actually can know. Today, the Catholic natural-law writers still give rational, natural arguments against abortion, biotechnological eugenics, sexual permissiveness, same-sex marriage, pornography, callous indifference to the poor, and capital punishment, as well as for genuine subsidiarity and religious liberty, appealing not just to believers but to all free men and women who rightly demand reasons. That's not to say their arguments are always airtight or even right, but they're arguments nonetheless. They mean to create the kind of disagreement in America that might be a prelude to shared understanding. They mean to restore Murray's view—which he shared with both our political and spiritual Fathers—that "the whole premise of the public argument . . . is . . . that among the people everything is not in doubt, but that there is a core of agreement. . . . We hold certain truths; therefore we can argue about them" (27).

We Hold These Truths at least offers the hope that Catholic natural-law thinking can bring together the religious devotion and moral concerns of the evangelicals with the devotion to reason and concern for scientific truth of the secular humanists. It offers the hope of getting Americans really arguing again, of holding again the truth that they are capable of engaging in the dialogue about the human good that is the foundation of any civil and civilized moral and political life.

INTRODUCTION

~

The Civilization of the Pluralist Society

The "free society" seems to be a phrase of American coinage. At least it has no comparable currency in any other language, ancient or modern. The same is true of the phrase "free government." This fact of itself suggests the assumption that American society and its form of government are a unique historical realization. The assumption is generally regarded among us as unquestionable.

However, we have tended of late to pronounce the phrase, "the free society," with a rising interrogatory inflection. The phrase itself, it seems, now formulates a problem. This is an interesting new development. It was once assumed that the American proposition, both social and political, was self-evident; that it authenticated itself on simple inspection; that it was, in consequence, intuitively grasped and generally understood by the American people. This assumption now stands under severe question.

What is the free society, in its "idea"? Is this "idea" being successfully realized in the institutions that presently determine the pattern of American life, social and personal? The web of American institutions has altered, rapidly and profoundly, even radically, over the past few generations. Has the "idea" of the free society perhaps been strangled by the tightening intricacies of the newly formed institutional network? Has some new and alien "idea" subtly and unsuspectedly assumed the role of an organizing force in American society? Do we understand not only the superficial facts of change in American life but also the underlying factors of change—those "variable constants" that forever provide the dynamisms of change in all human life?

The very fact that these questions are being asked makes it sharply urgent that they be answered. What is at stake is America's understanding of itself. Self-understanding is the necessary condition of a sense of self-identity and self-confidence, whether in the case of an individual or in the case of a people. If the American people can no longer base this sense on naive assumptions of self-evidence, it is imperative that they find other more reasoned grounds for their essential affirmation that they are uniquely a people, uniquely a free society. Otherwise the peril is great. The complete loss of one's identity is, with all propriety of theological definition, hell. In diminished forms it is insanity. And it would not be well for the American giant to go lumbering about the world today, lost and mad.

The Civil Multitude

At this juncture I suggest that the immediate question is not whether the free society is really free. This question may be unanswerable; it may even be meaningless as a question, if only for the reason that the norms of freedom seem to have got lost in a welter of confused controversy. Therefore I suggest that the immediate question is whether American society is properly civil. This question is intelligible and answerable, because the basic standard of civility is not in doubt: "Civilization is formed by men locked together in argument. From this dialogue the community becomes a political community." This statement, made by Thomas Gilby, O.P., in *Between Community and Society*,[1] exactly expresses the mind of St. Thomas Aquinas, who was himself giving refined expression to the tradition of classic antiquity, which in its prior turn had given first elaboration to the concept of the "civil multitude," the multitude that is not a mass or a herd or a huddle, because it is characterized by civility.

The specifying note of political association is its rational deliberative quality, its dependence for its permanent cohesiveness on argument among men. In this it differs from all other forms of association found on earth. The animal kingdom is held together simply by the material homogeneity of the species; all its unities and antagonisms are of the organic and biological order. Wolves do not argue the merits of running in packs. The primal human community, the family, has its own distinctive bonds of union. Husband and wife are not drawn into the marital association simply by the forces of reason but by the forces of life itself, importantly including the mysterious dynamisms of sex. Their association is indeed founded on a contract, which must be a rational and free act. But the substance and finality of the contract is both infra- and supra-rational; it is an engagement to become "two in one flesh." The marital relationship may at times be quarrelsome, but it is not argumentative. Similarly, the union of parents and children is not based on reason, justice, or power; it is based on kinship, love, and *pietas*.

It is otherwise with the political community. I am not, of course, maintaining that civil society is a purely rational form of association. We no longer believe, with Locke or Hobbes, that man escapes from a mythical "state of nature" by an act of will, by a social contract. Civil society is a need of human nature before it becomes the object of human choice. Moreover, every particular society is a creature of the soil; it springs from the physical soil of earth and from the more formative soil of history. Its existence is sustained by loyalties that are not logical; its ideals are expressed in legends that go beyond the facts and are for that reason vehicles of truth; its cohesiveness depends in no small part on the materialisms of property and interest. Though all this is true, nevertheless the distinctive bond of the civil multitude is reason, or more exactly, that exercise of reason which is argument.

Hence the climate of the City is likewise distinctive. It is not feral or familial but forensic. It is not hot and humid, like the climate of the animal kingdom. It lacks the cordial warmth of love and unreasoning loyalty that pervades the family. It is cool and dry, with the coolness and dryness that characterize good argument among informed and responsible men. Civic amity gives to this climate its vital quality. This form of friendship is a special kind of moral virtue, a thing of reason and intelligence, laboriously cultivated by the discipline of passion, prejudice, and narrow self-interest. It is the sentiment proper to the City. It has nothing to do with the cleavage of a David to a Jonathan, or with the kinship of the clan, or with the charity, *fortis ut mors,* that makes the solidarity of the Church. It is in direct contrast with the passionate fanaticism of the Jacobin: "Be my brother or I'll kill you!" Ideally, I suppose, there should be only one passion in the City—the passion for justice. But the will to justice, though it engages the heart, finds its measure as it finds its origin in intelligence, in a clear understanding of what is due to the equal citizen from the City and to the City from the citizenry according to the mode of their equality. This commonly shared will to justice is the ground of civic amity as it is also the ground of that unity which is called peace. This unity, qualified by amity, is the highest good of the civil multitude and the perfection of its civility.

The Public Argument

If then society is civil when it is formed by men locked together in argument, the question rises, what is the argument about? There are three major themes.

First, the argument is about public affairs, the *res publica*, those matters which are for the advantage of the public (in the phrase as old as Plato) and which call for public decision and action by government. These affairs have their origin in matters of fact; but their rational discussion calls for the Socratic dialogue, the close and easy use of the habit of cross-examination, that transforms brute facts into arguable issues.

Second, the public argument concerns the affairs of the commonwealth. This is a wider concept. It denotes the affairs that fall, at least in decisive part, beyond the limited scope of government. These affairs are not to be settled by law, though law may be in some degree relevant to their settlement. They go beyond the necessities of the public order as such; they bear upon the quality of the common life. The great "affair" of the commonwealth is, of course, education. It includes three general areas of common interest: the school system, its mode of organization, its curricular content, and the level of learning among its teachers; the later education of the citizen in the liberal art of citizenship; and the more general enterprise of the advancement of knowledge by research.

The third theme of public argument is the most important and the most difficult. It concerns the constitutional consensus whereby the people acquires its identity as a people and the society is endowed with its vital form, its entelechy, its sense of purpose as a collectivity organized for action in history. The idea of consensus has been classic since the Stoics and Cicero; through St. Augustine it found its way into the liberal tradition of the West: *"Res publica, res populi; populus autem non omnis hominum coetus quoquo modo congregatus, sed coetus multitudinis iuris consensu et utilitatis communione sociatus"* (Scipio).

The state of civility supposes a consensus that is constitutional, *sc.,* its focus is the idea of law, as surrounded by the whole constellation of ideas that are related to the *ratio iuris* as its premises, its constituent elements, and its consequences. This consensus is come to by the people; they become a people by coming to it. They do not come to it accidentally, without quite knowing how, but deliberatively, by the methods of reason reflecting on experience. The consensus is not a structure of secondary rationalizations erected on psychological data (as the behaviorist would have it) or on economic data (as the Marxist would have it). It is not the residual minimum left after rigid application of the Cartesian axiom, *"de omnibus dubitandum."* It is not simply a set of working hypotheses whose value is pragmatic. It is an ensemble of substantive truths, a structure of basic knowledge, an order of elementary affirmations that reflect realities inherent in the order of existence. It occupies an established position in society and excludes opinions alien or contrary to itself. This consensus is the intuitional a priori of all the rationalities and technicalities of constitutional and statutory law. It furnishes the premises of the people's action in history and defines the larger aims which that action seeks in internal affairs and in external relations.

The whole premise of the public argument, if it is to be civilized and civilizing, is that the consensus is real, that among the people everything is not in doubt, but that there is a core of agreement, accord, concurrence, acquiescence. We hold certain truths; therefore we can argue about them. It seems to have been one of the corruptions of intelligence by positivism to assume that argument ends when agreement is reached. In a basic sense the reverse is true. There can be no argument except on the premise, and within a context, of agreement. *Mutatis mutandis*, this is true of scientific, philosophical, and theological argument. It is no less true of political argument.

On its most imperative level the public argument within the City and about the City's affairs begins with the agreement that there is a reality called, in the phrase of Leo XIII, *patrimonium generis humani*, a heritage of an essential truth, a tradition of rational belief, that sustains the structure

of the City and furnishes the substance of civil life. It was to this patrimony that the Declaration of Independence referred: "These are the
truths we hold." This is the first utterance of a people. By it a people establishes its identity, and under decent respect to the opinions of
mankind declares its purposes within the community of nations.

In later chapters an effort will be made to state the contents of the public consensus in America. Briefly, its principles and doctrines are those of
Western constitutionalism, classic and Christian. This is our essential
patrimony, laboriously wrought out by centuries of thought, further refined and developed in our own land to fit the needs of the new American experiment in government. In addition, as will later appear, the consensus has a growing end, as American society itself has a growing end.
My point at the moment, however, is that there are two reasons why the
consensus furnishes the basic theme of the public argument whereby
American society hopes to achieve and maintain the mark of civility.

Initially, we hold these truths because they are a patrimony. They are
a heritage from history, through whose dark and bloody pages there runs
like a silver thread the tradition of civility. This is the first reason why the
consensus continually calls for public argument. The consensus is an intellectual heritage; it may be lost to mind or deformed in the mind. Its final depository is the public mind. This is indeed a perilous place to deposit what ought to be kept safe; for the public mind is exposed to the
corrosive rust of skepticism, to the predatory moths of deceitful *doxai* (in
Plato's sense), and to the incessant thieveries of forgetfulness. Therefore
the consensus can only be preserved in the public mind by argument.
High argument alone will keep it alive, in the vital state of being "held."

Second, we hold these truths because they are true. They have been
found in the structure of reality by that dialectic of observation and reflection which is called philosophy. But as the achievement of reason and
experience the consensus again presents itself for argument. Its vitality
depends on a constant scrutiny of political experience, as this experience
widens with the developing—or possibly the decaying—life of man in society. Only at the price of this continued contact with experience will a
constitutional tradition continue to be "held," as real knowledge and not
simply as a structure of prejudice. However, the tradition, or the consensus, is not a mere record of experience. It is experience illumined by principle, given a construction by a process of philosophical reflection. In the

public argument there must consequently be a continued recurrence to first principles. Otherwise the consensus may come to seem simply a projection of ephemeral experience, a passing shadow on the vanishing backdrop of some given historical scene, without the permanence proper to truths that are "held."

On both of these titles, as a heritage and as a public philosophy, the American consensus needs to be constantly argued. If the public argument dies from disinterest, or subsides into the angry mutterings of polemic, or rises to the shrillness of hysteria, or trails off into positivistic triviality, or gets lost in a morass of semantics, you may be sure that the barbarian is at the gates of the City.

The barbarian need not appear in bearskins with a club in hand. He may wear a Brooks Brothers suit and carry a ball-point pen with which to write his advertising copy. In fact, even beneath the academic gown there may lurk a child of the wilderness, untutored in the high tradition of civility, who goes busily and happily about his work, a domesticated and law-abiding man, engaged in the construction of a philosophy to put an end to all philosophy, and thus put an end to the possibility of a vital consensus and to civility itself. This is perennially the work of the barbarian, to undermine rational standards of judgment, to corrupt the inherited intuitive wisdom by which the people have always lived, and to do this not by spreading new beliefs but by creating a climate of doubt and bewilderment in which clarity about the larger aims of life is dimmed and the self-confidence of the people is destroyed, so that finally what you have is the impotent nihilism of the "generation of the third eye," now presently appearing on our university campuses. (One is, I take it, on the brink of impotence and nihilism when one begins to be aware of one's own awareness of what one is doing, saying, thinking. This is the paralysis of all serious thought; it is likewise the destruction of all the spontaneities of love.)

The barbarian may be the eighteenth-century philosopher, who neither anticipated nor desired the brutalities of the Revolution with its Committee on the Public Safety, but who prepared the ways for the Revolution by creating a vacuum which he was not able to fill. Today the barbarian is the man who makes open and explicit rejection of the traditional role of reason and logic in human affairs. He is the man who reduces all spiritual and moral questions to the test of practical results or to an analysis of language or to decision in terms of individual subjective feeling.

It is a Christian theological intuition, confirmed by all of historical experience, that man lives both his personal and his social life always more or less close to the brink of barbarism, threatened not only by the disintegrations of physical illness and by the disorganizations of mental imbalance, but also by the decadence of moral corruption and the political chaos of formlessness or the moral chaos of tyranny. Society is rescued from chaos only by a few men, not by the many. *Paucis humanum vivit genus*. It is only the few who understand the disciplines of civility and are able to sustain them in being and thus hold in check the forces of barbarism that are always threatening to force the gates of the City. To say this is not, of course, to endorse the concept of the fascist élite—a barbarous concept, if ever there was one. It is only to recall a lesson of history to which our own era of mass civilization may well attend. We have not been behind our forebears in devising both gross and subtle ways of massacring ancient civilities.

The Concept of Conversation

Barbarism is not, I repeat, the forest primeval with all its relatively simple savageries. Barbarism has long had its definition, resumed by St. Thomas after Aristotle. It is the lack of reasonable conversation according to reasonable laws. Here the word "conversation" has its twofold Latin sense. It means living together and talking together.

Barbarism threatens when men cease to live together according to reason, embodied in law and custom, and incorporated in a web of institutions that sufficiently reveal rational influences, even though they are not, and cannot be, wholly rational. Society becomes barbarian when men are huddled together under the rule of force and fear; when economic interests assume the primacy over higher values; when material standards of mass and quantity crush out the values of quality and excellence; when technology assumes an autonomous existence and embarks on a course of unlimited self-exploitation without purposeful guidance from the higher disciplines of politics and morals (one thinks of Cape Canaveral); when the state reaches the paradoxical point of being everywhere intrusive and also impotent, possessed of immense power and powerless to achieve rational ends; when the ways of men come under the sway of the instinctual, the impulsive, the compulsive. When things like this happen, barbarism is abroad, whatever the surface impressions of urbanity. Men have ceased to live together according to reasonable laws.

Barbarism likewise threatens when men cease to talk together according to reasonable laws. There are laws of argument, the observance of which is imperative if discourse is to be civilized. Argument ceases to be civil when it is dominated by passion and prejudice; when its vocabulary becomes solipsist, premised on the theory that my insight is mine alone and cannot be shared; when dialogue gives way to a series of monologues; when the parties to the conversation cease to listen to one another, or hear only what they want to hear, or see the other's argument only through the screen of their own categories; when defiance is flung to the basic ontological principle of all ordered discourse, which asserts that Reality is an analogical structure, within which there are variant modes of reality, to each of which there corresponds a distinctive method of thought that imposes on argument its own special rules. When things like this happen, men cannot be locked together in argument. Conversation becomes merely quarrelsome or querulous. Civility dies with the death of the dialogue.

All this has been said in order to give some meaning to the immediate question before us, sc., whether American society, which calls itself free, is genuinely civil. In any circumstances it has always been difficult to achieve civility in the sense explained. A group of men locked together in argument is a rare spectacle. But within the great sprawling City that is the United States the achievement of a civil society encounters a special difficulty—what is called religious pluralism.

The Experience of Religious Pluralism

The political order must borrow both from above itself and from below itself. The political looks upward to metaphysics, ethics, theology; it looks downward to history, legal science, sociology, psychology. The order of politics must reckon with all that is true and factual about man. The problem was complicated enough for Aristotle, for whom man in the end was only citizen, whose final destiny was to be achieved within the City, however much he might long to play the immortal. For us today man is still citizen; but at least for most of us his life is not absorbed in the City, in society and the state. In the citizen who is also a Christian there resides the consciousness formulated immortally in the second century Letter to Diognetes: "Every foreign land is a fatherland and every fatherland is a foreign land." This con-sciousness makes a difference, in ways upon which we need not dwell here. What makes the more important difference is the fact of religious divisions. Civil discourse would be hard enough if among us there prevailed conditions of religious unity; even in such conditions civic unity would be a compli-cated and laborious achievement. As it is, efforts at civil discourse plunge us into the twofold experience of the religiously pluralist society.

The first experience is intellectual. As we discourse on public affairs, on the affairs of the commonwealth, and particularly on the problem of consensus, we inevitably have to move upward, as it were, into realms of some theoretical generality—into metaphysics, ethics, theology. This movement does not carry us into disagreement; for disagreement is not an easy thing to reach. Rather, we move into confusion. Among us there is a plurality of universes of discourse. These universes are incommensu-rable. And when they clash, the issue of agreement or disagreement tends to become irrelevant. The immediate situation is simply one of confusion. One does not know what the other is talking about. One may distrust what the other is driving at. For this too is part of the problem—the dis-position amid the confusion to disregard the immediate argument, as made, and to suspect its tendency, to wonder what the man who makes it is really driving at.

This is the pluralist society as it is encountered on the level of intel-lectual experience. We have no common universe of discourse. In partic-ular, diverse mental equivalents attach to all the words in which the con-stitutional consensus must finally be discussed—truth, freedom, justice, prudence, order, law, authority, power, knowledge, certainty, unity, peace, virtue, morality, religion, God, and perhaps even man. Our intellectual experience is one of sheer confusion, in which soliloquy succeeds to argument.

The second experience is even more profound. The themes touched upon in any discussion of Religion and the Free Society have all had a long history. And in the course of discussing them we are again made aware that only in a limited sense have we severally had the same history. We more or less share the short segment of history known as America. But all of us have had longer histories, spiritual and intellectual.

These histories may indeed touch at certain points. But I, for instance, am conscious that I do not share the histories that lie behind many of my fellow citizens. The Jew does not share the Christian history, nor even the Christian idea of history. Catholic and Protestant history may be parallel in a limited sense but they are not coincident or coeval. And the secularist is a latecomer. He may locate his ancestry in the eighteenth or nineteenth centuries, or, if his historic sense is strong, he may go back to the fourteenth century, to the rise of what Lagarde has called *l'esprit laïque*. In any case, he cannot go back to Athens, Rome, or Alexandria; for his laicism is historically conditioned. It must situate itself with regard to the Christian tradition. It must include denials and disassociations that the secularism of antiquity did not have to make; and it also includes the affirmation of certain Christian values that antiquity could not have affirmed.

The fact of our discrepant histories creates the second experience of the pluralist society. We are aware that we not only hold different views but have become different kinds of men as we have lived our several histories. Our styles of thought and of interior life are as discrepant as our histories. The more deeply they are experienced and the more fully they are measured, the more do the differences among us appear to be almost unbridgeable. Man is not only a creature of thought but also a vibrant subject of sympathies; and in the realm of philosophy and religion today the communal experiences are so divergent that they create not sympathies but alienations as between groups.

Take, for instance, the question of natural law, of which there will be much discourse in the pages that follow. For the Catholic it is simply a problem in metaphysical, ethical, political, and juridical argument. He moves into the argument naturally and feels relatively at ease amid its complexities. For the Protestant, on the contrary, the whole doctrine of natural law is a challenge, if not an affront, to his entire style of moral thought and even to his religiosity. The doctrine is alien to him, unassimilable by him. He not only misunderstands it; he also distrusts it. "Thus," says Robert McAfee Brown in *American Catholics: A Protestant-Jewish View*,[2] "Catholic appeals to natural law remain a source of friction rather than a basis of deeper understanding" as between Protestant and Catholic.

Another example might be the argument that has been made by Catholics in this country for more than a century with regard to the distribution of tax funds for the support of the school system. The structure of the argument is not complex. Its principle is that the canons of distributive justice ought to control the action of government in allocating funds that it coercively collects from all people in pursuance of its legitimate interest in universal compulsory schooling. The fact is that these canons are presently not being observed. The "solution" to the School Question reached in the nineteenth century reveals injustice, and the legal statutes that establish the injustice are an abuse of power. So, in drastic brevity, runs the argument. I shall return to it in a later chapter. For my part, I have never heard a satisfactory answer to it.

This is a fairly serious situation. When a large section of the community asserts that injustice is being done, and makes a reasonable argument to substantiate the assertion, either the argument ought to be convincingly refuted and the claim of injustice thus disposed of, or the validity of the argument ought to be admitted and the injustice remedied. As a matter of fact, however, the argument customarily meets a blank stare, or else it is "answered" by varieties of the fallacy known as *ignoratio elenchi*. At the extreme, from the side of the more careerist type of anti-Catholic, the rejoinder takes this form, roughly speaking (sometimes the rejoinder is roughly spoken): "We might be willing to listen to this argument about the rights of Catholic schools if we believed that Catholic schools had any rights at all. But we do not grant that they have any rights, except to tolerance. Their existence is not for the advantage of the public; they offend against the integrity of the democratic community, whose warrant is fidelity to Protestant principle (or secularist principle, as the case may be)." This "answer" takes various forms, more or less uncomplimentary to the Catholic Church, according to the temper of the speaker. But this is the gist of it. The statement brings me to my next point.

A Structure of War

The fact is that among us civility—or civic unity or civic amity, as you will—is a thing of the surface. It is quite easy to break through it. And when you do, you catch a glimpse of the factual reality of the pluralist society. I agree with Prof. Eric Voegelin's thesis that our pluralist society has received its structure through wars and that the wars are still going on beneath a fragile surface of more or less forced urbanity. What Voegelin calls the "genteel picture" will not stand the test of confrontation with fact.

We are not really a group of men singly engaged in the search for truth, relying solely on the means of persuasion, entering into dignified communication with each other, content politely to correct opinions with which we do not agree. As a matter of fact, the variant ideas and allegiances among us are entrenched as social powers; they occupy ground; they have developed interests; and they possess the means to fight for them. The real issues of truth that arise are complicated by secondary issues of power and prestige, which not seldom become primary.

There are numerous well-known examples. What they illustrate is that the entrenched segments of American pluralism claim influence on the course of events, on the content of the legal order, and on the quality of American society. To each group, of course, its influence seems salvific; to other groups it may seem merely imperialist. In any case, the forces at work are not simply intellectual; they are also passionate. There is not simply an exchange of arguments but of verbal blows. You do not have to probe deeply beneath the surface of civic amity to uncover the structure of passion and war.

There is the ancient resentment of the Jew, who has for centuries been dependent for his existence on the good will, often not forthcoming, of a Christian community. Now in America, where he has acquired social power, his distrust of the Christian community leads him to align himself with the secularizing forces whose dominance, he thinks, will afford him a security he has never known. Again, there is the profound distrust between Catholic and Protestant. Their respective conceptions of Christianity are only analogous; that is, they are partly the same and totally different. The result is *odium theologicum,* a sentiment that not only enhances religious differences in the realm of truth but also creates personal estrangements in the order of charity.

More than that, Catholic and Protestant distrust each other's political intentions. There is the memory of historic clashes in the temporal order; the Irishman does not forget Cromwell any more readily than the Calvinist forgets Louis XIV. Neither Protestant nor Catholic is yet satisfied that the two of them can exist freely and peacefully in the same kind of City. The Catholic regards Protestantism not only as a heresy in the order of religion but also as a corrosive solvent in the order of civilization, whose intentions lead to chaos. The Protestant regards Catholicism not only as idolatry in the order of religion but as an instrument of tyranny in the order of civilization, whose intentions lead to clericalism. Thus an *odium civile* accrues to the *odium theologicum*.

This problem is particularly acute in the United States, where the Protestant was the native and the Catholic the immigrant, in contrast to Europe where the Catholic first held the ground and was only later challenged. If one is to believe certain socio-religious critics (Eduard Heimann, for instance), Protestantism in America has forged an identification of itself, both historical and ideological, with American culture, particularly with an indigenous secularist unclarified mystique of individual freedom as somehow the source of everything, including justice, order, and unity. The result has been Nativism in all its manifold forms, ugly and refined, popular and academic, fanatic and liberal. The neo-Nativist as well as the paleo-Nativist addresses to the Catholic substantially the same charge: "You are among us but you are not of us." (The neo-Nativist differs only in that he uses footnotes, apparently in the belief that reference to documents is a substitute for an understanding of them.) To this charge the Catholic, if he happens to set store, *pro forma*, on meriting the blessed adjective "sophisticated," will politely reply that this is Jacobinism, *nouveau style*, and that Jacobinism, any style, is out of style in this day and age. In contrast, the sturdy Catholic War Veteran is more likely to say rudely, "Them's fighten' words." And with this exchange of civilities, if they are such, the "argument" is usually over.

There is, finally, the secularist (I here use the term only in a descriptive sense). He too is at war. If he knows his own history, he must be. Historically his first chosen enemy was the Catholic Church, and it must still be the Enemy of his choice, for two reasons that will be further developed in a later chapter. First, it asserts that there is an authority superior to the authority of individual reason and of the political projection of individual reason, the state. But this assertion is the first object of the secularist's anathema. Second, it asserts that by divine ordinance this world is to be ruled by a dyarchy of authorities, within which the temporal is subordinate to the spiritual, not instrumentally but in dignity. This assertion is doubly anathema. It clashes with the socio-juridical monism that is always basic to the secularist position when it is consistently argued. In secularist theory there can be only one society, one law, one power, and one faith, a civic faith that is the "unifying" bond of the community, whereby it withstands the assaults of assorted pluralisms.

The secularist has always fought his battles under a banner on which is emblazoned his special device, "The Integrity of the Political Order." In the name of this thundering principle he would banish from the political order (and from education as an affair of the City) all the "divisive forces" of religion. At least in America he has traditionally had no quarrel with religion as a "purely private matter," as a sort of essence or idea or ambient aura that may help to warm the hidden heart of solitary man. He may even concede a place to religion-in-general, whatever that is. What alarms him is religion as a Thing, visible, corporate, organized, a community of thought that presumes to sit superior to, and in judgment on, the "community of democratic thought," and that is furnished somehow with an armature of power to make its thought and judgment publicly prevail. Under this threat he marshals his military vocabulary and speaks in terms of aggression, encroachment, maneuvers, strategy, tactics. He rallies to the defense of the City; he sets about the strengthening of the wall that separates the City from its Enemy. He too is at war.

The Conspiracies and Their Conspiracy

What it comes to then is that the pluralist society, honestly viewed under abdication of all false gentility, is a pattern of interacting conspiracies. There are chiefly four—Protestant, Catholic, Jewish, secularist, though in each camp, to continue the military metaphor, there are forces not fully broken to the authority of the high command.

I would like to relieve the word "conspiracy" of its invidious connotations. It is devoid of these in its original Latin sense, both literal and tropical. Literally it means unison, concord, unanimity in opinion and feeling, a "breathing together." Then it acquires inevitably the connotation of united action for a common end about which there is agreement; those who think alike inevitably join together in some manner of action to make their common thought or purpose prevail. The word was part of the Stoic political vocabulary; it was adopted by Cicero; and it has passed into my own philosophical tradition, the Scholastic tradition, that has been formative of the liberal tradition of the West. Civil society is formed, said Cicero, "*conspiratione hominum atque consensu*," that is by action in concert on the basis of consensus with regard to the purposes of the action. Civil society is by definition a conspiracy, "*conspiratio plurium in unum.*" Only by conspiring together do the many become one. *E pluribus unum.*

The trouble is that there are a number of conspiracies within American society. I shall not object to your calling Catholicism a conspiracy, provided you admit that it is only one of several. (Incidentally, I never have seen the validity of Prof. Sidney Hook's distinction: "Heresy, yes; conspiracy, no." The heresy that was not a conspiracy has not yet appeared on land or sea. One would say with greater propriety of word and concept: "Conspiracy, yes; heresy, no." Heresy, not conspiracy, is the bad word for the evil thing. No one would be bothered with the Communist conspiracy if its dynamism were not a civilizational heresy, or more exactly, an apostasy from civilization.)

Perhaps then our problem today is somehow to make the four great conspiracies among us conspire into one conspiracy that will be American society—civil, just, free, peaceful, one.

Can this problem be solved? My own expectations are modest and minimal. It seems to be the lesson of history that men are usually governed with little wisdom. The highest political good, the unity which is called peace, is far more an ideal than a realization. And the search for religious unity, the highest spiritual good, always encounters the "messianic necessity," so called: "Do you think that I have come to bring peace on earth? No, but rather dissension" (Luke 12:51). In the same text the dissension was predicted with terrible explicitness of the family. It has also been the constant lot of the family of nations and of the nations themselves. Religious pluralism is against the will of God. But it is the human condition; it is written into the script of history. It will not somehow marvelously cease to trouble the City.

Advisedly therefore one will cherish only modest expectations with regard to the solution of the problem of religious pluralism and civic unity. Utopianism is a Christian heresy (the ancient pagan looked backward, not forward, to the Golden Age); but it is a heresy nonetheless. We cannot hope to make American society the perfect conspiracy based on a unanimous consensus. But we could at least do two things. We could limit the warfare, and we could enlarge the dialogue. We could lay down our arms (at least the more barbarous kind of arms!), and we could take up argument.

Even to do this would not be easy. It would be necessary that we cease to project into the future of the Republic the nightmares, real or fancied, of the past. In Victorian England John Henry Newman noted that the Protestant bore "a stain upon the imagination," left there by the vivid images of Reformation polemic against the Church of Rome. Perhaps we all bear some stain or other upon our imaginations. It might be possible to cleanse them by a work of reason. The free society, I said at the outset, is a unique realization; it has inaugurated a new history. Therefore it might be possible within this new history to lay the ghosts of the past—to forget the ghettos and the autos-da-fé; the Star Chamber and the Committee on the Public Safety; Topcliffe with his "Bloody Question" and Torquemada with his rack; the dragonnades and the Black and Tans; Samuel F. B. Morse, the convents in Charleston and Philadelphia, the Know-Nothings and the Ku Klux Klan and what happened to Al Smith (whatever it was that did happen to him).

All this might be possible. It certainly would be useful. I venture to say that today it is necessary. This period in American history is critical, not organic (to use Prof. Toynbee's distinction). We face a crisis that is new in history. We would do well to face it with a new cleanliness of imagination, in the realization that internecine strife, beyond some inevitable human measure, is a luxury we can no longer afford. Serious issues confront us on all the three levels of public argument. Perhaps the time has come when we should endeavor to dissolve the structure of war that underlies the pluralistic society, and erect the more civilized structure of the dialogue. It would be no less sharply pluralistic, but rather more so, since the real pluralisms would be clarified out of their present confusion. And amid the pluralism a unity would be discernible—the unity of an orderly conversation. The pattern would not be that of ignorant armies clashing by night but of informed men locked together in argument in the full light of a new dialectical day. Thus we might present to a "candid world" the spectacle of a civil society.

Notes

1. New York: Longmans, Green & Co., 1953.
2. New York: Sheed and Ward, 1959.

PART I

THE AMERICAN PROPOSITION

~

CHAPTER ONE

E Pluribus Unum:
The American Consensus

As it arose in America, the problem of pluralism was unique in the modern world, chiefly because pluralism was the native condition of American society. It was not, as in Europe and in England, the result of a disruption or decay of a previously existent religious unity. This fact created the possibility of a new solution; indeed, it created a demand for a new solution. The possibility was exploited and the demand was met by the American Constitution.

The question here concerns the position of the Catholic conscience in the face of the new American solution to a problem that for centuries has troubled, and still continues to trouble, various nations and societies. A new problem has been put to the universal Church by the fact of America—by the uniqueness of our social situation, by the genius of our newly conceived constitutional system, by the lessons of our singular national history, which has molded in a special way the consciousness and temper of the American people, within whose midst the Catholic stands, sharing with his fellow citizens the same national heritage. The Catholic community faces the task of making itself intellectually aware of the conditions of its own coexistence within the American pluralistic scene. We have behind us a lengthy historical tradition of acceptance of the special situation of the Church in America, in all its differences from the situations in which the Church elsewhere finds herself. But it is a question here of pursuing the subject, not in the horizontal dimension of history but in the vertical dimension of theory.

The argument readily falls into two parts. The first part is an analysis of the American Proposition with regard to political unity. The effort is to make a statement, later to be somewhat enlarged, of the essential contents of the American consensus, whereby we are made "e pluribus unum," one society subsisting amid multiple pluralisms. Simply to make this statement is to show why American Catholics participate with ready conviction in the American consensus. The second part of the argument, to be pursued in the next chapter, is an analysis of the American Proposition with regard to religious pluralism, especially as this proposition is embodied in our fundamental law. Again, simply to make this analysis is to lay bare the reasons why American Catholics accept on principle the unique American solution to the age-old problem.

The Nation Under God

The first truth to which the American Proposition makes appeal is stated in that landmark of Western political theory, the Declaration of Independence. It is a truth that lies beyond politics; it imparts to politics a fundamental human meaning. I mean the sovereignty of God over nations as well as over individual men. This is the principle that radically distinguishes the conservative Christian tradition of America from the Jacobin laicist tradition of Continental Europe. The Jacobin tradition proclaimed the autonomous reason of man to be the first and the sole principle of political organization. In contrast, the first article of the American political faith is that the political community, as a form of free and ordered human life, looks to the sovereignty of God as to the first principle of its organization. In the Jacobin tradition religion is at best a purely private concern, a matter of personal devotion, quite irrelevant to public affairs. Society as such, and the state which gives it legal form, and the government which is its organ of action are by definition agnostic or atheist. The statesman as such cannot be a believer, and his actions as a statesman are immune from any imperative or judgment higher than the will of the people, in whom resides ultimate and total sovereignty (one must remember that in the Jacobin tradition "the people" means "the party"). This whole manner of thought is altogether alien to the authentic American tradition.

From the point of view of the problem of pluralism this radical distinction between the American and the Jacobin traditions is of cardinal importance. The United States has had, and still has, its share of agnostics and unbelievers. But it has never known organized militant atheism on the Jacobin, doctrinaire Socialist, or Communist model; it has rejected parties and theories which erect atheism into a political principle. In 1799, the year of the Napoleonic *coup d'état* which overthrew the Directory and established a dictatorship in France, President John Adams stated the first of all American first principles in his remarkable proclamation of March 6:

> . . . it is also most reasonable in itself that men who are capable of social arts and relations, who owe their improvements to the social state, and who derive their enjoyments from it, should, as a society, make acknowledgements of dependence and obligation to Him who hath endowed them with these capacities and elevated them in the scale of existence by these distinctions. . . .

President Lincoln on May 30, 1863, echoed the tradition in another proclamation:

> Whereas the Senate of the United States, devoutly recognizing the supreme authority and just government of Almighty God in all the affairs of men and nations, has by a resolution requested the President to designate and set apart a day for national prayer and humiliation; And whereas it is the duty of nations as well as of men to own their dependence upon the overruling power of God, to confess their sins and trespasses in humble sorrow, yet with the assured hope that genuine repentance will lead to mercy and pardon. . . .

The authentic voice of America speaks in these words. And it is a testimony to the enduring vitality of this first principle—the sovereignty of God over society as well as over individual men—that President Eisenhower in June, 1952, quoted these words of Lincoln in a proclamation of similar intent. There is, of course, dissent from this principle, uttered by American secularism (which, at that, is a force far different in content and purpose from Continental laicism). But the secularist dissent is clearly a dissent; it illustrates the existence of the American affirmation.

And it is continually challenged. For instance, as late as 1952 an opinion of the United States Supreme Court challenged it by asserting: "We are a religious people whose institutions presuppose a Supreme Being." Three times before in its history—in 1815, 1892, and 1931—the Court had formally espoused this same principle.

The Tradition of Natural Law

The affirmation in Lincoln's famous phrase, "this nation under God," sets the American proposition in fundamental continuity with the central political tradition of the West. But this continuity is more broadly and importantly visible in another, and related, respect. In 1884 the Third Plenary Council of Baltimore made this statement: "We consider the establishment of our country's independence, the shaping of its liberties and laws, as a work of special Providence, its framers 'building better than they knew,' the Almighty's hand guiding them." The providential aspect of the matter, and the reason for the better building, can be found in the fact that the American political community was organized in an era when the tradition of natural law and natural rights was still vigorous. Claiming no sanction other than its appeal to free minds, it still commanded universal acceptance. And it furnished the basic materials for the American consensus.

The evidence for this fact has been convincingly presented by Clinton Rossiter in his book, *Seedtime of the Republic*,[1] a scholarly account of the "noble aggregate of 'self-evident truths' that vindicated the campaign of resistance (1765–1775), the resolution for independence (1776), and the establishment of the new state governments (1776–1780)." These truths, he adds, "had been no less self-evident to the preachers, merchants, planters, and lawyers who were the mind of colonial America." It might be further added that these truths firmly presided over the great time of study, discussion, and decision which produced the Federal Constitution. "The great political philosophy of the Western world," Rossiter says, "enjoyed one of its proudest seasons in this time of resistance and revolution." By reason of this fact the American Revolution, quite unlike its French counterpart, was less a revolution than a conservation. It conserved, by giving newly vital form to, the liberal tradition of politics, whose ruin in Continental Europe was about to be consummated by the first great modern essay in totalitarianism.

The force for unity inherent in this tradition was of decisive importance in what concerns the problem of pluralism. Because it was conceived in the tradition of natural law the American Republic was rescued
from the fate, still not overcome, that fell upon the European nations in
which Continental Liberalism, a deformation of the liberal tradition,
lodged itself, not least by the aid of the Lodges. There have never been
"two Americas," in the sense in which there have been, and still are, "two
Frances," "two Italys," "two Spains." Politically speaking, America has always been one. The reason is that a consensus was once established, and
it still substantially endures, even in the quarters where its origins have
been forgotten.

Formally and in the first instance this consensus was political, that is,
it embraced a whole constellation of principles bearing upon the origin
and nature of society, the function of the state as the legal order of society, and the scope and limitations of government. "Free government"—
perhaps this typically American shorthand phrase sums up the consensus.
"A free people under a limited government" puts the matter more exactly.
It is a phrase that would have satisfied the first Whig, St. Thomas
Aquinas.

To the early Americans government was not a phenomenon of force,
as the later legal positivists would have it. Nor was it a "historical category," as Marx and his followers were to assert. Government did not mean
simply the power to coerce, though this power was taken as integral to
government. Government, properly speaking, was the right to command.
It was authority. And its authority derived from law. By the same token
its authority was limited by law. In his own way Tom Paine put the matter when he said, "In America Law is the King." But the matter had been
better put by Henry of Bracton (d. 1268) when he said, "The king ought
not to be under a man, but under God and under the law, because the law
makes the king." This was the message of Magna Charta; this became the
first structural rib of American constitutionalism.

Constitutionalism, the rule of law, the notion of sovereignty as purely
political and therefore limited by law, the concept of government as an
empire of laws and not of men—these were ancient ideas, deeply im-
planted in the British tradition at its origin in medieval times. The major
American contribution to the tradition—a contribution that imposed itself on all subsequent political history in the Western world—was the

written constitution. However, the American document was not the *constitution octroyée* of the nineteenth-century Restorations—a constitution graciously granted by the King or Prince-President. Through the American techniques of the constitutional convention and of popular ratification, the American Constitution is explicitly the act of the people. It embodies their consensus as to the purposes of government, its structure, the extent of its powers and the limitations on them, etc. By the Constitution the people define the areas where authority is legitimate and the areas where liberty is lawful. The Constitution is therefore at once a charter of freedom and a plan for political order.

The Principle of Consent

Here is the second aspect of the continuity between the American consensus and the ancient liberal tradition; I mean the affirmation of the principle of the consent of the governed. Sir John Fortescue (d. 1476), Chief Justice of the Court of King's Bench under Henry VI, had thus stated the tradition, in distinguishing between the absolute and the constitutional monarch: "The secounde king [the constitutional monarch] may not rule his people by other laws than such as thai assenten to. And therefore he may set uppon thaim non imposicions without their consent." The principle of consent was inherent in the medieval idea of kingship; the king was bound to seek the consent of his people to his legislation. The American consensus reaffirmed this principle, at the same time that it carried the principle to newly logical lengths. Americans agreed that they would consent to none other than their own legislation, as framed by their representatives, who would be responsible to them. In other words, the principle of consent was wed to the equally ancient principle of popular participation in rule. But, since this latter principle was given an amplitude of meaning never before known in history, the result was a new synthesis, whose formula is the phrase of Lincoln, "government by the people."

Americans agreed to make government constitutional and therefore limited in a new sense, because it is representative, republican, responsible government. It is limited not only by law but by the will of the people it represents. Not only do the people adopt the Constitution; through the techniques of representation, free elections, and frequent rotation of administrations they also have a share in the enactment of all subsequent statutory legislation. The people are really governed; American political theorists did not pursue the Rousseauist will-o'-the-wisp: how shall the individual in society come to obey only himself? Nevertheless, the people are governed because they consent to be governed; and they consent to be governed because in a true sense they govern themselves.

The American consensus therefore includes a great act of faith in the capacity of the people to govern themselves. The faith was not unrealistic. It was not supposed that everybody could master the technical aspects of government, even in a day when these aspects were far less complex than they now are. The supposition was that the people could understand the general objectives of governmental policy, the broad issues put to the decision of government, especially as these issues raised moral problems. The American consensus accepted the premise of medieval society, that there is a sense of justice inherent in the people, in virtue of which they are empowered, as the medieval phrase had it, to "judge, direct, and correct" the processes of government.

It was this political faith that compelled early American agreement to the institutions of a free speech and a free press. In the American concept of them, these institutions do not rest on the thin theory proper to eighteenth-century individualistic rationalism, that a man has a right to say what he thinks merely because he thinks it. The American agreement was to reject political censorship of opinion as unrightful, because unwise, imprudent, not to say impossible. However, the proper premise of these freedoms lay in the fact that they were social necessities. "Colonial thinking about each of these rights had a strong social rather than individualistic bias," Rossiter says. They were regarded as conditions essential to the conduct of free, representative, and responsible government. People who are called upon to obey have the right first to be heard. People who are to bear burdens and make sacrifices have the right first to pronounce on the purposes which their sacrifices serve. People who are summoned to contribute to the common good have the right first to pass their own judgment on the question, whether the good proposed be truly a good, the people's good, the common good. Through the technique of majority opinion this popular judgment becomes binding on government.

A second principle underlay these free institutions—the principle that the state is distinct from society and limited in its offices toward society.

This principle too was inherent in the Great Tradition. Before it was cancelled out by the rise of the modern omnicompetent society-state, it had found expression in the distinction between the order of politics and the order of culture, or, in the language of the time, the distinction between *studium* and *imperium*. The whole order of ideas in general was autonomous in the face of government; it was immune from political discipline, which could only fall upon actions, not ideas. Even the medieval Inquisition respected this distinction of orders; it never recognized a crime of opinion, *crimen opinionis*; its competence extended only to the repression of organized conspiracy against public order and the common good. It was, if you will, a Committee on un-Christian Activities; it regarded activities, not ideas, as justiciable.

The American Proposition, in reviving the distinction between society and state, which had perished under the advance of absolutism, likewise renewed the principle of the incompetence of government in the field of opinion. Government submits itself to judgment by the truth of society; it is not itself a judge of the truth in society. Freedom of the means of communication whereby ideas are circulated and criticized, and the freedom of the academy (understanding by the term the range of institutions organized for the pursuit of truth and the perpetuation of the intellectual heritage of society) are immune from legal inhibition or government control. This immunity is a civil right of the first order, essential to the American concept of a free people under a limited government.

A Virtuous People

"A free people": this term too has a special sense in the American Proposition. America has passionately pursued the ideal of freedom, expressed in a whole system of political and civil rights, to new lengths; but it has not pursued this ideal so madly as to rush over the edge of the abyss, into sheer libertarianism, into the chaos created by the nineteenth-century theory of the "outlaw conscience," *conscientia exlex*, the conscience that knows no law higher than its own subjective imperatives. Part of the inner architecture of the American ideal of freedom has been the profound conviction that only a virtuous people can be free. It is not an American belief that free government is inevitable, only that it is possible, and that its possibility can be realized only when the people as a whole are inwardly governed by the recognized imperatives of the universal moral law.

The American experiment reposes on Acton's postulate, that freedom is the highest phase of civil society. But it also reposes on Acton's further postulate, that the elevation of a people to this highest phase of social life supposes, as its condition, that they understand the ethical nature of political freedom. They must understand, in Acton's phrase, that freedom is "not the power of doing what we like, but the right of being able to do what we ought." The people claim this right, in all its articulated forms, in the face of government; in the name of this right, multiple limitations are put upon the power of government. But the claim can be made with the full resonance of moral authority only to the extent that it issues from an inner sense of responsibility to a higher law. In any phase civil society demands order. In its highest phase of freedom it demands that order should not be imposed from the top down, as it were, but should spontaneously flower outward from the free obedience to the restraints and imperatives that stem from inwardly possessed moral principle. In this sense democracy is more than a political experiment; it is a spiritual and moral enterprise. And its success depends upon the virtue of the people who undertake it. Men who would be politically free must discipline themselves. Likewise institutions which would pretend to be free with a human freedom must in their workings be governed from within and made to serve the ends of virtue. Political freedom is endangered in its foundations as soon as the universal moral values, upon whose shared possession the self-discipline of a free society depends, are no longer vigorous enough to restrain the passions and shatter the selfish inertia of men. The American ideal of freedom as ordered freedom, and therefore an ethical ideal, has traditionally reckoned with these truths, these truisms.

Human and Historical Rights

This brings us to the threshold of religion, and therefore to the other aspect of the problem of pluralism, the plurality of religions in America. However, before crossing this threshold one more characteristic of the American Proposition, as implying a consensus, needs mention, namely, the Bill of Rights. The philosophy of the Bill of Rights was also tributary to the tradition of natural law, to the idea that man has certain original responsibilities precisely as man, antecedent to his status as citizen. These responsibilities are creative of rights which inhere in man antecedent to any act of government; therefore they are not granted by government and they cannot be surrendered to government. They are as inalienable as they are inherent. Their proximate source is in nature, and in history insofar as history bears witness to the nature of man; their ultimate source, as the Declaration of Independence states, is in God, the Creator of nature and the Master of history. The power of this doctrine, as it inspired both the Revolution and the form of the Republic, lay in the fact that it drew an effective line of demarcation around the exercise of political or social authority. When government ventures over this line, it collides with the duty and right of resistance. Its authority becomes arbitrary and therefore nil; its act incurs the ultimate anathema, "unconstitutional."

One characteristic of the American Bill of Rights is important for the subject here, namely, the differences that separate it from the Declaration of the Rights of Man in the France of 1789. In considerable part the latter was a parchment-child of the Enlightenment, a top-of-the-brain concoction of a set of men who did not understand that a political community, like man himself, has roots in history and in nature. They believed that a state could be simply a work of art, a sort of absolute beginning, an artifact of which abstract human reason could be the sole artisan. Moreover, their exaggerated individualism had shut them off from a view of the organic nature of the human community; their social atomism would permit no institutions or associations intermediate between the individual and the state.

In contrast, the men who framed the American Bill of Rights understood history and tradition, and they understood nature in the light of both. They too were individualists, but not to the point of ignoring the social nature of man. They did their thinking within the tradition of freedom that was their heritage from England. Its roots were not in the top of anyone's brain but in history. Importantly, its roots were in the medieval notion of the *homo liber et legalis*, the man whose freedom rests on law, whose law was the age-old custom in which the nature of man expressed itself, and whose lawful freedoms were possessed in association with his fellows. The rights for which the colonists contended against the English Crown were basically the rights of Englishmen. And these were substantially the rights written into the Bill of Rights.

Of freedom of religion there will be question later. For the rest, freedom of speech, assembly, association, and petition for the redress of grievances, security of person, home, and property—these were great historical as well as civil and natural rights. So too was the right to trial by jury, and all the procedural rights implied in the Fifth- and later in the Fourteenth-Amendment provision for "due process of law." The guarantee of these and other rights was new in that it was written, in that it envisioned these rights with an amplitude, and gave them a priority, that had not been known before in history. But the Bill of Rights was an effective instrument for the delimitation of government authority and social power, not because it was written on paper in 1789 or 1791, but because the rights it proclaims had already been engraved by history on the conscience of a people. The American Bill of Rights is not a piece of eighteenth-century rationalist theory; it is far more the product of Christian history. Behind it one can see, not the philosophy of the Enlightenment but the older philosophy that had been the matrix of the common law. The "man" whose rights are guaranteed in the face of law and government is, whether he knows it or not, the Christian man, who had learned to know his own personal dignity in the school of Christian faith.

The American Consensus Today

Americans have been traditionally proud of the earlier phases of their history—colonial and Revolutionary, constitutional and Federalist. This pride persists today. The question is, whether the American consensus still endures—the consensus whose essential contents have been sketched in the foregoing. A twofold answer may be given. The first answer is given by Professor Rossiter:

> Perhaps Americans could achieve a larger measure of liberty and prosperity and build a more successful government if they were to abandon the language and assumptions of men who lived almost two centuries ago. Yet the feeling cannot be downed that rude rejection of the past, rather than level-headed respect for it, would be the huge mistake. Americans may eventually take the advice of their advanced philosophers and adopt a political theory that pays more attention to groups, classes, public opinion, power-élites, positive law, public administration, and other realities of twentieth-century

America. Yet it seems safe to predict that the people, who occasionally prove themselves wiser than their philosophers, will go on thinking about the political community in terms of unalienable rights, popular sovereignty, consent, constitutionalism, separation of powers, morality, and limited government. The political theory of the American Revolution—a theory of ethical, ordered liberty—remains the political tradition of the American people.

This is a cheerful answer. I am not at all sure that it is correct, if it be taken to imply that the tradition of natural law, as the foundation of law and politics, has the same hold upon the mind of America today that it had upon the "preachers, merchants, planters, and lawyers who were the mind of colonial America." There is indeed talk today about a certain revival of this great tradition, notably among more thoughtful men in the legal profession. But the talk itself is significant. One would not talk of reviving the tradition, if it were in fact vigorously alive. Perhaps the American people have not taken the advice of their advanced philosophers. Perhaps they are wiser than their philosophers. Perhaps they still refuse to think of politics and law as their philosophers think—in purely positivist and pragmatist terms. The fact remains that this is the way the philosophers think. Not that they have made a "rude rejection of the past." They are never rude. And they can hardly be said to have rejected what they never knew or understood, because it was never taught to them and they never learned it. The tradition of natural law is not taught or learned in the American university. It has not been rejected, much less refuted. We do not refute our adversaries, said Santayana; we quietly bid them goodbye. I think, as I shall later say, that the American university long since bade a quiet goodbye to the whole notion of an American consensus, as implying that there are truths that we hold in common, and a natural law that makes known to all of us the structure of the moral universe in such wise that all of us are bound by it in a common obedience.

There is, however, a second answer to the question, whether the original American consensus still endures. It is certainly valid of a not inconsiderable portion of the American people, the Catholic community. The men of learning in it acknowledge certain real contributions made by positive sociological analysis of the political community. But both they and their less learned fellows still adhere, with all the conviction of intelligence, to the tradition of natural law as the basis of free and ordered political life. Historically, this tradition has found, and still finds, its intellectual home within the Catholic Church. It is indeed one of the ironies of history that the tradition should have so largely languished in the so-called Catholic nations of Europe at the same time that its enduring vigor was launching a new Republic across the broad ocean. There is also some paradox in the fact that a nation which has (rightly or wrongly) thought of its own genius in Protestant terms should have owed its origins and the stability of its political structure to a tradition whose genius is alien to current intellectualized versions of the Protestant religion, and even to certain individualistic exigencies of Protestant religiosity. These are special questions, not to be pursued here. The point here is that Catholic participation in the American consensus has been full and free, unreserved and unembarrassed, because the contents of this consensus— the ethical and political principles drawn from the tradition of natural law—approve themselves to the Catholic intelligence and conscience. Where this kind of language is talked, the Catholic joins the conversation with complete ease. It is his language. The ideas expressed are native to his own universe of discourse. Even the accent, being American, suits his tongue.

Another idiom now prevails. The possibility was inherent from the beginning. To the early American theorists and politicians the tradition of natural law was an inheritance. This was its strength; this was at the same time its weakness, especially since a subtle alteration of the tradition had already commenced. For a variety of reasons the intellectualist idea of law as reason had begun to cede to the voluntarist idea of law as will. One can note the change in Blackstone, for instance, even though he still stood within the tradition, and indeed drew whole generations of early American lawyers into it with him. (Part of American folklore is Sandburg's portrait of Abraham Lincoln, sitting barefoot on his woodpile, reading Blackstone.) Protestant Christianity, especially in its left wing (and its left wing has always been dominant in America), inevitably evolved away from the old English and American tradition. Grotius and the philosophers of the Enlightenment had cast up their secularized versions of the tradition. Their disciples were to better their instruction, as the impact of the methods of empirical science made itself felt even in those areas of human thought in which knowledge is noncumulative and to that extent recalcitrant to the methods of science. Seeds of dissolution were already present in the ancient heritage as it reached the shores of America.

Perhaps the dissolution, long since begun, may one day be consummated. Perhaps one day the noble many-storeyed mansion of democracy will be dismantled, levelled to the dimensions of a flat majoritarianism, which is no mansion but a barn, perhaps even a tool shed in which the weapons of tyranny may be forged. Perhaps there will one day be wide dissent even from the political principles which emerge from natural law, as well as dissent from the constellation of ideas that have historically undergirded these principles—the idea that government has a moral basis; that the universal moral law is the foundation of society; that the legal order of society—that is, the state—is subject to judgment by a law that is not statistical but inherent in the nature of man; that the eternal reason of God is the ultimate origin of all law; that this nation in all its aspects— as a society, a state, an ordered and free relationship between governors and governed—is under God. The possibility that widespread dissent from these principles should develop is not foreclosed. If that evil day should come, the results would introduce one more paradox into history. The Catholic community would still be speaking in the ethical and political idiom familiar to them as it was familiar to their fathers, both the Fathers of the Church and the Fathers of the American Republic. The guardianship of the original American consensus, based on the Western heritage, would have passed to the Catholic community, within which the heritage was elaborated long before America was. And it would be for others, not Catholics, to ask themselves whether they still shared the consensus which first fashioned the American people into a body politic and determined the structure of its fundamental law.

What has been said may suffice to show the grounds on which Catholics participate in the American consensus. These grounds are drawn from the materials of the consensus itself. It has been a greatly providential blessing that the American Republic never put to the Catholic conscience the questions raised, for instance, by the Third Republic. There has never been a schism within the American Catholic community, as there was among French Catholics, over the right attitude to adopt toward the established polity. There has never been the necessity for nice distinctions between the regime and the legislation; nor has there ever been the need to proclaim a policy of *ralliement*. In America the *ralliement* has been original, spontaneous, universal. It has been a matter of conscience and conviction, because its motive was not expediency in the narrow sense—the need to accept what one is powerless to change. Its motive was the evident coincidence of the principles which inspired the American Republic with the principles that are structural to the Western Christian political tradition.

Note

1. New York: Harcourt, Brace and Co., 1953.

CHAPTER TWO

~

Civil Unity and Religious Integrity: The Articles of Peace

The unity asserted in the American device, "E pluribus unum" (as I have adapted its meaning) is a unity of a limited order. It does not go beyond the exigencies of civil conversation, taken in the sense already defined. This civil unity therefore must not hinder the various religious communities in American society in the maintenance of their own distinct identities. Similarly, the public consensus, on which civil unity is ultimately based, must permit to the differing communities the full integrity of their own religious convictions. The one civil society contains within its own unity the communities that are divided among themselves; but it does not seek to reduce to its own unity the differences that divide them. In a word, the pluralism remains as real as the unity. Neither may undertake to destroy the other. Each subsists in its own order. And the two orders, the religious and the civil, remain distinct, however much they are, and need to be, related. All this, I take it, is integral to the meaning attached in America to the doctrine of religious freedom and to its instrumental companion-doctrine called (not felicitously) separation of church and state. I use the word "doctrine" as lawyers or political philosophers, not theologians, use it.

We come therefore to the second question. It concerns the American solution to the problem put by the plurality of conflicting religions within the one body politic. In its legal form (there are other forms, as I shall later say) the solution is deposited in the First Amendment to the Federal Constitution: "Congress shall make no law respecting an establishment of religion or prohibiting the free exercise thereof. . . ." What then is the Catholic view of this constitutional proviso?

A Matter of Prejudice

In 1790 Edmund Burke published his *Reflections on the Revolution in France*. When he comes to his defense of English institutions ("an established Church, an established monarchy, an established aristocracy, and an established democracy"), he says: "First I beg leave to speak of our Church Establishment, which is the first of our prejudices—not a prejudice destitute of reason, but involving in it profound and extensive wisdom. I speak of it first. It is first, and last, and midst in our minds." In that same year the people of the states newly formed into the American Federal Republic were debating the ten amendments to the Constitution, submitted to them for ratification. The ratification was complete in 1791, and in that year the legal rule against any establishment of religion was on its way to becoming, where it had not already become, the first of our prejudices. There is a contrast here, a clash of prejudices, which still endures. The clash ought to be mentioned at the outset of our present question, primarily because it should teach one the dangers of doctrinaire judgments. Such judgments are always in peril of falsity; they are particularly so in the delicate matter of the legal regulation of religion in society. We have a special prejudice in this matter, which is specifically American, because its origins are in our particular context and its validity has been demonstrated by the unique course of American history.

The subject might almost be left right here, if it could be generally admitted that the First Amendment expresses simply an American prejudice, in Burke's sense of the word. A prejudice is not necessarily an error; to be prejudiced is not necessarily to be unreasonable. Certain prejudgments are wholesome. Normally, they are concrete judgments of value, not abstract judgments of truth. They are not destitute of reason, but their chief corroboration is from experience. They are part of the legacy of wisdom from the past; they express an ancestral consensus. Hence they supply in the present, as Russell Kirk puts it, "the half-intuitive knowledge which enables men to meet the problems of life without logic-chopping." The American Catholic is entirely prepared to accept our constitutional concept of freedom of religion and the policy of no establishment as the first of our prejudices. He is also prepared to admit that other prejudices may obtain elsewhere—in England, in Sweden, in Spain. Their validity in their own context and against the background of the history that generated them does not disturb him in his conviction that his own prejudice, within his own context and against the background of his own history, has its own validity.

American Catholics would even go as far as to say of the provisions of the First Amendment what Burke, in his *Reflections*, said of the English Church Establishment, that they consider it as "essential to their state; not as a thing heterogeneous and separable, something added from accommodation, what they may either keep up or lay aside, according to their temporary ideas of convenience. They consider it as the foundation of their whole Constitution, with which, and with every part of which, it holds an indissoluble union." The prejudice formulated in the First Amendment is but the most striking aspect of the more fundamental prejudice that was the living root of our constitutional system—the prejudice in favor of the method of freedom in society and therefore the prejudice in favor of a government of limited powers, whose limitations are determined by the consent of the people. The American people exempted from their grant of power to government any power to establish religion or to prohibit the free exercise thereof. The Catholic community, in common with the rest of the American people, has historically consented to this political and legal solution to the problem created by the plurality of religious beliefs in American society. They agree that the First Amendment is by no means destitute of reason; that it involves profound and extensive wisdom; that its wisdom has been amply substantiated by history. Consequently, they share the general prejudice which it states; often enough both in action and in utterances they have made this fact plain. And that should be the end of the matter.

Theologies of the First Amendment

But, as it happens, one is not permitted thus simply to end the matter. I leave aside the practical issues that have arisen concerning the application of the First Amendment. The question here is one of theory, the theory of the First Amendment in itself and in its relation to Catholic theories of freedom of religion and the church-state relation. It is customary to put to Catholics what is supposed to be an embarrassing question: Do you really believe in the first two provisions of the First Amendment? The question calls to mind one of the more famous among the multitudinous queries put by Boswell to Dr. Johnson, "whether it is necessary to believe all the Thirty-Nine Articles." And the Doctor's answer has an applicable point: "Why, sir, that is a question which has been much agitated. Some have held it necessary that all be believed. Others have considered them to be only articles of peace, that is to say, you are not to preach against them."

An analogous difference of interpretation seems to exist with regard to the first two articles of the First Amendment.

On the one hand, there are those who read into them certain ultimate beliefs, certain specifically sectarian tenets with regard to the nature of religion, religious truth, the church, faith, conscience, divine revelation, human freedom, etc. In this view these articles are invested with a genuine sanctity that derives from their supposed religious content. They are dogmas, norms of orthodoxy, to which one must conform on pain of some manner of excommunication. They are true articles of faith. Hence it is necessary to believe them, to give them a religiously motivated assent.

On the other hand, there are those who see in these articles only a law, not a dogma. These constitutional clauses have no religious content. They answer none of the eternal human questions with regard to the nature of truth and freedom or the manner in which the spiritual order of man's life is to be organized or not organized. Therefore they are not invested with the sanctity that attaches to dogma, but only with the rationality that attaches to law. Rationality is the highest value of law. In further consequence, it is not necessary to give them a religious assent but only a rational civil obedience. In a word, they are not articles of faith but articles of peace, that is to say, you may not act against them, because they are law and good law.

Those who dogmatize about these articles do not usually do so with all the clarity that dogmas require. Nor are they in agreement with one another. The main difference is between those who see in these articles certain Protestant religious tenets and those who see in them certain ultimate suppositions of secular liberalism. The differences between those two groups tend to disappear in a third group, the secularizing Protestants, so called, who effect an identification of their Protestantism with American secular culture, consider the church to be true in proportion as its organization is commanded by the norms of secular democratic society, and bring about a coincidence of religious and secular-liberal concepts of freedom.

All three of these currents of thought have lengthy historical roots; the first, predominantly in the modified Puritan Protestantism of the "free church" variety; the second, in early American deism and rationalism; the third, in less specific sources, but importantly in the type of Protestantism, peculiar to America, whose character was specified during the Great Awakening, when the American climate did as much to influence Protestantism as Protestantism did to influence the American climate. This more radical secularizing Protestantism has in common with the later Puritan tradition the notion that American democratic institutions are the necessary secular reflection of Protestant anti-authoritarian religious individualism and its concept of the "gathered" church. Protestantism and Americanism, it is held, are indissolubly wedded as respectively the religious and the secular aspects of the one manner of belief, the one way of life.

This is not the place to argue the question, whether and how far any of these views can be sustained as a historical thesis. What matters here is a different question, whether any of them can serve as a rule of interpretation of the First Amendment. What is in question is the meaning and the content of the first of our American prejudices, not its genesis. Do these clauses assert or imply that the nature of the church is such that it inherently demands the most absolute separation from the state? Do they assert or imply that the institutional church is simply a voluntary association of like-minded men; that its origins are only in the will of men to associate freely for purposes of religion and worship; that all churches, since their several origins are in equally valid religious inspirations, stand on a footing of equality in the face of the divine and evangelical law; that all ought by the same token to stand on an equal footing in the face of civil law? In a word, does separation of church and state in the American sense assert or imply a particular sectarian concept of the church?

Further, does the free-exercise clause assert or imply that the individual conscience is the ultimate norm of religious belief in such wise that an external religious authority is inimical to Christian freedom? Does it hold that religion is a purely private matter in such wise that an ecclesiastical religion is inherently a corruption of the Christian Gospel? Does it maintain that true religion is religion-in-general, and that the various sects in their dividedness are as repugnant religiously as they are politically dangerous? Does it pronounce religious truth to be simply a matter of personal experience, and religious faith to be simply a matter of subjective impulse, not related to any objective order of truth or to any structured economy of salvation whose consistence is not dependent on the human will?

The questions could be multiplied, but they all reduce themselves to two. Is the no-establishment clause a piece of ecclesiology, and is the free-exercise clause a piece of religious philosophy? The general Protestant tendency, visible at its extreme in the free-church tradition, especially among the Baptists, is to answer affirmatively to these questions. Freedom of religion and separation of church and state are to be, in the customary phrase, "rooted in religion itself." Their substance is to be conceived in terms of sectarian Protestant doctrine. They are therefore articles of faith; not to give them a religious assent is to fall into heterodoxy.

The secularist dissents from the Protestant theological and philosophical exegesis of the first of our prejudices. But it is to him likewise an article of faith (he might prefer to discard the word, "faith," and speak rather of ultimate presuppositions). Within this group also there are differences of opinion. Perhaps the most sharpened view is taken by those who in their pursuit of truth reject not only the traditional methods of Christian illumination, both Protestant and Catholic, but also the reflective methods of metaphysical inquiry.

These men commit themselves singly to the method of scientific empiricism. There is therefore no eternal order of truth and justice; there are no universal verities that require man's assent, no universal moral law that commands his obedience. Such an order of universals is not empirically demonstrable. Truth therefore is to be understood in a positivistic sense; its criteria are either those of science or those of practical life, i.e., the success of an opinion in getting itself accepted in the market place. With this view of truth there goes a corresponding view of freedom. The essence of freedom is "non-committalism." I take the word from Gordon Keith Chalmers. He calls it a "sin," but in the school of thought in question it is the highest virtue. To be uncommitted is to be in the state of grace; for a prohibition of commitment is inherent in the very notion of freedom. The mind or will that is committed, absolutely and finally, is by definition not free. It has fallen from grace by violating its own free nature. In the intellectual enterprise the search for truth, not truth itself or its possession, is the highest value. In the order of morals the norm for man is never reached by knowledge. It is only approximated by inspired guesses or by tentative practical rules that are the precipitate of experience, substantiated only by their utility.

This school of thought, which is of relatively recent growth in America, thrusts into the First Amendment its own ultimate views of truth, freedom, and religion. Religion itself is not a value, except insofar as its ambiguous reassurances may have the emotional effect of conveying reassurance. Roman Catholicism is a disvalue. Nevertheless, religious freedom, as a form of freedom, is a value. It has at least the negative value of an added emancipation, another sheer release. It may also have the positive value of another blow struck at the principle of authority in any of its forms; for in this school authority is regarded as absolutely antinomous to freedom.

Furthermore, this school usually reads into the First Amendment a more or less articulated political theory. Civil society is the highest societal form of human life; even the values that are called spiritual and moral are values by reason of their reference to society. Civil law is the highest form of law and it is not subject to judgment by prior ethical canons. Civil rights are the highest form of rights; for the dignity of the person, which grounds these rights, is only his civil dignity. The state is purely the instrument of the popular will, than which there is no higher sovereignty. Government is to the citizen what the cab-driver is to the passenger (to use Yves Simon's descriptive metaphor). And since the rule of the majority is the method whereby the popular will expresses itself, it is the highest governing principle of statecraft, from which there is no appeal. Finally, the ultimate value within society and state does not consist in any substantive ends that these societal forms may pursue; rather it consists in the process of their pursuit. That is to say, the ultimate value resides in the forms of the democratic process itself, because these forms embody the most ultimate of all values, freedom. There are those who pursue this theory to paradoxical lengths—perhaps more exactly, to the lengths of logical absurdity—by maintaining that if the forms of democracy perish through the use of them by men intent on their destruction, well then, so be it.

Given this political theory, the churches are inevitably englobed within the state, as private associations organized for particular purposes. They possess their title to existence from positive law. Their right to freedom is a civil right, and it is respected as long as it is not understood to include any claim to independently sovereign authority. Such a claim must be disallowed on grounds of the final and indivisible sovereignty of the democratic process over all the associational aspects of human life. The notion that any church should acquire status in public life as a society in its own right is per se absurd; for there is only one society, civil society, which may so exist. In this view, separation of church and state, as ultimately implying a subordination of church to state, follows from the very nature of the state and its law; just as religious freedom follows from the very nature of freedom and of truth.

The foregoing is a sort of anatomical description of two interpretations of the religion clauses of the First Amendment. The description is made anatomical in order to point the issue. If these clauses are made articles of faith in either of the described senses, there are immediately in this country some 35,000,000 dissenters, the Catholic community. Not being either a Protestant or a secularist, the Catholic rejects the religious position of Protestants with regard to the nature of the church, the meaning of faith, the absolute primacy of conscience, etc.; just as he rejects secularist views with regard to the nature of truth, freedom, and civil society as man's last end. He rejects these positions as demonstrably erroneous in themselves. What is more to the point here, he rejects the notion that any of these sectarian theses enter into the content or implications of the First Amendment in such wise as to demand the assent of all American citizens. If this were the case the very article that bars any establishment of religion would somehow establish one. (Given the controversy between Protestant and secularist, there would be the added difficulty that one could not know just what religion had been established.)

If it be true that the First Amendment is to be given a theological interpretation and that therefore it must be "believed," made an object of religious faith, it would follow that a religious test has been thrust into the Constitution. The Federal Republic has suddenly become a voluntary fellowship of believers either in some sort of free-church Protestantism or in the tenets of a naturalistic humanism. The notion is preposterous. The United States is a good place to live in; many have found it even a sort of secular sanctuary. But it is not a church, whether high, low, or broad. It is simply a civil community, whose unity is purely political, consisting in "agreement on the good of man at the level of performance without the necessity of agreement on ultimates" (to adopt a phrase from the 1945 Harvard Report on General Education in a Free Society). As regards important points of ultimate religious belief, the United States is pluralist. Any attempt at reducing this pluralism by law, through a process of reading certain sectarian tenets into the fundamental law of the land, is prima facie illegitimate and absurd.

Theologians of the First Amendment, whether Protestant or secularist, are accustomed to appeal to history. They stress the importance of ideological factors in the genesis of the American concept of freedom of religion and separation of church and state. However, these essays in theological history are never convincing. In the end it is always Roger Williams to whom appeal is made. Admittedly, he was the only man in pre-Federal America who had a consciously articulated theory. The difficulty is that the Williams who is appealed to is a Williams who never was. Prof. Perry Miller's book, *Roger Williams*,[1] is useful in this respect. Its citations and analyses verify the author's statement: "I have long been persuaded that accounts written in the last century create a figure admirable by the canons of modern secular liberalism, but only distantly related to the actual Williams." The unique genius of Master Roger has been badly obscured by historians of a long-dominant school, now in incipient decline, who tended to see early American history through the climate of opinion generated by the Enlightenment. Their mistake lay in supposing that the haze of this climate actually hung over the early American landscape, whereas in fact it only descended, long after, upon the American universities within which the historians did their writing.

Professor Miller's book enhances the moral grandeur and human attractiveness of Roger Williams. It further makes clear, largely by letting him speak for himself, that he was no child of the Enlightenment born before his time. He was a seventeenth-century Calvinist who somehow had got hold of certain remarkably un-Calvinist ideas on the nature of the political order in its distinction from the church. He then exaggerated this distinction in consequence of his special concept of the discontinuity of the Old and New Testaments and of the utter transcendence of the church in the New Testament, which forbids it to maintain any contacts with the temporal order. In any event, Williams's premises and purposes were not those of the secular liberal democrat, any more than his rigidly orthodox Calvinist theology is that of his Baptist progeny. (One can imagine his horror were he to hear an outstanding Baptist spokesman utter with prideful satisfaction the phrase, "the Americanization of the churches.")

However, this is not the place to explore Williams's ideas, ecclesiastical or political. The point is that his ideas, whatever their worth, had no genetic influence on the First Amendment. Professor Miller makes the point: "Hence, although Williams is celebrated as the prophet of religious freedom, he actually exerted little or no influence on institutional developments in America; only after the conception of liberty for all denominations had triumphed on wholly other grounds did Americans look back on Williams and invest him with his ill-fitting halo." Williams therefore is to be ruled out as the original theologian of the First Amendment. In fact, one must rule out the whole idea that any theologians stood at the origin of this piece of legislation. The truth of history happens to be more prosaic than the fancies of the secular liberals. In seeking an understanding of the first of our prejudices we have to abandon the poetry of those who would make a religion out of freedom of religion and a dogma out of separation of church and state. We have to talk prose, the prose of the Constitution itself, which is an ordinary legal prose having nothing to do with doctrinaire theories.

Articles of Peace

From the standpoint both of history and of contemporary social reality the only tenable position is that the first two articles of the First Amendment are not articles of faith but articles of peace. Like the rest of the Constitution these provisions are the work of lawyers, not of theologians or even of political theorists. They are not true dogma but only good law. That is praise enough. This, I take it, is the Catholic view. But in thus qualifying it I am not marking it out as just another "sectarian" view. It is in fact the only view that a citizen with both historical sense and common sense can take.

That curiously clairvoyant statesman, John C. Calhoun, once observed that "this admirable federal constitution of ours is superior to the wisdom of any or all the men by whose agency it was made. The force of circumstances and not foresight or wisdom induced them to adopt many of its wisest provisions." The observation is particularly pertinent to the religion clauses of the First Amendment. If history makes one thing clear it is that these clauses were the twin children of social necessity, the necessity of creating a social environment, protected by law, in which men of differing religious faiths might live together in peace. In his stimulating book, *The Genius of American Politics*,[2] Prof. Daniel Boorstin says: "The impression which the American has as he looks about him is one of the inevitability of the particular institutions under which he lives." This mark of inevitability is an index of goodness. And it is perhaps nowhere more strikingly manifest than in the institutions which govern the relation of government to religion. These institutions seem to have been preformed in the peculiar conditions of American society. It did indeed take some little time before the special American solution to the problem of religious pluralism worked itself out; but it is almost inconceivable that it should not have worked itself out as it did. One suspects that this would have been true even if there had been no Williamses and Penns, no Calverts and Madisons and Jeffersons. The theories of these men, whatever their merits, would probably have made only literature not history, had it not been for the special social context into which they were projected. Similarly, the theories of these men, whatever their defects, actually made history because they exerted their pressure, such as it was, in the direction in which historical factors were already moving the new American society.

To say this is not of course to embrace a theory of historical or social determinism. It is only to say that the artisans of the American Republic and its Constitution were not radical theorists intent on constructing a society in accord with the a priori demands of a doctrinaire blueprint, under disregard for what was actually "given" in history. Fortunately they were, as I said, for the most part lawyers. And they had a strong sense of that primary criterion of good law which is its necessity or utility for the preservation of the public peace, under a given set of conditions. All law looks to the common good, which is normative for all law. And social peace, assured by equal justice in dealing with possibly conflicting groups, is the highest integrating element of the common good. This legal criterion is the first and most solid ground on which the validity of the First Amendment rests.

Every historian who has catalogued the historical factors which made for religious liberty and separation of church and state in America would doubtless agree that these institutions came into being under the pressure of their necessity for the public peace. Four leading factors, contributory to this necessity, are usually listed.

First, there was the great mass of the unchurched. They were either people cut off from religion by the conditions of frontier life; or people careless of religion in consequence of preoccupation with the material concerns of this world; or people concerned with religion as indispensable to morality and therefore to ordered civil life, but unconcerned with, or even hostile toward, what is called organized religion. The fact may be embarrassing to the highminded believer, but it is nevertheless a fact that the development of religious freedom in society bears a distinct relationship to the growth of unbelief and indifference. Our historical good fortune lay in the particular kind of unbelief that American society has known. It was not Continental laicism, superficially anticlerical, fundamentally antireligious, militant in its spirit, active in its purpose to destroy what it regarded as hateful. Unbelief in America has been rather easy-going, the product more of a naive materialism than of any conscious conviction. The American unbeliever is usually content to say, "I am not personally a religious man," and let the subject drop there. American unbelief is usually respectful of belief, or at least respectful of the freedom to believe. And this fact has been important in influencing the general climate in which our institutions work.

The second factor was the multiplicity of denominations. This was Protestantism's decisive contribution to the cause of religious freedom—decisive because made at a time when the rapidly proliferating denominations were less disposed than they now are to live together in peace. This fact made it necessary to seek a basis for political unity other than the hitherto prevailing one, agreement in religious faith and ecclesiastical polity. Figgis's famous dictum, "Political liberty is the residuary legatee of ecclesiastical animosities," is a historical half-truth. It is not the whole of the truth even in the matter of religious liberty. But the truth in it cannot be denied. In this sense the Cottons and the Mathers made their contribution to American freedom of religion no less, and perhaps more, than the Williamses and Penns. The sheer fact of dissent and sectarian antagonisms was a particularly important motive of the Federal constitutional arrangements; for at that time four states still retained establishments of various kinds. One recalls John Adams's testy reluctance to hear any argument about disestablishment in Massachusetts.

Thirdly, the economic factor was by no means unimportant. It was present in the somewhat impenetrable thinking of the two Calverts. The merchants of New Jersey, New York, Virginia, and the more southern colonies were as emphatically on the side of religious freedom as on the side of commercial profits. Persecution and discrimination were as bad for business affairs as they were for the affairs of the soul.

A fourth factor of lesser importance was the pressure, not indeed very great but real enough, exerted by the widening of religious freedom in England. This growth had been fostered by the same factors that were operating more strongly in America. Anglicanism and Nonconformism were engaged in a struggle whose issue was already becoming clear. It was not to be disestablishment; Burke's prejudice, widely shared, would be too strong to permit that. But it would at least be religious freedom (except for Catholics), conjoined with establishment. In America, where the ground was clear for the creation of a new prejudice, the development could go all the way.

These four factors, taken as a sociological complex, made it sufficiently clear to all reasonable men that under American conditions any other course but freedom of religion and separation of church and state would have been disruptive, imprudent, impractical, indeed impossible. The demands of social necessity were overwhelming. It remains only to insist that in regarding the religion clauses of the First Amendment as articles of peace and in placing the case for them on the primary grounds of their social necessity, one is not taking low ground. Such a case does not appeal to mean-spirited expediency nor does it imply a reluctant concession to *force majeure*. In the science of law and the art of jurisprudence the appeal to social peace is an appeal to a high moral value. Behind the will to social peace there stands a divine and Christian imperative. This is the classic and Christian tradition.

Roger Williams himself was a powerful spokesman of it. "Sweet peace" (the phrase he uses in *The Bloudy Tenent*) stands at the center of his doctrine; and he adds in the same context that "if it be possible, it is the express command of God that peace be kept." In a letter of 1671 to John Cotton the younger he recalls with satisfaction that his second great work, *The Bloudy Tenent Still More Bloudy*, was received in England "with applause and thanks" as "professing that of necessity, yea, of Christian equity, there could be no reconciliation, pacification, or living together but by permitting of dissenting consciences to live amongst them." There is also, along with others, the strong statement with which he concludes his pamphlet, *The Hireling Ministry None of Christ's*. As the sum of the matter he proclaims the duty of the civil state in the current conditions of religious division "to proclaim free and impartial liberty to all the people of the three nations to choose and maintain what worship and ministry their souls and consciences are persuaded of; which act, as it will prove an act of mercy and righteousness to the enslaved nations, so it is a binding force to engage the whole and every interest and conscience to preserve the common freedom and peace." This is the way whereby "civil peace and the beauty of civilty and humanity [may] be obtained among the chief opposers and dissenters."

Roger Williams was no partisan of the view that all religions ought to be equally free because, for all anybody knows, they may all be equally true or false. He reckons with truth and falsity in honest fashion. Yet even in the case of a "false religion (unto which the civil magistrate dare not adjoin)" he recommends as the first duty of the civil magistrate "permission (for approbation he owes not what is evil) and this according to Matthew 13:30, for public peace and quiet's sake." The reference is to the parable of the tares.

It is interesting that this same parable is referred to by Pius XII in his discourse to a group of Italian jurists on December 6, 1953. This discourse is a strong affirmation of the primacy of the principle of peace (or "union," which is the Pope's synonymous word) when it comes to dealing with the "difficulties and tendencies" which arise out of mankind's multiple pluralisms and dissensions. The "fundamental theoretical principle," says the Pope (and one should underscore the word, "theoretical"; it is not a question of sheer pragmatism, much less of expediency in the low sense), is this: "within the limits of the possible and the lawful, to promote everything that facilitates union and makes it more effective; to remove everything that disturbs it; to tolerate at times that which it is impossible to correct but which on the other hand must not be permitted to make shipwreck of the community from which a higher good is looked for." This higher good, in the context of the whole discourse, is "the establishment of peace."

From this firm footing of traditional principle the Pope proceeds to reject the view that would "solve" the problem of religious pluralism on the ultimate basis of this doctrinaire argument: Religious and moral error have no rights and therefore must always be repressed when repression of them is possible. In contradiction of this view the Pope says, after quoting the parable of the tares: "The duty of repressing religious and moral error cannot therefore be an ultimate norm of action. It must be subordinated to higher and more general norms which in some circumstances permit, and even perhaps make it appear the better course of action, that error should not be impeded in order to promote a greater good." The Pope makes a clear distinction between the abstract order of ethics or theology, where it is a question of qualifying doctrines or practices as true or false, right or wrong, and the concrete order of jurisprudence, where it is a question of using or not using the coercive instrument of law in favor of the true and good, against the false and wrong. In this latter order the highest and most general norm is the public peace, the common good in its various aspects. This is altogether a moral norm.

Roger Williams had many a quarrel with the Roman papacy; in fact, he wanted it abolished utterly. It is therefore piquant in itself, and also a testimony to the strength of the hold that the central Christian tradition had upon him, to read this basic principle of Catholic teaching in the *Bloudy Tenent*: "It must be remembered that it is one thing to command, to conceal, to approve evil; and another thing to permit and suffer evil with protestation against it or dislike of it, at least without approbation of it. This sufferance or permission of evil is not for its own sake but for the sake of the good, which puts a respect of goodness upon such permission." The "good" here is the public peace. Williams concludes the passage thus: "And therefore, when it crosseth not an absolute rule to permit and tolerate (as in the case of the permission of the souls and consciences of all men of the world), it will not hinder our being holy as He is holy in all manner of conversation." In substance Pius XII says the same thing, that it crosseth not an absolute rule to permit within the civil community, as he says, "the free exercise of a belief and of a religious and moral practice which possess validity" in the eyes of some of its members.

In fact, the Pope goes much further when he flatly states that "in certain circumstances God does not give men any mandate, does not impose any duty, and does not even communicate the right to impede or to repress what is erroneous and false." The First Amendment is simply the legal enunciation of this papal statement. It does not say that there is no distinction between true and false religion, good and bad morality. But it does say that in American circumstances the conscience of the community, aware of its moral obligations to the peace of the community, and speaking therefore as the voice of God, does not give government any mandate, does not impose upon it any duty, and does not even communicate to it the right to repress religious opinions or practices, even though they are erroneous and false.

On these grounds it is easy to see why the Catholic conscience has always consented to the religion clauses of the Constitution. They conform to the highest criterion for all legal rulings in this delicate matter. The criterion is moral; therefore the law that meets it is good, because it is for the common good. Therefore the consent given to the law is given on grounds of moral principle. To speak of expediency here is altogether to misunderstand the moral nature of the community and its collective moral obligation toward its own common good. The origins of our fundamental law are in moral principle; the obligations it imposes are moral obligations, binding in conscience. One may not, without moral fault, act against these articles of peace.

The Distinction of Church and State

If the demands of social necessity account for the emergence in America of religious freedom as a fact, they hardly account for certain peculiarities of the first of our prejudices and for the depth of feeling that it evokes. Another powerful historical force must be considered, namely, the dominant impulse toward self-government, government by the people in the most earnest sense of the word. Above all else the early Americans wanted political freedom. And the force of this impulse necessarily acted as a corrosive upon the illegitimate "unions" of church and state which the post-Reformation era had brought forth. The establishments of the time were, by and large, either theocratic, wherein the state was absorbed in the church, or Erastian, wherein the church was absorbed in the state. In both cases the result was some limitation upon freedom, either in the form of civil disabilities imposed in the name of the established religion, or in the form of religious disabilities imposed in the name of the civil law of the covenanted community. The drive toward popular freedom would with a certain inevitability sweep away such establishments. Men might share the fear of Roger Williams, that the state would corrupt the church, or the fear of Thomas Jefferson, that the church would corrupt the state. In either case their thought converged to the one important conclusion, that an end had to be put to the current confusions of the religious and political orders. The ancient distinction between church and state had to be newly reaffirmed in a manner adapted to the American scene. Calvinist theocracy, Anglican Erastianism, Gallican absolutism—all were vitiated by the same taint: they violated in one way or another this traditional distinction.

The dualism of mankind's two hierarchically ordered forms of social life had been Christianity's cardinal contribution to the Western political tradition, as everyone knows who has looked into the monumental work of the two Carlyles, *Medieval Political Thought in the West*. Perhaps equally with the very idea of law itself it had been the most fecund force for freedom in society. The distinction had always been difficult to maintain in practice, even when it was affirmed in theory. But when it was formally denied the result was an infringement of man's freedom of religious faith or of his freedom as a citizen—an infringement of either or both. Hence the generalized American impulse toward freedom inevitably led to a new and specially emphatic affirmation of the traditional distinction.

The distinction lay readily within the reach of the early American lawyers and statesmen; for it was part of the English legal heritage, part of the patrimony of the common law. One can see it appearing, for instance, in Madison's famous *Memorial and Remonstrance*, where it is interpreted in a manner conformable to the anti-ecclesiasticism which he had in common with Jefferson. But the interesting figure here is again Roger Williams. Reading him, the Catholic theorist is inclined to agree with those "juditious persons" whose verdict was reluctantly and belatedly recorded by Cotton Mather. They "judged him," said Mather, "to have the root of the matter in him."

In the present question the root of the matter is this distinction of the spiritual and temporal orders and their respective jurisdictions. One is tempted to think that he got hold of this root at least partly because of his early acquaintance with English law. He was for a time secretary to the great Sir Edward Coke and it is at least not unlikely that he continued his legal interests at Cambridge. In any event, this distinction was a key principle with Williams. He had his own special understanding of it, but at least he understood it. What is more, in 1636 he felt in his own flesh, so to speak, the effects of its violations in the Massachusetts colony. Of his banishment from Massachusetts in that year he later wrote: "Secondly, if he (John Cotton) means this civil act of banishing, why should he call a civil sentence from a civil state, within a few weeks execution in so sharp a time of New England's cold, why should he call this a banishment from the churches except he silently confess that the frame or constitution of their churches is implicitly national (which yet they profess against)? For otherwise, why was I not yet permitted to live in the world or commonweal except for this reason, that the commonweal and church is yet but one, and he that is banished from the one must necessarily be banished from the other also?" This was his constant accusation against the New England Way. He says on another occasion: "First, it will appear that in spiritual things they make the garden and the wilderness (as I often have intimated), I say, the garden and the wilderness, the church and the world are all one." The same charge is lodged against "holy men, emperors and bishops" throughout history, that "they made the garden of the church and the field of the world to be all one. . . ."

However erroneously Williams may have understood the "garden," the church, as having no relation whatsoever to the "wilderness," at least he knew that church and civil society are not one but two. To make them "all one" is to violate the nature of the church and also the nature of civil society, as this latter had been understood in the liberal Christian political tradition.

As has been said, Roger Williams was not a Father of the Federal Constitution. He is adduced here only as a witness, in his own way, to the genuine Western tradition of politics. The point is that the distinction of church and state, one of the central assertions of this tradition, found its way into the Constitution. There it received a special embodiment, adapted to the peculiar genius of American government and to the concrete conditions of American society.

How this happened need not concern us here. Certainly it was in part because the artisans of the Constitution had a clear grasp of the distinction between state and society, which had been the historical product of the distinction between church and state, inasmuch as the latter distinction asserted the existence of a whole wide area of human concerns which were remote from the competence of government. Calhoun's "force of circumstances" also had a great deal of influence; here again it was a matter of the Fathers building better than they knew. Their major concern was sharply to circumscribe the powers of government. The area of state—that is, legal— concern was limited to the pursuit of certain enumerated secular purposes (to say that the purposes are secular is not to deny that many of them are also moral; so for instance the establishment of justice and peace, the promotion of the general welfare, etc.). Thus made autonomous in its own sphere, government was denied all competence in the field of religion. In this field freedom was to be the rule and method; government was powerless to legislate respecting an establishment of religion and likewise powerless to prohibit the free exercise of religion. Its single office was to take legal or judicial steps necessary on given occasions to make effective the general guarantee of freedom.

The concrete applications of this, in itself quite simple, solution have presented great historical and legal difficulties. This has been inevitable, given the intimacy with which religion is woven into the whole social fabric, and given, too, the evolution of government from John Adams's "plain, simple, intelligible thing, quite comprehensible by common sense," to the enormously complicated and sprawling thing which now organizes a great part of our lives, handles almost all education, and much social welfare. In particular, we have not yet found an answer to the question whether government can make effective the primary intention of the First Amendment, the guarantee of freedom of religion, simply by attempting to make more and more "impregnable" what is called, in Rogers Williams' fateful metaphor, the "wall of separation" between church and state. However, what concerns us here is the root of the matter, the fact that the American Constitution embodies in a special way the traditional principle of the distinction between church and state.

For Catholics this fact is of great and providential importance for one major reason. It serves sharply to set off our constitutional system from the system against which the Church waged its long-drawn-out fight in the nineteenth century, namely, Jacobinism, or (in Carlton Hayes's term) sectarian Liberalism, or (in the more definitive term used today) totalitarian democracy.

It is now coming to be recognized that the Church opposed the "separation of church and state" of the sectarian Liberals because in theory and in fact it did not mean separation at all but perhaps the most drastic unification of church and state which history had known. The Jacobin "free state" was as regalist as the *ancien régime*, and even more so. Writing as a historian, de Tocqueville long ago made this plain. And the detailed descriptions which Leo XIII, writing as a theologian and political moralist, gave of the Church's "enemy" make the fact even more plain. Within this "free state" the so-called "free church" was subject to a political control more complete than the Tudor or Stuart or Bourbon monarchies dreamed of. The evidence stretches all the way from the Civil Constitution of the Clergy in 1790 to the Law of Separation in 1905.

In the system sponsored by the sectarian Liberals, as has been well said, "The state pretends to ignore the Church; in reality it never took more cognizance of her." In the law of 1905, the climactic development, the Church was arrogantly assigned a juridical statute articulated in forty-four articles, whereby almost every aspect of her organization and action was minutely regulated. Moreover, this was done on principle—the principle of the primacy of the political, the principle of "everything within the state, nothing above the state." This was the cardinal thesis of sectarian Liberalism, whose full historical development is now being witnessed in the totalitarian "people's democracies" behind the Iron Curtain. As the Syllabus and its explicatory documents—as well as the multitudinous writings of Leo XIII—make entirely clear, it was this thesis of the juridical omnipotence and omnicompetence of the state which was the central object of the Church's condemnation of the Jacobin development. It was because freedom of religion and separation of church and state were predicated on this thesis that the Church refused to accept them as a thesis.

This thesis was utterly rejected by the founders of the American Republic. The rejection was as warranted as it was providential, because this thesis is not only theologically heterodox, as denying the reality of the Church; it is also politically revolutionary, as denying the substance of the liberal tradition. The American thesis is that government is not juridically omnipotent. Its powers are limited, and one of the principles of limitation is the distinction between state and church, in their purposes, methods, and manner of organization. The Jacobin thesis was basically philosophical; it derived from a sectarian concept of the autonomy of reason. It was also theological, as implying a sectarian concept of religion and of the church. In contrast, the American thesis is simply political. It asserts the theory of a free people under a limited government, a theory that is recognizably part of the Christian political tradition, and altogether defensible in the manner of its realization under American circumstances.

It may indeed be said that the American constitutional system exaggerates the distinction between church and state by its self-denying ordinances. However, it must also be said that government rarely appears to better advantage than when passing self-denying ordinances. In any event, it is one thing to exaggerate a traditional distinction along the lines of its inherent tendency; it is quite another thing to abolish the distinction. In the latter case the result is a vicious monistic society; in the former, a faultily dualistic one. The vice in the Jacobin system could only be condemned by the Church, not in any way condoned. The fault in the American system can be recognized as such, without condemnation. There are times and circumstances, Chesterton jocosely said, when it is necessary to exaggerate in order to tell the truth. There are also times and circumstances, one may more seriously say, when some exaggeration of the restrictions placed on government is necessary in order to insure freedom. These circumstances of social necessity were and are present in America.

The Freedom of the Church

Here then is the second leading reason why the American solution to the problem of religious pluralism commends itself to the Catholic conscience. In the discourse already cited Pius XII states, as the two cardinal purposes of a Concordat, first, "to assure to the Church a stable condition of right and of fact within society," and second, "to guarantee to her a full independence in the fulfillment of her divine mission." It may be maintained that both of these objectives are sufficiently achieved by the religious provisions of the First Amendment. It is obvious that the Church in America enjoys a stable condition in fact. That her status at law is not less stable ought to be hardly less obvious, if only one has clearly in mind the peculiarity of the American affirmation of the distinction between church and state. This affirmation is made through the imposition of limits on government, which is confined to its own proper ends, those of temporal society. In contrast to the Jacobin system in all its forms, the

American Constitution does not presume to define the Church or in any way to supervise her exercise of authority in pursuit of her own distinct ends. The Church is entirely free to define herself and to exercise to the full her spiritual jurisdiction. It is legally recognized that there is an area which lies outside the competence of government. This area coincides with the area of the divine mission of the Church, and within this area the Church is fully independent, immune from interference by political authority.

The juridical result of the American limitation of governmental powers is the guarantee to the Church of a stable condition of freedom as a matter of law and right. It should be added that this guarantee is made not only to the individual Catholic but to the Church as an organized society with its own law and jurisdiction. The reason is that the American state is not erected on the principle of the unity and indivisibility of sovereignty which was the post-Renaissance European development. Nowhere in the American structure is there accumulated the plenitude of legal sovereignty possessed in England by the Queen in Parliament. In fact, the term "legal sovereignty" makes no sense in America, where sovereignty (if the alien term must be used) is purely political. The United States has a government, or better, a structure of governments operating on different levels. The American state has no sovereignty in the classic Continental sense. Within society, as distinct from the state, there is room for the independent exercise of an authority which is not that of the state. This principle has more than once been affirmed by American courts, most recently by the Supreme Court in the *Kedroff* case. The validity of this principle strengthens the stability of the Church's condition at law.

Perhaps the root of the matter, as hitherto described, might be seen summed up in an incident of early American and Church history. This is Leo Pfeffer's account of it in his book, *Church, State and Freedom:*[3]

> In 1783 the papal nuncio at Paris addressed a note to Benjamin Franklin suggesting that, since it was no longer possible to maintain the previous status whereunder American Catholics were subject to the Vicar Apostolic at London, the Holy See proposed to Congress that a Catholic bishopric be established in one of the American cities. Franklin transmitted the note to the [Continental] Congress, which directed Franklin to notify the nuncio that "the subject of his application to Doctor Franklin being purely

spiritual, it is without the jurisdiction and powers of Congress, who have no authority to permit or refuse it, these powers being reserved to the several states individually." (Not many years later the several states would likewise declare themselves to "have no authority to permit or refuse" such a purely spiritual exercise of ecclesiastical jurisdiction.)

The good nuncio must have been mightily surprised on receiving this communication. Not for centuries had the Holy See been free to erect a bishopric and appoint a bishop without the prior consent of government, without prior exercise of the governmental right of presentation, without all the legal formalities with which Catholic states had fettered the freedom of the Church. In the United States the freedom of the Church was completely unfettered; she could organize herself with the full independence which is her native right. This, it may be confidently said, was a turning point in the long and complicated history of church-state relations.

The American Experience

One final ground for affirming the validity of the religion clauses of the First Amendment as good law must be briefly touched on. Holmes's famous dictum, "The life of the law is not logic but experience," has more truth in it than many other Holmesian dicta. When a law ceases to be supported by a continued experience of its goodness, it becomes a dead letter, an empty legal form. Although pure pragmatism cannot be made the philosophy of law, nonetheless the value of any given law is importantly pragmatic. The First Amendment surely passes this test of good law. In support of it one can adduce an American experience. One might well call it *the* American experience in the sense that it has been central in American history and also unique in the history of the world.

This experience has three facets, all interrelated.

First, America has proved by experience that political unity and stability are possible without uniformity of religious belief and practice, without the necessity of any governmental restrictions on any religion. Before the days of the Federal Republic some men had tried to believe that this could be so; thus for instance the *politiques* in France, in their attack upon the classic Gallican and absolutist thesis, "One law, one faith, one king." But this thesis, and its equivalents, had not been disproved.

This event was accomplished in the United States by an argument from experience. For a century and a half the United States has displayed to the world the fact that political unity and stability are not necessarily dependent on the common sharing of one religious faith.

The reach of this demonstration is, of course, limited. Granted that the unity of the commonwealth can be achieved in the absence of a consensus with regard to the theological truths that govern the total life and destiny of man, it does not follow that this necessary civic unity can endure in the absence of a consensus more narrow in its scope, operative on the level of political life, with regard to the rational truths and moral precepts that govern the structure of the constitutional state, specify the substance of the common weal, and determine the ends of public policy. Nor has experience yet shown how, if at all, this moral consensus can survive amid all the ruptures of religious division, whose tendency is inherently disintegrative of all consensus and community. But this is a further question, for the future to answer. I shall have occasion in later chapters to discuss this whole question of the American consensus and its present condition among us.

The second American experience was that stable political unity, which means perduring agreement on the common good of man at the level of performance, can be strengthened by the exclusion of religious differences from the area of concern allotted to government. In America we have been rescued from the disaster of ideological parties. They are a disaster because, where such parties exist, power becomes a special kind of prize. The struggle for power is a partisan struggle for the means whereby the opposing ideology may be destroyed. It has been remarked that only in a disintegrating society does politics become a controversy over ends; it should be simply a controversy over means to ends already agreed on with sufficient unanimity. The Latin countries of Europe have displayed this spectacle of ideological politics, a struggle between a host of "isms," all of which pretend to a final view of man and society, with the twin results of governmental paralysis and seemingly irremediable social division. In contrast, the American experience of political unity has been striking. (Even the Civil War does not refute this view; it was not an ideological conflict but simply, in the more descriptive Southern phrase, a war between the states, a conflict of interests.) To this experience of political unity the First Amendment has made a unique contribution; and in doing so it has qualified as good law.

The third and most striking aspect of the American experience consists in the fact that religion itself, and not least the Catholic Church, has benefited by our free institutions, by the maintenance, even in exaggerated form, of the distinction between church and state. Within the same span of history the experience of the Church elsewhere, especially in the Latin lands, has been alternately an experience of privilege or persecution. The reason lay in a particular concept of government. It was alternatively the determination of government to ally itself either with the purposes of the Church or with the purposes of some sect or other (sectarian Liberalism, for instance) which made a similar, however erroneous, claim to possess the full and final truth. The dominant conviction, whose origins are really in pagan antiquity, was that government should represent transcendent truth and by its legal power make this truth prevail. However, in the absence of social agreement as to what the truth really was, the result was to involve the Catholic truth in the vicissitudes of power. It would be difficult to say which experience, privilege or persecution, proved in the end to be the more damaging or gainful to the Church.

In contrast, American government has not undertaken to represent transcendental truth in any of the versions of it current in American society. It does indeed represent the commonly shared moral values of the community. It also represents the supreme religious truth expressed in the motto on American coins: "In God we trust." The motto expresses the two truths without which, as the Letter to the Hebrews says, "nobody reaches God's presence," namely, "to believe that God exists and that he rewards those who try to find him" (Hebrews 11:6). For the rest, government represents the truth of society as it actually is; and the truth is that American society is religiously pluralist. The truth is lamentable; it is nonetheless true. Many of the beliefs entertained within society ought not to be believed, because they are false; nonetheless men believe them. It is not the function of government to resolve the dispute between conflicting truths, all of which claim the final validity of transcendence. As representative of a pluralist society, wherein religious faith is—as it must be—free, government undertakes to represent the principle of freedom.

In taking this course American government would seem to be on the course set by Pius XII for the religiously pluralist international community, of which America offers, as it were, a pattern in miniature. In the discourse already cited he distinguishes two questions: "The first concerns the objective truth and the obligation of conscience toward that which is objectively true and good." This question, he goes on, "can hardly be made the object of discussion and ruling among the individual states and their communities, especially in the case of a plurality of religious confessions within the same community." In other words, government is not a judge of religious truth; parliaments are not to play the theologian. In accord with this principle American government does not presume to discuss, much less rule upon, the objective truth or falsity of the various religious confessions within society. It puts to itself only Pius XII's second question, which concerns "the practical attitude" of government in the face of religious pluralism. It answers this question by asserting that in the given circumstances it has neither the mandate nor the duty nor the right to legislate either in favor of or against any of the religious confessions existent in American society, which in its totality government must represent. It will therefore only represent their freedom, in the face of civil law, to exist, since they do in fact exist. This is precisely the practical attitude which Pius XII recognizes as right, as the proper moral and political course.

In consequence of this American concept of the representative function of government the experience of the Church in America, like the general American experience itself, has proved to be satisfactory when one scans it from the viewpoint of the value upon which the Church sets primary importance, namely, her freedom in the fulfillment of her spiritual mission to communicate divine truth and grace to the souls of men, and her equally spiritual mission of social justice and peace. The Church has not enjoyed a privileged status in public life; at the same time she has not had to pay the price of this privilege. A whole book could be written on the price of such legal privilege. Another book could be written on the value of freedom without privilege. In fact, both books have been written, on the metaphorical pages of history. And looking over his own continually unrolling historical manuscript the American Catholic is inclined to conclude that his is a valid book.

It does not develop a doctrinal thesis, but it does prove a practical point. The point is that the goodness of the First Amendment as constitutional law is manifested not only by political but also by religious experience. By and large (for no historical record is without blots) it has been good for religion, for Catholicism, to have had simply the right of freedom. This right is at the same time the highest of privileges, and it too has its price. But the price has not been envy and enmity, the coinage in which the Church paid for privilege. It has only been the price of sacrifice, labor, added responsibilities; and these things are redemptive.

Conclusion

In the final analysis any validation of the First Amendment as good law—no matter by whom undertaken, be he Protestant, Catholic, Jew, or secularist—must make appeal to the three arguments developed above—the demands of social necessity, the rightfulness within our own circumstances of the American manner of asserting the distinction between church and state, and the lessons of experience. Perhaps the last argument is the most powerful. It is also, I may add, the argument which best harmonizes with the general tone which arguments for our institutions are accustomed to adopt.

In a curiously controlling way this tone was set by the *Federalist* papers. These essays were not political treatises after the manner of Hobbes and Hegel, Rousseau and Comte, or even John Locke. It has been remarked that in America no treatises of this kind have been produced; and it is probably just as well. The authors of the *Federalist* papers were not engaged in broaching a political theory universal in scope and application, a plan for an Ideal Republic of Truth and Virtue. They were arguing for a particular Constitution, a special kind of governmental structure, a limited ensemble of concrete laws, all designed for application within a given society. They were in the tradition of the Revolutionary thinkers who led a colonial rebellion, not in the name of a set of flamboyant abstractions, but in the name of the sober laws of the British Constitution which they felt were being violated in their regard. It has been pointed out that the only real slogan the Revolution produced was: "No taxation without representation." It has not the ring of a trumpet; its sound is more like the dry rustle of a lawyer's sheaf of parchment.

It is in the tone of this tradition of American political writing that one should argue for the First Amendment. The arguments will tend to be convincing in proportion as their key of utterance approaches a dry rustle and not a wild ring. The arguments here presented are surely dry enough. Perhaps they will not satisfy the American doctrinaire, the theologizer. But they do, I think, show that the first of our prejudices is "not a prejudice destitute of reason, but involving in it profound and extensive wisdom." This is all that need be shown; it is likewise all that can be shown.

The Catholic Church in America is committed to this prejudice by the totality of her experience in American history. As far as I know, the only ones who doubt the firmness, the depth, the principled nature of this commitment are not Catholics. They speak without knowledge and without authority; and the credence they command has its origins in emotion. If perhaps what troubles them is the fact that the commitment is limited, in the sense that it is not to the truth and sanctity of a dogma but only to the rationality and goodness of a law, they might recall the story of Pompey. After the capture of Jerusalem in 63 B.C. he went to the Temple and forced his way into the Holy of Holies. To his intense astonishment he found it empty. He should not have been astonished; for the emptiness was the symbol of the absence of idolatry. It symbolized the essential truth of Judaism, that One is the Lord. Professor Boorstin, who recounts the tale, adds: "Perhaps the same surprise awaits the student of American culture [or, I add, the American Constitution] if he finally manages to penetrate the arcanum of our belief. And for a similar reason. Far from being disappointed, we should be inspired that in an era of idolatry, when so many nations have filled their sanctuaries with ideological idols, we have had the courage to refuse to do so."

The American Catholic is on good ground when he refuses to make an ideological idol out of religious freedom and separation of church and state, when he refuses to "believe" in them as articles of faith. He takes the highest ground available in this matter of the relations between religion and government when he asserts that his commitment to the religion clauses of the Constitution is a moral commitment to them as articles of peace in a pluralist society.

Notes

1. Indianapolis: Bobbs-Merrill, 1953.
2. Chicago: University of Chicago Press, 1953.
3. Boston: Beacon Press, 1953.

~

CHAPTER THREE

Two Cases for the Public Consensus: Fact or Need

Previous chapters have raised the issue of the American consensus, or, what comes to the same thing, the public philosophy of America. (I shall use the terms pretty much synonymously, though there is a nuance of meaning. The term "public philosophy" emphasizes an objectivity of content; the term "consensus" emphasizes a subjectivity of persuasion.) There is no doubt that the issue is today alive in the American mind, in itself and in its relation to broad public problems, notably that of the "national purpose." However, from some experience on lecture platforms and in conversations I have found that the very notion of an American consensus or public philosophy meets considerable opposition.

There are two possible approaches to the subject. First, one can raise the question, does the United States have a public philosophy, or not? When the question is put in this way, it has been my experience that the argument tends to run out in futility. I am therefore inclined to think that the form of the question should be altered. One should ask, whether the United States needs a public philosophy or not. If the question is asked in this way, there may be the possibility of constructive argument.

The Case That Fails

The affirmative case on the question, as put in its first form, can be made in four steps. I shall run through them briefly, since some of the materials of argument have been stated already. The starting point, as I have indicated, is the forthright statement of the Declaration of Independence: "We hold these truths. . . ." That is to say, we have a public philosophy; as a people, we have come to a consensus. This philosophy is the foundation of our public life; by coming to this consensus we have come to be a people, possessed of an identity.

The truths we hold, as a people, belong to the order of philosophical and political truth. (Here I presume that God Himself belongs to the order of reason, in the sense that His existence and sovereignty as the Author of the universe are not inaccessible to human reason.) The truths are the product of reason reflecting on human experience. They are not simply a codification or registration of experience; they are reached by an act of abstraction from experience, which carries the mind of man above the level of experience. Hence the affirmation of these truths pretends to and possesses a certain universal validity. Not only do *we* hold these truths; they are human truths of a sort that man as such is bound to hold.

The second step is to explain the three-fold function of the ensemble of truths that make up the public consensus or philosophy. The first function is to determine the broad purposes of our nation, as a political unity organized for action in history. This determination of purposes is, as always, a moral act. Second, the public philosophy furnishes the standards according to which judgment is to be passed on the means that the nation adopts to further its purposes. These means, in general, are what is called policy. Third, the consensus or public philosophy furnishes the basis of communication between government and the people and among the people themselves. It furnishes a common universe of discourse in which public issues can be intelligibly stated and intelligently argued.

The third step would be to indicate the ideas that form the object of the consensus, the content of the public philosophy. Since the consensus is constitutional, its focal concept is the idea of law. We hold in common a concept of the nature of law and its relationships to reason and to will, to social fact and to political purpose. We understand the complex relationship between law and freedom. We have an idea of the relation between the order of law and the order of morals. We also have an idea of the uses of force in support of law. We have criteria of good law, norms of jurisprudence that judge the necessity of law and determine the limits of its usefulness. We have an idea of justice, which is at once the basis of law and its goal. We have an ideal of social equality and of social unity and of the value of law for the achievement of both. We believe in the principle of consent, in terms of which the order of coercive law makes contact with the freedom of the public conscience. We distinguish between state and society, between the relatively narrow order of law as such and the wider order of the total public good. We understand the relation between law and social progress; we grasp the notion of law as a force for orderly change as well as for social stability. We understand the value of law as a means of educating the public conscience to higher viewpoints on matters of public morality. All these ideas, and others too, of which there will be question in a later chapter, form the essential contents of the consensus.

The argument here should be made to include the notion that the whole consensus has its ultimate root in the idea of the sacredness of man, *res sacra homo*. Man has a sacredness of personal dignity which commands the respect of society in all its laws and institutions. His sacredness guarantees him certain immunities and it also endows him with certain empowerments. He may make certain demands upon society and the state which require action in their support, and he may also utter certain prohibitions in the face of society and state. He may validly claim assistance, and with equal validity he may claim to be let alone.

In its fourth step the case reaches the question of dissent from the consensus. Here the essential point is that the consensus does not "exterminate" dissent, in the ancient sense of the word, *scil.*, by putting dissent or the dissenter beyond the pale of social or civil rights. On the contrary, the consensus supposes and implies dissent. But it remains the function of the consensus to identify dissent as dissent. As for dissent, its function is not to destroy or undermine the consensus but to solidify it and make it more conscious and articulate. This has always been the historical function of error, to contribute to the development of truth. Dissent from the public philosophy serves to stimulate public argument about the philosophy and thus keep the philosophy alive, bring it to refinement, and maintain it in its vital contact with new questions that are always arising under the pressure of constant social change.

These then are the four essential points I should develop in making the affirmative case on the question: Is there or is there not an American consensus, a public philosophy on which the whole order of the Republic rests? The case is only outlined here; these bones would need to be clothed with flesh. And the full case would have to be made both by philosophical and by historical argument.

I have tried to take this affirmative case on more than one public occasion. What is usually the result? Briefly, when the result is not simply a blank stare, it is emphatic negation. The sort of thing that happens may be indicated as follows.

Someone is sure to rise with this question: Sir, you refer to "these truths" as the product of reason; the question is, whose reason? I reply that it is not a question of whose reason but of right reason. But, says the questioner, whose reason is right? And with that question the whole footing is cut from under any discussion of the public philosophy. For the implication is that there can be no philosophy which is public. Philosophy, like religion, is a purely private affair. Indeed, there is no philosophy; there are only philosophies, or better, philosophers. And for all anyone knows or could possibly tell, any of them may be right, or none of them.

Someone else then rises to say that all talk of a public philosophy in America is idle and irrelevant. The argument is that ours is an industrial and technological society; it acknowledges only one value in the end; that value is success; and success in this society can only be defined and measured in material terms. Therefore let there be no talk of philosophy. Such problems as confront us were created by technology, and they are to be solved by technology, either by more technology or by less. The business of America is business, and philosophy has nothing to do with it.

Then a more sophisticated form of resistance is manifested. There are truths and we hold them? Well, yes, says the positivist, provided you understand clearly what "truth" is and how it is to be "held." There is no other truth but scientific truth, reached by the methods of science, whether classical or statistical. And one holds truths only tentatively; one is never committed to them. Such commitment spells the death of the free mind. Your public philosophy—it may be myth or fancy, poetry or symbol; but, as described, it cannot pretend to be permanent truth.

The pragmatist will also join the argument. If there is to be talk of ideas, he says, you must remember that all ideas were born free and equal; that all of them are to be thrown into the competition of the market place; that the ideas which are bought are true, or the ideas that work are true, or at least the ideas that survive are true. But the ideas in your public philosophy are no longer bought; they are no longer operative; they have not even survived. The forces of history have made a vacuum where once there was a public philosophy, if indeed there ever was a public philosophy. Why then bother to talk about it?

Since the word "morality" was used in making the affirmative case, another speaker will rise to say that there may indeed be an American morality, but it is hardly more than tribal, a matter of the national mores, having no greater warrant than custom or fashion or the necessity of convention and even hypocrisy in any manner of social life. If the speaker is a philosopher, his proposition will be that all morality is contextualistic. Or he may choose to say that all morality is existentialist, a situation-ethics, a problem of individual decisions in whose making no appeal may be made to a moral order, since there is no moral order. In a word, the argument about the public philosophy gets involved in all the confusions about the idea of morality that are today current (a subject to which I shall return in a later chapter).

In the end, someone will surely advance the view that the American consensus contains only one tenet—an agreement to disagree. With this agreement all agreement ends; and this agreement is hardly sufficient to constitute a philosophy.

Against these varied but converging lines of argument I customarily fall back on a historical point, that no society in history has ever achieved and maintained an identity and a vigor in action unless it has had some substance, unless it has been sustained and directed by some body of substantive beliefs. The rejoinder is that we are a new kind of society, a "free society," a democracy. And the consensus proper to this kind of society is purely procedural. It involves no agreement on the premises and purposes of political life and legal institutions; it is solely an agreement with regard to the method of making decisions and getting things done, whatever the things may be. The substance of American society is our "democratic institutions," conceived as purely formal categories. These institutions have no content; they are simply channels through which any kind of content may flow. In the end, the only life-or-death question for American society is that it should live or die under punctilious regard for correct democratic procedures.

My experience has been that the foregoing represents the general range of response that one gets to the affirmation that there is an American public philosophy. This sort of response is pitched on the intellectual level.

There is, of course, a more heated response on the level of emotion. Usually, the outcry is raised: But this is orthodoxy! Thus the great word of anathema is hurled. The limits of tolerance have been reached. We will tolerate all kinds of ideas, however pernicious; but we will not tolerate the idea of an orthodoxy. That is, we refuse to say, as a people: There are truths, and we hold them, and these are the truths.

So the argument runs down and out. It ends in negation. On the question as put, is there an American public philosophy? the Noes will have it. I have about come to the conclusion that they do have it. Their negation of a public philosophy seems to be valid on the two levels on which the question itself is validly asked.

First, there is the level of the people at large. On this popular level the public philosophy would appear as a wisdom, possessed almost intuitively, in the form of a simple faith rather than an articulate philosophy. To this wisdom the people are heir by tradition; it is their patrimony. It gives them an identity as a people by relating them to their own history within which their identity was shaped. Even in simple form this wisdom would be adequate to its function, which is to enable the people to "judge, direct, and correct" the moral bearing of courses of government (I use the famous three words of medieval political theory). The ancient example from the field of religious faith is valid here. The simple people of Alexandria caught the resonances of heresy in the preaching of Arius before the clerics caught them, entangled as these latter were in the subtleties of emanationist theory that confused the simple issue: The Word of God—is He God or not? Analogously, the body politic by reason of its patrimony of political wisdom should be able to sense in some instinctive fashion the basic errors in governmental policy, even when the politicians themselves get lost in their technical arguments and partisan feelings.

Second, there is the level of the "clerks," the intellectuals. I mean, of course, not only the academicians—the professional students of philosophy, politics, economics, history, etc.—but also the politicians, the writers, the journalists, the clergy, the whole range of men and women equipped by formal education and training to take an intelligent interest in public affairs, in the res publica. These are the people who are supposed to be in conscious possession of the public philosophy as a philosophy; for them it would be a personal acquisition and not simply a patrimony.

On both these levels I am inclined to think that the Noes have it. Say there is no public philosophy in America. By one cause or another it has been eroded. And the sign of the vacuum, especially on the intellectual level, is the futility of argument on the question as put in its first form, whether there is a public philosophy or not.

The Case That May Succeed

Nonetheless, I am unwilling to relinquish the argument. But the form of the question must be changed to read: Do we or do we not need a public philosophy? Can we or can we not achieve a successful conduct of our national affairs, foreign and domestic, in the absence of a consensus that will set our purposes, furnish a standard of judgment on policies, and establish the proper conditions for political dialogue?

To argue the question in this form I would recur to the truth that lies at the heart of the philosophical error of pragmatism. It is false to say that what works is true. But it is an altogether sound proposition that what is not true will somehow fail to work. I think it is possible to prove America's present need of a public philosophy by using this principle as the key to the method of demonstration. The demonstration would be concrete; the materials for it would be drawn from the facts concerning public affairs.

Briefly, the argument would be that, if public affairs today are going badly, the basic reason is the absence of a public philosophy. In other words, it is not true to say that America does not need a public philosophy, for the fundamental reason that this assertion will fail to work. It is failing to work; it is daily proving its own falsity. The further conclusion will be that there is today a need for a new moral act of purpose and a new act of intellectual affirmation, comparable to those which launched the American constitutional commonwealth, that will newly put us in possession of the public philosophy, the basic consensus that we need.

Obviously, this kind of demonstration cannot be undertaken here. But I might make a rapid statement of the lines along which it would proceed.

The starting point is the obvious fact that the United States is doing badly in this moment of historical crisis. I would myself accept the view of Mr. Max Ways, for instance, as stated in his book, *Beyond Survival*, that America today is more insecure than it has ever been in its history—more insecure than in the darkest days of the Civil War, more insecure than in the perilous time that followed Pearl Harbor. These were moments of crisis. But at least a goal was clear before us in both of them—a victory to be won, whose symbol would be the capture of a place, Richmond, Berlin, Tokyo. Today what is the goal, the victory to be won? Surely it has no such simple symbol. So baffling has the problem of our national purpose become that it is now the fashion to say that our purpose is simply "survival." The statement, I think, indicates the depth of our political bankruptcy. This is not a purpose worthy of the world's most powerful nation. It utterly fails to measure the meaning of the historical moment or to estimate the opportunities for greatness inherent in the moment. Worst of all, if we pursue only the small-souled purpose of survival, we shall not even achieve survival.

From this comment on our current insecurity I should go on to say that the reason for the insecurity is not Communism, whether as an external threat or (much less) as an internal threat. I would not be misunderstood. If the menace of Communism is properly understood, it would be almost impossible to exaggerate it, so massive is it, and so fundamental. Moreover, if the menace is not understood, it becomes all the greater. And this, I fear, is the current situation. However, postponing to a later chapter an analysis of the exact nature of the Communist challenge, I would here maintain that Communism is not the basic cause of our present confusions, uncertainties, insecurities, falterings and failures of purpose. I would go so far as to maintain that, if the Communist empire were to fall apart tomorrow, and if Communist ideology were to distintegrate with it, our problems would not be solved. In fact, they would be worse in many ways.

I can here suggest only one general reason for this assertion. Having finally, and much too slowly, reached a consensus that Communism is an evil thing, we have resolved to be "against" it. We reject the Communist idea of world order; we object to a Communist organization of the world. The trouble is that, after you have rejected the Communist order, you are still stuck with the sheer fact of the world's disorder. It is the fact of the century. Communism did not create the fact, though it exploits it. The disorder would persist, or be rendered even more chaotic, if Communist ideas and power vanished into thin air this very moment. Facing the massive fact of world disorder, the United States faces the question: What kind of order in the world do you want? What are its premises and principles? What is to be the form of its institutions—political, legal, economic? How do you propose to help organize this disorganized world? Or do you propose not to help? Or do you perhaps think an order of peace, freedom, justice, and prosperity will come about in the world simply by accident, or by sheer undirected technological progress, or by the power of prayer, or by what? Order is, by definition, the work of the wise man: *sapientis est ordinare*. It is the work of men and peoples who are able to say: There are truths and we hold them. Hence the disordered state of the world itself puts to America the question: What are your truths? With a decent respect to the opinions of a mankind that is groping for a civilized order, speak these truths.

It is, I think, the absence of any convinced and convincing answers to these questions, and others of the same tenor, that explains our present insecurity, the fact of it and the sense of it. The questions are not answered simply by saying that we are against Communism. I am pleased that the American people have agreed to be against Communism, though I could wish that the opposition to this enemy were more intelligent than it is. However, anti-Communism is not a public philosophy. This negative consensus is no firm guide to public policy. In fact, it has its dangers, since it can furnish a pseudo-justification for misguided policies. It can distort the issues in public debate. It can distract attention from issues that are less visible but no less urgent.

Having got the issue of Communism and anti-Communism in proper perspective, subordinate to the problem of our positive intentions with regard to the organization of the world, the next problem would be to examine the various areas of American policy to see whether the confusions and ineffectivenesses in them are not due to the absence of a public philosophy. I shall assume that our major problems are in the field of foreign, not domestic, policy. I shall further assume that foreign policy embraces two broad areas, military policy and economic policy.

A Public Philosophy of Force

On the matter of military policy I was impressed by the *Rockefeller Report on International Security: The Military Aspect*.[1] Four broad problems were distinguished in an order of ascending importance. First, there are all the technological problems involved in our enormously spreading defense establishment. Second, there is the problem of the economic burden imposed on the people by the necessities of national defense. Third, there is the problem of doctrine and strategy with regard to the military uses of the force at our command. Finally, there is the problem of the political and moral ends for which we are prepared to use force. This is the ultimate problem. It is an issue of political and moral judgment. It is finally determinative. We can quite literally do anything we want to do in the matter of creating and using force. The question is, what do we want to do?

This is the problem we have refused—the moral problem of the use of force as an instrument of justice and political order. What is worse, we seem to think that we have solved the problem. We have said that we shall never shoot first. That seems to be the first and the last thing we have to say about the morality of war. Having said it, we think that the moral issue is settled. This, of course, is sheer nonsense. Or else we say, as President Eisenhower said, that we are making weapons not to wage but to prevent war. Thus we think to have put a moral basis under the whole gigantic operation of Cape Canaveral, Los Alamos, the Livermore laboratory, etc., etc. We seem not to be aware that the unacknowledged half-falsity of this half-truth again represents a blindness to the complexity of the moral problem. The premise of the statement seems to be that the prevention of war through the creation of armaments is an exercise in morality, whereas the waging of war, if the preventive effort fails, is not an exercise in morality at all.

This premise is brought to view when the two controlling American policies are seen in their logical relation: We shall never shoot first, but if anybody shoots at us the answer will be "massive retaliation" by weapons of indiscriminate mass slaughter. These are, I take it, the two correlative policies, of the highest order, that embody the most profound thought about war that our government has been able to elaborate. I take it so, because as a member of the public, I have never been informed to the contrary. It seems to be the deepest conviction of American government and its people too that war and peace are two completely discontinuous universes, between which no moral connection exists. When you step out of the universe of peace, which is the universe of morality, you step into the universe of war, in which morality is irrelevant. The prevention of war is a moral effort. War itself is simply a problem in technology.

I think it fair to say that there is no consensus in America with regard to the answer to the fourth and climactic problem raised by the Rockefeller Report. It has been raised in other sources too. An example would be the chapter entitled, "The Need of Doctrine," in Henry Kissinger's book, *Nuclear Weapons and Foreign Policy*;[2] this chapter most unfortunately has got overlooked in the course of the technical debates over Kissinger's concept of limited war. One should read, in contrast, Raymond L. Garthoff's book, *Soviet Strategy in the Nuclear Age*.[3] The Soviet Union does not need a public philosophy with regard to the uses of force; as I shall later point out, it has one. The philosophy, you may say, is damnable. The trouble is that even a damnable philosophy is more effective than no philosophy at all.

The argument here does not stop with the fact that there is no American public philosophy with regard to the uses of force. The point is that we need such a philosophy. Otherwise there is no real solution to what are usually called the "practical problems" pointed to by the Rockefeller panel. The technological, economic and strategic aspects of the total problem are involved in enormous confusions because there is not available in a public philosophy, shared by government and people alike, a higher viewpoint from which ordered solutions might be seen. What is not true will somehow fail to work. And it is not true that America can intelligently construct, and morally put to use, a defense establishment in the absence of a public philosophy concerning the use of force as a moral and political act.

It is along these lines, but with more complete analysis and detail, that an argument can be constructed to show the need of a public philosophy in order to "judge, direct, and correct" the structure, content and orientation of military policies.

A Philosophy of Foreign Aid

The same sort of argument could be made with regard to foreign economic policy. This too is a problem of enormous technical difficulty; there are many aspects to it, and not all of them are purely economic. However, the argument would undertake to show that the prior and primatial problem regards the lack, and therefore the need, of a consensus with respect to the broad purposes of foreign economic aid. In other words, the technical problems cannot be successfully solved in a vacuum of philosophy with regard to this vital area of American action abroad.

The validity of this proposition might be illustrated, if not demon-strated, by a look at the classic argument for foreign economic aid since the inception of programs of aid in the post-war period. The classic argu-ment, I take it, has asserted that foreign economic aid is necessary in or-der to counter the Communist threat, to stop the advance of Commu-nism. There have been other arguments indeed; but this is the one that "comes through" to the public and seems to be decisive. Moreover, it is being made all the more insistently now that Communist imperialism is increasingly taking on an economic form. Hence I call the argument clas-sic. I would not deny it some validity. The trouble is that this basic argu-ment contains a basic fallacy, sc., the notion that it is the basic argument.

The fact is that the United States would confront a massive problem in foreign economic policy, even if there were no Communism around the lot. Even if no imperialist advances were being made from Moscow, the United States would have to have a world economic policy, of a ra-tional kind, based on a coherent philosophy. The need for it is there, in the economic facts. Moscow did not create the need. It is simply trying to fill the need in its own way. We do not like the Communist idea of eco-nomic order, in itself and in its relation to political forms. But our dislike of the Communist solution does not cancel the problem itself. Nor can we sensibly say that our solution is to stop the Communist solution. This negativism of policy, evident in the classic argument, is no good, certainly not good enough. We have got to meet head on, with a policy whose in-tentions are positive, the disorderly situation that presently exists.

Its existence is not accounted for by Communism. More basic dy-namisms are at work. There is the economic dynamism that looks towards betterment of the material conditions of life. This dynamism is not sheerly materialist. It also has a political character; a prosperous economy is regarded as a means to political status. And this latter is the higher value in those regions now emerging from colonial status. Moreover, eco-nomic and political hopes and desires are now sharpened to the point of passion by the great vision that technology has created. Science and technology, in themselves and by the spectacle of their achievements both in the "capitalist" world and in the Communist world, have made it clear to the peoples of the world that it is now altogether possible for them to realize their hopes and desires. This is the new thing. It is no longer necessary to endure all that history has understood by poverty, in the way of wretched (or widely unequal) material conditions or in the way of political dependence. Regions and countries are "poor" only because they are "underdeveloped." But the means of development are within reach. And the world's peoples are determined to reach them.

These, I should think, are the underlying factors that are creating current economic, political, and social unrest—what is sometimes called the "revolution of rising expectations." In the face of these factors the classic argument for American foreign economic aid misses the main point. I cannot but believe that American policy makers realize that it misses the point. But, they may say, it is the only argument that finds an echo in the present negative American consensus, anti-Communism. The State Department knows the argument to be basically fallacious; but it has to use it in order to get appropriations through Congress. Congress too understands the fallacy; but the Congressman has his eye on his constituents who will approve his affirmative vote for foreign aid only because it is good for America, and it is good for America only because it is bad for the Communists. If this whole curious situation were further analyzed, the vacuum in public life would come into view. It is a vacuum of philosophy, a public philosophy with affirmative tenets that determine positive goals. The need is for this kind of philosophy, in government circles and among the people, in terms of which government and people could communicate with one another and consent intelligently to one another.

I know, of course, that there is something of a search for bases of foreign economic policy other than sheer anti-Communism. But the arguments for them tend to go out, as most public arguments today go out, in futility. Moral altruism, for instance, is advanced as a basis; economic aid is the generous duty of the rich nation. But this argument, usually made quite fuzzily and with soft sentimental overtones, awakes no resonance in the public mind. And it collides with the "tough" argument that self-interest is the final controlling factor of political or economic policy. This latter argument does not lack validity; and it certainly has popularity.

The search for other criteria of aid has no better issue. Is "the greatest need" to be the criterion? But it may be that aid will be put to least efficient use where most needed. Is foreign aid to be a reward or a bribe? But this is perilously close to trickery. Is it to be only an emergency program, or a permanent element in American policy? Others could trace these confusions better than I. The Report of Panel III of the Rockefeller Special Studies

Project on *Foreign Economic Policy in the Twentieth Century*[4] adverted to some of them. It firmly rejected the notion that our policy structure can or should be designed "merely to prevent an expansion of the Soviet's sphere." It added: "The free world confronts a deeper challenge than mere survival." It went on: "We should consider its efforts not as an act of benevolence but of partnership." A sensible remark, if one only knew what it meant. And it concluded: "The challenge therefore is to our sense of purpose and to our values." But there it concluded. It left the questions hanging: What is our purpose? And what are our values? These are the crucial questions. They are not being answered. They need to be answered.

Quod erat demonstrandum. That is, I set out to indicate the lines of an argument, whose materials would be taken from public affairs, whereby one might demonstrate America's need of a public philosophy, a consensus that could find utterance beginning with the words: There are truths and we hold them. Until we can make this utterance, public policies will continue to be projected out of a vacuum in the governmental mind into a vacuum in the popular mind. But it is not true that public policies can be so projected, and yet be successful.

I might add a final remark, even though it may bring these comments to a close on a "down beat." Until we can articulate an American consensus with regard to our truths, our purposes, and our values, it may be that there is much instinctive wisdom in raising the issue of survival. In the circumstances the issue is most real. It may possibly be true to say that an individual man can survive the tests of human life without religion; I mean, of course, the tests of terrestrial life, not the definitive tests put by ultimate truth, which are met in the internal forum of the mind and the moral conscience. In any case, it is not true to say that a nation can survive the tests of terrestrial life without a public philosophy, least of all in this our day when the very bases even of terrestrial life are being called into question. And what is not true will somehow fail to work. Hence one does well in America today to raise the issue of survival.

Notes

1. New York: Doubleday and Co., 1958.
2. New York: Harper and Brothers, 1957.
3. New York: Praeger, 1958.
4. New York: Doubleday and Co., 1958.

~

CHAPTER FOUR

The Origins and Authority of the Public Consensus: A Study of the Growing End

It has been pointed out to me more than once, in discussions on the subject of the American consensus, that the word is misleading. In current speech connotations have clustered round the word that form a barrier to an understanding of its classic sense. This is unfortunately true. Nevertheless, I am unwilling to relinquish the word. It is the apt word. It is also the historical word, whose use goes back to the origins of the Western constitutional tradition. From the Roman jurists, through St. Augustine, it passed into the Western political vocabulary. If it has now become colored by misleading connotations, it deserves to be redeemed unto right usage.

Today, of course, the word is often taken to mean simply "majority opinion," which is the supreme category in which men have lately come to think, when there is question of the political order. There is also the frequent meaning, reflected in Webster's Dictionary, where the word is defined: "Agreement in matters of opinion, testimony, etc.; accord; also, loosely, the convergent trend, as of opinion." These usages, however valid elsewhere, are departures from the technical constitutional sense that the word bears within the Western tradition.

I would maintain, for instance, that the public consensus of the West, and of the United States as a historic participant in the Western style of civilization, would remain the public consensus, even if it were held, as perhaps it is held, only by a minority within the West. The validity of the consensus is radically independent of its possible status as either majority or minority opinion. Moreover, the Declaration of Independence did not hazard the conjecture: "This is the convergent trend of opinion among us. . . ." It made the affirmation: "We hold these truths. . . ." Or in the equivalent formula: "This is the public consensus. . . ."

The current ambiguity of the word is indicative of a deeper conceptual difficulty. Two related questions are usually raised. Do we hold these truths because they are true, or are these truths true because we hold them? Do the propositions included in the consensus acquire validity through the sheer fact of their general acceptance, or conversely, does the inherent validity of these propositions require that they be generally accepted? Does the consensus, as an agreement, constitute the truth, or does the truth command the agreement which is the consensus? In a word, what is the precise nature of the consensus, as revealed in its origins? This is the first question.

The second question follows. If the warrant for the validity of the propositions that form the consensus is not the sheer fact of their general acceptance, what is this warrant? Where is it to be sought? Why, in the end, do we hold these truths to be true? Why are we obliged to make these affirmations? Whence is their necessity? And whence is the quality that transforms them from naked abstractions into operative imperatives that furnish the premises of more particular judgments of "right" and "wrong," passed on details of constitutional structure, legal enactment, and political action? In a word, whence comes the authority of the consensus?

Both of these questions could be answered by an analysis of the classical contents of the consensus, that is, the truths about law and government, related to the nature of man, that have come to be consciously held, in some manner of explicit formulation, as the basis for a commonwealth and a polity in the Western style. For a variety of reasons, however, it may be useful here to approach both questions from the standpoint of the "growing end" of the consensus.

The Origins and Growth of the Consensus

It is well, first, to emphasize that the consensus does have a growing end. It is indeed a legacy from the past, but not in the form of a deposit that is closed to all change and addition. It is never finished, complete, and perfect, beyond need or possibility of further development. What we call the West is a historical concept, or better, a historical process. It is therefore an open-ended action. There is always the possibility and need of progress in the consensus that sustains its life, as there is likewise the possibility and the danger of decadence. The virtualities of human freedom, for good and for evil, are never exhausted. Man's free existence, the philosophers say, is a forward-looking historicity, whose structure, which has been conditioned by the historic past, is the matrix of projects for the future. This is true of the free society, as it is true of the free man. One must expect therefore that the public consensus, in terms of which the free society defines its identity, will not be a static quantity. It must obey one or the other of the alternative laws of history, which are growth or decline, fuller integrity or disintegration.

The most obvious growing end of the free society has been its business system in the complex meaning of the term. Behind its enormous growth has lain the pressure of the people's needs, wants, desires, dreams, passions, and illusions, which have all grown more demanding as it has become clear that the demands can be satisfied by science, technology, financial acumen, productive enterprise, and the skills of business management, all bound in alliance with one another. The result has been the great sprawling Thing known as the American economy, which is now coming to be recognized as also a strange and new sort of polity. I have no competence to describe the Thing, nor is this necessary for the present purpose.

The first essential point is that the American industrial or business system is a power system. The power of which it is the vehicle is unprecedented in its magnitude. And this power is not diffused throughout the system but concentrated in a relatively few great corporations—more exactly, in their managements, or concretely, in the hands of a few men, who in effect direct the activities of the economic-political system, determine its forms, create and distribute its profits, and select the path of future growth. The second essential point is that the power of this immense economy and polity, or political economy, is an omnipresence in American society. No institution—certainly not government, or the university, and not even the Church—is immune from the touch of it, nor is any family or individual.

In consequence, the question has arisen with great urgency, is this omnipresent power also somehow an omnipotence? Are there any limitations that it freely recognizes, or that it can at least be forced to accept? More basically, how does this power establish its legitimacy, as all power must, if it is not to be indicted as a usurpation? Finally, before what bench or bar may this power be summoned for judgment on its uses, to know if perhaps they be not abuses, and therefore an exercise of tyranny?

In the forefront of those who have been occupying themselves with these difficult and important questions has stood Prof. Adolf A. Berle. In his Stafford Little Lectures at Princeton in 1958, later published in the book, *Power Without Property*,[1] he presented his latest thought with wonted lucidity and force. One major thesis of the book is pertinent to our purpose here. It is thus stated: "Observing the American scene you note that, as power goes, the present concentration has in recent years been (on the whole) relatively free from the excesses which often make concentrated power odious. Certainly this was not because historical chance had located American economic power in a collection of saints. Checks (not 'balances') appeared in the form of periodic political interventions demanded by American public opinion. To explain this it becomes necessary to import a political conception—the 'public consensus' —familiar to political scientists and brilliantly explained a few years ago by Mr. Walter Lippmann. So, it seems, the ultimate protection of individuals lies not in the play of economic forces in free markets, but in a set of value judgments so widely accepted and deeply held in the United States that public opinion can energize political action when needed to prevent power from violating these values."

My interest here is in Mr. Berle's concept of the public consensus. He enters the disclaimer: "It is not within the scope of this essay to examine the nature of 'public consensus' though the subject is passionately interesting and needs intensive thought." Despite this modesty, however, he gives the most significant development to the notion of the public consensus, on its "growing end," that I have come across. I shall first undertake simply to report it.

In the first place, what is the public consensus? It is "a set of ideas, widely held by the community, and often by the (business) organization itself and the men who direct it, that certain uses of power are 'wrong,' that is, contrary to the established interest and value system of the community." It is "essentially a body of doctrine which has attained wide, if not general, acceptance." This body of doctrine contains "principles," "tenets," "rules," "standards," and "criteria" of judgment on individual cases or situations.

In the second place, how does the public consensus originate? It is "not a spontaneous fact in the minds of many individuals. It is the product of a body of thought and experience." In it there is "nothing abstract or assumed." Were it codified, it would be seen as a "systematized recording of experience and attitudes."

In the third place, how and in what form does the public consensus exist? "Public consensus, though it is indefinite, almost completely unorganized, and without traceable form, nonetheless is a hard-core fact. Every corporation executive knows this." As a body of thought and experience, it is "sufficiently expressed in one form or another so that its principles are familiar to and have become accepted by those members of the community interested in the relevant field." Again: "The principles of the public consensus, some of which are well enough defined as to be inchoate law, have never been stated. Yet men in each industry are fairly well aware of them. With time, effort, and thought, they could manage a quite tolerable outline of the public consensus as it applies to them." Though presently there is a reluctance to be completely explicit about the principles, "the time will come when manuals will be needed and will be produced."

In the fourth place, the public consensus is not a finished, but a developing, body of doctrine. "It is not omniscient; it constantly absorbs new thinking and draws new lessons from experience." It is "subject to constant examination, criticism, and evolution. Individuals, more advanced in thinking and insight, can, should, and do insist that the consensus on any subject shall change, expand, or raise its standards." The occasion for this insistence is the perception of a "margin" intervening between the existent consensus and the ongoing economic life of society.

In the fifth place, what is the relation between the public consensus and public opinion? They are not identical, but distinct and related. "'Public opinion' is sometimes misleadingly used as a synonym. Actually, public opinion is a shorthand phrase expressing the fact that a large body of the community has reached or may reach specific conclusions in some particular situation. These conclusions are spontaneously, perhaps emotionally, reached, usually from some unstated but very real premises. The 'public consensus' is the body of these general, unstated premises which has come to be accepted. It furnishes the basis for public opinion. Public opinion is the specific application of tenets embodied in the public consensus to some situation which has come into general consciousness."

In the sixth place, who are the depositaries of the consensus and the agents of its development and application? Development is effected by those who work on the "margin": "There is a margin here upon which students, writers, financial analysts, businessmen, economists must work. In their studies and discussions the results of (particular business practices) for good or evil are examined and stated. Presently doctrine solidifies; consensus is reached. A new criterion of judgment has been set up; in the next emergency it will be enforced by public opinion." In applying the consensus and translating it into public opinion the business community may play a limited role, but its judgments are likely to be self-interested. "Of greater force are the conclusions of careful university professors, the reasoned opinions of specialists, the statements of responsible journalists, and at times the solid pronouncements of respected politicians. . . . These, and men like them, are thus the real tribunal to which the American system is finally accountable." Their judgments are principled, free, disinterested, informed. "Collectively they are developers of public consensus, the men first sought to guide the formation of public opinion to any given application." These men, in Berle's favorite image, are the "logical recipients of the mantle of the historical Lord's Spiritual," who of old "erected generally accepted standards or criteria of judgment (in these studies represented rather than described by the symbol 'public consensus') . . ." and "also determined, somewhat crudely but sufficiently, whether the holder of temporal power had measured up to these standards."

In the seventh place, what are the public functions of the consensus? Chiefly, it acts as "final arbiter" of the legitimacy of economic power and of the rightfulness of its uses. "In a democratic society no instrument other than this 'public consensus' has been devised." The consensus also "furnishes the basis for public opinion," and validates the sanctions imposed by public opinion on uses of power judged to be wrongful, whether because they are "dangerous" or because they are "inherently bad or illegitimate." Thus the consensus furnishes the "reality of the corporate conscience," as it recognizes limits on corporate power and submits uses of economic power to public judgment. Finally, because concentrated economic power is checked by, and responsible to, the public consensus, the American economy qualifies as "democratic." This is the supreme function of the consensus—to determine the nature of the economy, to specify its style, and thus to insure that the style of the economy accords with the whole larger style of life that the American people has adopted as its own—the "democratic style" that identifies the American people as a people and characterizes its action.

In the eighth place, what is the relation between the public consensus and the order of government and law? The consensus itself "does include settled principles of law applicable to economic power. But it also includes capacity to criticize that law. From time to time it may demand changes in existing law. It also carries capacity to insist that principles heretofore comprised only within the consensus must be added to statute or common law, enforceable by courts as well as by public opinion." Therefore the reach of the consensus goes "over and beyond the accepted or enacted provisions of law"; it imposes standards of performance and conduct whose violation may lead to political or legal intervention. In this sense these standards are "inchoate law," which may become "explicit law in case of abuse of power." Thus the consensus furnishes the premises that justify governmental intervention in the economy, whether in the form of "investigation, enactment of a relevant statute, or emergence of a new rule through the common-law courts."

This exposition of the public consensus may lack full definition here and there; and it is not entirely free of inconsistencies. Nevertheless, the concept is constructed with remarkable firmness. Certain things seem to be clear. I hope I may state them without seeming to force Mr. Berle's thought, which I have no wish to do.

The consensus is not "majority opinion," certainly not in its origins; the Lords Spiritual are not a majority. Again, the consensus is not the "convergent trend of opinion." It supposes a process of thought and argument; but it is itself the term of this process, reached when "doctrine solidifies," and "consensus is reached." Moreover, the doctrine is the rational term of the argument, a proper conclusion; it is not simply the least-common-denominator residue of a collation of opinions. And it looks for its validity, not to the sheer fact that the Lords Spiritual, or the people at large, agree on it, but to the evidence adduced to show that it is true or good or just or equitable or useful or necessary. The agreement is consequent on the constitution of the doctrine. It is expected that men who examine the evidence will come to an agreement on the doctrine. In the end, of course, the consensus implies public agreement, though its origins may lie in the reasoned affirmation of one man or of a university seminar; but the consensus itself, formally considered, is not sheerly the public agreement. It is a doctrine or a judgment that commands public agreement on the merits of the arguments for it.

Again, the consensus supposes experience and the analysis of economic fact; but it is something more than a mere registry of experience, and its contents are not simply facts. They are ideas and principles—or better, judgments and imperatives. These judgments and imperatives are not abstractions or assumptions, as law itself, whether inchoate or explicit, is not an abstraction or an assumption. The consensus is doctrine—not, however, in the sense of Platonic dogma, but in the sense that the word carries when used by a lawyer or by a military strategist. The doctrine bears on the order of action, not on the ultimate order of beings and purposes, which is the order of metaphysics. On the other hand, the principles of the consensus are cast in a certain mode of generality, in such wise that they are capable of application to cases.

Furthermore, these practical rules of action are not proposed simply as techniques, or as sheerly procedural rules prescribed in the single interest of success in economic operations. They are the premises of moral judgments whereby economic action is qualified in the moral categories of "right" and "wrong."

Finally, it may be well to say that the consensus is not in any sense an ideology. Its close relation to concrete experience rescues it from that fate. The thought it embodies is not visionary or doctrinaire. Nor does it reveal any trace of class-consciousness or partisan group interest. And it makes no attempt to do what ideologies always do, which is to thrust themselves upon reality, in violation of reality's own dynamisms and structures, in an attempt to actuate some more or less utopian scheme. The consensus leaves completely intact what Berle calls the "non-dogmatic quality of American political economic action," which permits the uses of pragmatism their full legitimate scope in the devising of economic policies.

In summary, we are invited, I take it, to imagine some such utterance as this, in four propositions, being made by the American people "to a candid world": (1) There are truths (or principles of action or standards of judgment) that command the structure and the courses of the political-economic system of the United States. (2) We hold these truths; our Lords Spiritual have come to them, and We, the People, assent and consent to them; and we could, if we wanted, show a "decent respect to the opinions of mankind" and declare them. (3) These truths, in their application, join harmoniously with other truths in imparting a special character and identity to the American people in what concerns the economic order of their life, which they bring into accord, in general style, with the American idea of a free people democratically organized. (4) The life of these truths (or principles or standards) is sustained, as it was born, of argument and persuasion, which appeal for their validity to experience and reflective thought.

Although Mr. Berle disclaims the intention to "examine the nature of 'public consensus,'" it should be gratefully admitted that he has carried the subject a considerable distance. The questions that remain are of a philosophical order. In addressing myself to them it is my intention to speak for myself. It would be out of place to impute to Mr. Berle ideas or theories that he might wish to disavow.

The Authority of the Consensus

The initial questions are clear enough. The public consensus appears as the systematization of experience. The difficulty is that economic experience does not systematize itself; nor are the elements whereby to systematize it, introduce order into it, and make it intelligible, contained within the ambit of the sheer experience. Whence then do these elements derive?

Again, the consensus presents itself as a body of thought. But what is the relation between the consensual thought and the economic experience? Is the experience totally productive of the thought, or is there perhaps some thought that is prior to, and normative of, the experience?

Furthermore, simply as experienced, economic life, like all life, is no more than a stream of successive "facts." And all the facts are contingent; there is no experience, as the philosophical empiricists see quite well, except of what is contingent. On the other hand, there would seem to be within the consensus an element of thought that is not contingent. The consensus is not simply "the facts." It is a set of principles or standards in terms of which to pass judgment on the facts. The question then recurs: what is this non-contingent element of thought, in terms of which the economic facts are transformed into issues that may be argued, and then decided, in a form of decision that assumes the status of a principle, a criterion of permanent judgment on passing situations of fact?

Finally, as the function of the consensus is to furnish standards of judgment on economic events, so also it is to correct the processes of the economy, and to direct them in purposeful fashion toward selected ends. The selection of these ends is itself among the functions of the consensus—in the case, the larger consensus that determines the substance, and specifies the general style, of the community life of the American people, and therefore requires that the action of the economy conform to this style. The economy itself does not decide that it shall be a "democratic" economy. It could decide otherwise, and in fact tends to do so; the native tendency of an industrial economy is towards oligarchic organization and towards independence of all political, not to say popular, control. The decision for economic democracy is not an economic decision. It is political. More profoundly, since the issue affects the substance of society, the decision is ultimately moral. Therefore the consensus that forms the decision in the public mind, and enforces it on economic action, contains an element of moral thought.

Only this moral element will enable the consensus to transcend sheer experience, and impart some system to it, and do this in terms of non-contingent principle that is capable of coping with the issue of ends as well as of means. In a word, the very conception, "public consensus," is a moral conception. Morality and the consensus have at least this in common, that they are not simply reflections of fact, as if whatever is must be considered right; nor are they mere techniques of success, as if whatever works must be considered true and good.

There is not likely to be much resistance to the notion that the public consensus has the character of a moral experience that is public. There is, however, the further question, in terms of what theory of morality is this moral experience, and its publicity, to be understood and explained. Every moral experience assumes intelligibility only in terms of a moral theory. And a moral theory, if it is to be any good, must be able to give an account of every manner of moral experience.

My proposition is that only the theory of natural law is able to give an account of the public moral experience that is the public consensus. The consensus itself is simply the tradition of reason as emergent in developing form in the special circumstances of American political-economic life.

The Doctrine of Natural Law

In a later chapter I shall present a historical and theoretical discussion of what is meant by natural law. For the moment, in view of the particular question in hand, it will be sufficient to sketch the general structure and style of this mode of moral thought. It is sometimes said that one cannot accept the doctrine of natural law unless one has antecedently accepted "its Roman Catholic presuppositions." This, of course, is quite wrong. The doctrine of natural law has no Roman Catholic presuppositions. Its only presupposition is threefold: that man is intelligent; that reality is intelligible; and that reality, as grasped by intelligence, imposes on the will the obligation that it be obeyed in its demands for action or abstention. Even these statements are not properly "presuppositions," since they are susceptible of verification.

The permeability of reality, especially moral reality, to intelligence is limited, as human intelligence itself is limited. But the limitations do not destroy the capacity of intelligence to do three things, in an order of diminishing ease and certainty. As these three things are done in orderly fashion, the structure of natural-law thought rises, and its style of argument appears.

First, intelligence can grasp the ethical a priori, the first principle of the moral consciousness, which does not originate by argument, but which dawns, as it were, as reason itself emerges from the darkness of infant animalism. Human reason that is conscious of itself is also conscious of the primary truths both of the intellectual and of the moral consciousness that what is true cannot at the same time and under the same respect be false, and that what is good is to be done and what is evil avoided. This latter truth is what I call the ethical a priori. Second, after some elementary experience of the basic situations of human life, and upon some simple reflection on the meaning of terms, intelligence can grasp the meaning of "good" and "evil" in these situations and therefore know what is to be done or avoided in them. For instance, to know the meaning of "parent" and of "disrespect" is to know a primary principle of the natural law, that disrespect to parents is evil, intrinsically and antecedent to any human prohibition. Third, as the experience of reality unfolds in the unfolding of the various relationships and situations that are the reality of human life, intelligence, with the aid of simple reasoning, can know, and know to be obligatory, a set of natural-law principles that are derivative. These, in general, are the Ten Commandments, the basic moral laws of human life, sanctioned by reason, and also sanctioned by their inclusion in the Jewish and Christian codes (the third, to "keep holy the sabbath," is of course positive divine law).

These three achievements requiring, as they do, only common human experience and only a modicum of reflection and reasoning are within the powers of human intelligence as such, at least *ut in pluribus*, in the case of most men. This is St. Thomas Aquinas's repeated qualification. The qualification means that rational human nature works competently in most men, but in particular instances it may fail. In other words, man is not an animal, ruled by unerring instinct. His guide to moral action is practical judgment; and this act of reason may go astray, for discernible causes, here and there, now and then.

There is a fourth area of achievement open to the moral reason of man. It concerns particular principles which represent the requirements of rational human nature in more complex human relationships and amid the institutional developments that accompany the progress of civilization. This area is reserved for those whom St. Thomas calls "the wise" (*sapientes*). The reason for the reservation is clear. The further the human mind advances toward apprehending the particulars of morals, the greater is the part that knowledge, experience, reflection, and dispassionateness of judgment must play. To grasp the bearing of fundamental moral truth on particular human relations and on concrete social institutions requires a prior understanding of these relations and these institutions. They are, in the case, the "reality" in whose dense depths the demands of reason must be discerned, and then stated as dictates to be obeyed. Little reflection on experience is needed to know the principle of justice, "*Suum cuique*" ("to each what is his"). But an extensive scientific analysis of the functioning of economic cooperation is needed to know what a just settlement of a wage-dispute might be.

The elaboration of these particular and detailed—or, in traditional language, "remote"—principles of natural law falls therefore to the wise. One might even better say, in George Washington's famous phrase, "the wise and honest." Not only knowledgeability but rectitude of judgment is required. In farthest antiquity the wise were the lawgivers, who declared the law—that is, the customs—to the community and thus brought to consciousness the moral principles of community life which otherwise would not or perhaps could not be grasped by the individual. This is still the function of civil legislation, which has not lost its character as a moral discipline, even though so much legislation is now technical. In the course of human evolution the wise came to include the philosophers as well as the jurists. And in the growing complexity of the full human reality which is the characteristic of advanced civilization, these wise men have come to depend more and more on other scientific disciplines for aid in that analysis of reality which is the condition of all moral judgment. The dynamism behind the whole process was stated by St. Thomas: "Since a rational soul is the proper form of man, there is in every man a natural inclination to act according to reason; and this is to act according to virtue." To act against reason is to act against nature, that is, to sin.

St. Thomas, of course, had quite clearly in mind that "man" is not an abstract essence but a historical existent, who does not act in a vacuum of time and space, at the same time that he must always act as a man, and not as an animal or an angel. The fundamental structure of man's nature is, of course, permanent and unchanging; correlatively constant are the elementary human experiences. Every man, simply because he is a man, has to "meet" himself, others, and God. In these relationships he must avoid the evil and do the good that come home to him as evidently evil or good, if he at all understands the situation, as he must—*ut in pluribus*. This is the general truth that the ethical relativists go to great trouble to avoid in their theories, however little trouble they have in recognizing it in their own practical lives. Normally they are men who keep to moderation and avoid extremes; who render to others their due; who fulfill their contracts; who love their wives and cherish their children; who flee ignorance and seek truth; who honor their God, or at least their idols; and who otherwise conduct themselves as well-behaved natural-law jurists, even though they would be horrified to be called such. History does not alter the basic structure of human nature, nor affect the substance of the elementary human experiences, nor open before man wholly new destinies. Therefore history cannot alter the natural law, in so far as the natural law is constituted by the ethical a priori, by the primary principles of the moral reason, and by their immediate derivatives. History has not, for instance, abolished the Ten Commandments.

But history, as any history book shows, does change what I have called the human reality. It evokes situations that never happened before. It calls into being relationships that had not existed. It involves human life in an increasing multitude of institutions of all kinds, which proliferate in response to new human needs and desires, as well as in consequence of the creative possibilities that are inexhaustibly resident in human freedom. History has spread mankind over all the earth in a variety of climates and conditions that call for some adaptation of human reality. History has here halted, and there hastened, the progress of civilization. It has done the fateful thing of dividing men into nations, thus creating areas of collective self-interest whose harmony is by no means automatic. History, too, has set afoot the great enterprise of science, which has altered the relationship of man to the forces of cosmic nature and imparted to the whole concept of power a qualitatively new dimension. In a word, it has been abundantly proved in history that the nature of man is a historical nature. "The nature of man is susceptible of change," St. Thomas repeatedly states. History continually changes the community of mankind and alters the modes of communication between man and man, as these take form "through external acts," as St. Thomas says. In this sense, the nature of man changes in history, for better or for worse; at the same time that the fundamental structure of human nature, and the essential destinies of the human person, remain untouched and intact.

As all this happens, continually new problems are being put to the wisdom of the wise; at the same time, the same old problems are being put to every man, wise or not. The basic issue remains unchanged: what is man or society to do, here and now, in order that personal or social action may fulfill the human inclination to act according to reason. The same old problems get the same old answers, in terms of the same old primary principles of the natural law which, as primary, follow on the permanent structure of the nature of man and furnish the norms whereby man must always act in the constant recurrent basic human situations. In the case of the new problems, however, which are created by the changing structure of human social living, and which concern the particulars of morals, the answers may contain new specifications of old principles: "Things that are just and good may be considered in two ways. There is the formal consideration; and in this sense they are always and every-where the same, because the principles of right, which are in the natural reason, do not change. There is also the material consideration; and in this sense the same things are not always and everywhere good and just. They have to be determined by the law [he means 'by custom,' or 'by the declaration of the wise']. This happens on account of the mutability of human nature, and the diverse conditions of men and affairs according to the diversity of times and places."

This brief account of the structure and style of natural-law thought, and of the various areas in which it operates, will suffice for the moment. I come now to my proposition.

The Consensus and Natural Law

Only the theory of natural law, I said, can give an account of the moral ex-perience which is the public consensus, and thus lift it from the level of sheer experience to the higher level of intelligibility toward which, I take, the mind of man aspires. The structure of principle in terms of which this account is to be given, and this intelligibility achieved, is sufficiently de-posited in two texts of St. Thomas. Their essential point is the one that I have already made, that there are three areas of moral principle and three modes of moral judgment, all dependent on the one standard.

The first text occurs in a discussion of the way in which all moral pre-cepts belong to the law of nature. "In human action," he says, "there are certain things so explicit that they can immediately, on some slight re-flection, be accepted as good or repudiated as evil on grounds of the common and first principles." The reference is to the principles of action that govern what I have called the basic human situations that are con-stant and relatively uncomplicated. As the moral reason reaches these principles without difficulty, so too they find their way on obvious title into the criminal code of society; there are laws against perjury, theft, murder, adultery, etc. St. Thomas continues: "There are, however, other matters for whose judgment much reflection is required, bearing on di-versities of circumstance. The careful consideration of these circum-stances is not the province of anybody at all, but of the wise." Here it is a question of relatively complicated human situations in which the good and the evil—that is to say, the inherent demands of reason—are not so readily discerned, and the principles of right action are not evident to the man in the street.

Both sets of moral principles and judgment belong to the natural law, but in different ways: "There are certain things which the natural reason of every man, immediately and of itself, discerns and judges, as to be done or not to be done; for instance, honor your father and mother, do not kill, do not steal. Things of this sort are of the natural law in absolute fashion." That is to say, not only is their obligation unrestricted, but the perception of the obligation is common and easy to all men. He goes on: "There are, however, other matters which those who are wise judge, after rather subtle reflection, to be matters of necessary observance. These things are of the natural law indeed, but in such a way that they are matters for instruction. The wise must teach them to those of lesser reflectiveness; for instance, come to your feet in the presence of white hair, honor the prerogatives of age, and other such things." The examples may seem quaint, but they are apt to make the point, which is the moral thoughtlessness or obtuseness of the unreflective man.

The second text deals with the fact that certain precepts find place in the Decalogue and others do not; in explaining the fact fuller distinctions are made. First, the primary and common principles do not find place in this explicit statement of moral law, for the reason that "they need no declaration other than their inscription in natural reason as self-evident principles; for instance, that a man ought not to injure another, and that sort of thing." There are, however, two other classes of principles.

As the prelude to explaining the distinction between them St. Thomas cites the Old Testament history, according to which the basic and general moral principles (the Decalogue) were given directly to the people by God himself, whereas others of more particular import reached the people through the lawgiver, Moses. In terms of philosophical explanation, those precepts find place in the Decalogue, "the knowledge of which each man of himself has from God. These are the precepts that can be known, immediately and on slight reflection, from the first common principles." Here is the basic natural-law assertion, that the dictates of common human reason are the dictates of God, who is Eternal Reason, the Logos. This is the final explanation of their obligatory character. Their ultimate origin is divine, though the mode of their knowing is human and rational. The remaining category of principle does not find place in the Decalogue, because a "lawgiver" must intervene. This category includes those principles and rules "which the careful inquiries of the wise have found to be in accord with reason. These come from God to the people through the medium of the instruction of the wise." Their ultimate origin is the same, from God. Their mode of knowing is the same, through reason. But the "reason" here is tutored by experience and reflection. To use the term that arrived only lately, it is a "responsible" reason. It is not mere knowledgeability, or cleverness, or skill in dialectic, or the "viewiness" that Newman scorned. It is not a thing of intellect alone; it implies a love of truth, and a developed instinct for the right and good that are of the "heart," in the Hebrew sense of the word. The reason of the wise and good is dispassionate, but not cold. It is a disinterested reason that has, nonetheless, one supreme interest, the essential human interest, which is that man should do good and avoid evil. Finally, it is a reason that has penetrated, and come to understand, the complexities of the developing human situation.

Obviously, St. Thomas did not anticipate the multiform complexities of our contemporary industrial society with its maze of complicated interlocking institutions, political and socio-economic, national and international. In social matters he was, as a man of his time, extremely conservative. Like Aristotle, he viewed with foreboding, for instance, the fate of a city "that needs for its maintenance a great number of commercial dealings." This was, he thought, the way to the corruption of a city's identity through the introduction into it of alien customs and mores. The result would be to throw into disorder what he untranslatably called "civilis conversatio." This was his highest civic value—a whole manner of living together and talking together, in terms of which a city establishes its identity. Was he so very far wrong? Perhaps not, if one considers today's anxious questions about our own *civilis conversatio*. The "open society" today faces the question, how open can it afford to be, and still remain a society; how many barbarians can it tolerate, and still remain civil; how many "idiots" can it include (in the classical Greek sense of the "private person" who does not share in the public thought of the City), and still have a public life; how many idioms, alien to one another, can it admit, and still allow the possibility of civil conversation?

In any case, the present point is that St. Thomas did construct with firmness and delicacy a system of moral thought that renders a remarkable account of the origins and structure of the public consensus that today we have been told governs the industrial society and imparts to the processes and results of its economic action some quality of morality and humanity. The account may be set out under five headings.

The first point concerns the contents of the consensus. Technically, its principles and rules are "remote precepts of natural law." They are "removed" from the primary common precepts and from the immediately derivative precepts as particular conclusions are "removed" from the generality of the premises that engender them. These remote precepts bear on situations that might best be called "historical." That is, they are human situations indeed, but their creation requires a process of historical development, as original human situations do not. For instance, the situation that relates corporation stockholders to corporation management is more remote from the springs of nature than the situation that relates husband and wife. The former "got here" in time; the latter always substantially "is."

In consequence, the principles and standards of the consensus are by no means self-evident. They are reached by "careful inquiries." They suppose a thorough analysis of "circumstances," that is, of the existent reality in its full complexity in a given historical moment. They are formulated after "much reflection." Then they are proposed as "matters of necessary observance." They cover a certain span of cases and have therefore a measure of generality. It is the mode of generality that attaches to law; like law, the consensus covers what happens *ut in pluribus*, in most cases. The rules of the consensus may therefore be said to be *in genere legis*, a sort of law, even though they are not legal enactments. Between a legal enactment and a remote principle of natural law there intervenes all the difference that distinguishes the moral from the legal.

The second point concerns the elaboration of the consensus. This is not the work of the people at large. It is not the job for sheer common sense. The public consensus is not formally public opinion. Its elaboration is the task of the wise and honest. The "careful inquiries," the "rather subtle reflection," the analysis of "circumstances," the exact formulation of the "precept"—these tasks lie beyond the competence of the generality. It is for the wise, who develop the consensus, to give "instruction" to the generality, in the meaning of its principles as "matters of necessary observance," and also in the manner of their application. Public opinion, thus instructed by the wise, conspires to effect these applications. Thus the consensus exists in the public mind; but it exists in two forms or on two levels. In consciously articulated and reasoned form it exists among the wise. In the form of simple affirmation or accepted conviction it exists among the people.

The third point concerns the inherent authority of the consensus, the quality that makes its principles and rule to be "matters of necessary observance." If the public consensus comes into being at all, and wins the assent of the public mind, and actually sets a controlling hand, as it were, not hidden but visible, on the political-economic action of society, it is only because its principles "have been found, by the careful inquiry of the wise, to be in accord with reason." Behind the whole conception of the consensus there lies the single indisputable dynamism that is the root of the doctrine of natural law: "Since the rational soul is the proper form of man, there is in every man a natural inclination to act according to reason, that is, according to virtue." In the wise and honest this dynamism is more fully released and more purified; that is why they are honored as being wise and honest.

This quality of being in accord with reason is the non-contingent element in the body of thought that constitutes the consensus. Brute fact or sheer experience have no virtue to elaborate themselves into controlling rules of public conduct. The transcendence of experience and the transformation of fact into principle is the work of reason. The act whereby the doctrine of the consensus is formulated is not the act of inquiry into the facts, nor the act of reflection on the experience. It is an act of judgment, an exercise in moral affirmation or denial.

In summary of this account of the consensus in its relation to natural law, the contents of the consciousness of the wise may thus be stated: "Having come to know the situation of fact, and having reflected on it, we discern and decide that there is inherent in the factual situation a demand, which our reason perceives, that this action be commanded or that action forbidden. What our reason assents and consents to, as a rational demand of the situation, is a matter of necessary observance. It is not necessary simply as a matter of fact; nor is it necessary simply as a consequence of experience. The necessity of its observance decisively derives only from our understanding that in the given situation of fact this concrete demand is according to reason. Out of the situation itself, as factually known and rationally examined, this demand presents itself as the dictate, in the end, of reason. Therefore, it presents itself as a matter of necessary observance, in final virtue of the principle that what is in accord with reason is good (right, just, equitable, prudent, useful) and therefore is to be done. In so judging, we who are wise are right; that is, our judgment is the dictate of right reason. So we shall instruct the people of its rightness. So we, in alliance with the people, shall require that this dictate of reason be obeyed by the members of society, by the social 'forces,' by the economic 'powers.' And if obedience fails or is not forthcoming, we shall invoke the discipline of coercion in the aid of the dictate of reason. We shall require that this moral dictate be made public law."

Here then is the high warrant on which the writ of the consensus runs. Here too is the explanation of the consensus as a moral experience that is public. The reasonableness of its doctrine is the basis of the publicity of the experience. Once they have been instructed, those who are "of lesser reflective capacity" can grasp the reasonableness of the conclusions reached by the wise, even though they are incapable of the "careful inquiry" that led the wise to these conclusions. Here, finally, is the key to the most curious aspect of the whole matter, namely, that the economic powers in society accept the judgments, directions, and corrections of the public consensus, at times to their own disadvantage, even when these moral dictates are not backed by the coercive force of the supreme public power.

There is in men, even when they are powerful, some natural inclination to act according to reason in what concerns their power. That is, they naturally seek to establish the legitimacy of their power and also to have their uses of it publicly recognized as legitimate. They are naturally disinclined to appear to themselves or to others as unreasonable. They do not want their economic action to be judged "evil," not according to virtue, as virtue is concretely estimated by public judgment in the circumstances. In a word, they are somehow inclined to be "natural" men, who recognize and obey the remote principles of natural law that constitute the public consensus. Or, if this moral inclination fails, as it is likely to fail, in the face of the contrary imperatives of self-interest, these men of power are at least "natural" enough to submit to the just interventions of the public power in support of the public consensus.

If therefore there is, as Mr. Berle suggests, a public consensus constantly forming on the growing end of American life, its formation, I suggest, is a testimony to the slow and subtle operation of that rational dynamism, inherent in human nature, which is called natural law. This is the source from which human affairs acquire whatever quality of humanity may attach to them in any age of history. Again, the processes whereby the public consensus is formed are those characteristic of natural-law thinking. Finally, the social authority of the rules and standards that the consensus constantly develops is none other than the authority of natural law itself, that is, the high authority of right reason.

I must append a note. It concerns the architects or artisans of the public consensus. I do not myself care for the phrase, "Lords Spiritual," to designate them. The phrase has a historical flavor; but to my taste it has the wrong flavor. It tends to confuse two bodies and functions that were historically distinct. I mean *sacerdotium* and *studium*, the Church and the University. It is not the function of the Church as such to elaborate the public consensus, which is a body of rational knowledge, a structure of rational imperatives, that sustain and direct the action of the People Temporal and of their secular rulers. The proper task of the Church is the custody and development of the deposit of faith, which is a body of revealed truth, a structure of mystery, that sustains and directs the action of the People Spiritual. The public consensus is the property of the *studium*. This is the institution that, together with the Church, stood between the People and the Princes, the men of power, who bore the responsibility of using their power in the high service of justice and the freedom of the people. It is the function of the University, which has a care both for the princes and for the people, to see that this duty is wisely performed, chiefly by defining what justice is, and what the freedom of the people requires, in changing circumstances. The University assembles these definitions and requirements into the public consensus, whereby the prince's use of his power in respect of the people may be judged, directed, and corrected. The *sapientes* of whom St. Thomas speaks made their residence in the University, not in the Curia. They were not *domini*, but *magistri*, not Lords, but Masters. This is dignity enough; at least it was in those older days.

In the fulfillment of its function the University often had the support of the Church, since freedom and justice are integral to the *res sacra* that is committed to her. The Second Lateran Council, for instance, in 1139 blasted "the insatiable rapacity of money-lenders," and threatened them with the denial of Christian burial. But the argument about usury was carried on by the Masters. It was they who elaborated the fencing restrictions to be thrown about the growing power of money, in the name of justice. They did the work of reason, of reflection on the changing economic facts. It was not a "spiritual," but an "intellectual," task. The spiritual task was done by the Church, when she supported by her authority the work of reason. Sitting in Council, the Lords Spiritual confirmed the work of the Masters, who sat in the Study.

At that, the medieval analogy, rightly understood, may be of some assistance in answering the difficult question that always comes up when there is talk of the "wise and honest." Concretely, who are these men today? In regard of any given social, political, or economic issue that arises in our highly competitive society, in which power struggles are forever seething, who are the Masters, the Men of Reason, to whom both "princes" and "people" may look for judgment? In point of principle, and in dependence on the medieval diagram of forces (Church, Study, People, Princes), all one can say is that they are the men who have a "care," but who are not "interested parties" (in the usual sense of the latter phrase).

There was, for instance, a Jeremiah S. Black, who in 1883 refused a retainer to argue the railroad case against public regulation of railroads, because (he said) he was "pledged to the people on the issues at stake." There was a Louis D. Brandeis; when asked to represent the interests of a great investment banking group in a proxy fight involving the Illinois Central Railroad, he "required" (he said) to be "satisfied of the justness" of the bankers' position. This is the style of man one seeks, whose "care" is not an "interest."

Note

1. New York: Harcourt, Brace and Co., 1959.

CHAPTER FIVE

~

Creeds at War Intelligibly: Pluralism and the University

The articles of peace which are the religion-clauses of the First Amendment designed a framework for the solution to the problem of religious pluralism in America, in so far as this problem admits and requires a solution in terms of constitutional law. Whether this legal solution, genial in principle, is satisfactory in its current application to the major area of difficulty, the historic School Question, is a matter for later discussion. In any case, religious pluralism is far more than a problem in law. It does indeed present itself to the state, to constitutional assemblies, legislatures, and courts. But these institutions have only a severely limited function, since they can do no more than bring the directive and coercive force of law to bear on the order of external social action—what is called the public order—in the interests of a necessary minimum of public peace.

In its deeper implications religious pluralism is a problem in the order of truth. It goes without saying that it presents itself to the mind and conscience of every individual who is concerned, as every individual must be concerned, to know the truth and to find God in peace. This, however, is not the aspect of the problem that claims my attention here. My narrower point is that the problem of religious pluralism presents itself to society. More exactly, it presents itself to the university. By the university I mean here that social institution whose function it is to bring the resources of reason and intelligence to bear, through all the disciplines of learning and teaching, on the problems of truth and understanding that confront society because they confront the mind of man himself.

What then is the competence, and what is the function, of the university with regard to the social problem of religious pluralism? The question is not easy to answer. This may be a major reason why it is so seldom asked.

Religious Pluralism and Modernity

It must first be noted that religious pluralism in America today has its own distinctive historical quality. Our society is not the ancient Christian Empire, with its divisions between Arian (or Nestorian) and Catholic Christianity. It is not the medieval commonwealth, with its many schools of contrasting philosophical and legal thought, whose conflicts were often sharpened by involvement in the constant polemic between the imperial power and the authority of the Church. It is not the post-Reformation Continental nation-state, with its religious wars between Catholic and Protestant. Nor is it the post-Revolution "Catholic nation," with its pluralism of attitudes towards Catholicism, ranging from the most devout fidelity all the way to the extremes of anti-clericalism in the Latin Continental sense. Religious pluralism in American society is basically related to the kind of Ultimate Questions that have become the typical concern of modernity, as modernity has run its historic course and, in the process, carried the perennial human argument to ever more fundamental issues.

The Basic Question that modernity has come to ask is, of course, what is man? From this question all the others proliferate; to it, in one way or another, they all return.

What is the rank of man within the order of being, if there is an order of being? Is the nature of man simply continuous with the nature of the cosmic universe, to be understood in terms of its laws, whatever they may be? Or is there a discontinuity between man and the rest of nature, in that the nature of man is spiritual in a unique sense? Whence is man's origin? And what is his destiny? Is it to be found and fulfilled within terrestrial history or does it lie beyond time in "another world"? What is the "sense" of man's history, its direction and meaning and finality? Or is the category of "finality" meaningless? What can a man know? What do you mean when you say, "I know"? What manner of certitude or certainty attaches to human knowledge? Is knowledge a univocal term or are there diverse modes and degrees of knowledge, discontinuous one from another? What mental equivalents attach to all the words that have long been the currency of civilized discourse—freedom, justice, order, law, authority, power, peace, virtue, morality, religion? Can man's knowledge and his love reach to realities that transcend the world of matter, space, and time? Is there a God? What is God? A Person, or a Power, or only a Projection—whether of man's consciousness or of his unconscious? Does God have a care for man? How has He shown it? Has God entered the world of human history? Has He undertaken to accomplish a "redemption" of man? Does man need to be redeemed from sin or only from anxiety? Is man to be rescued from death or only from the fear of death? Is "salvation" only a reassuring ambiguity, an illusion and not a hope? If it is a hope, is there a plan of salvation? And if there is, does it include the Church? What is the Church? Is it a human thing, the work of man himself? Or is it a divine gift to man—not a "gathered" but a "given" Church? Since the Church somehow looks to Christ, who is this "man, Christ Jesus"? By whom was the truth about him stated—by Arius or Nestorius or Eutyches, or by Chalcedon? Was Chalcedon only Hellenism, a human accomplishment, or was the Holy Spirit in assistance to the assembled Fathers? And, farther back, since the Fathers appealed to the Bible, what is the Bible? Is it singly the work of men or is God Himself somehow its "author"? Do its books tell simply a human story or do they record the *magnalia Dei*, the wonderful deeds and words of God?

All these questions, and others related to them, concern the essentials of human existence. Through all of them there runs the continuous thread of modernity's basic question, what is man? The multiplicity of answers to all these questions, and the multiple ways of refusing the questions themselves, are in general what we mean by the religious pluralism of the modern age. Integral to the pluralism is the skeptic or agnostic view that it is useless or illegitimate even to ask Ultimate Questions.

If the university takes its function seriously, it ought to find itself in the characteristically modern situation of religious conflict, which is at once intellectual and passionate, a clash of individual minds and of organized opinions. Any refusal on the part of the university (and the university sometimes makes this refusal) to recognize its own spiritual and intellectual situation would be a flight from reality. The university would succumb to a special type of neurotic disorder if it were to cultivate an "inflated image" of itself as somehow standing in all serenity "above" the religious wars that rage beneath the surface of modern life and as somehow privileged to disregard these conflicts as irrelevant to its "search for truth." The only inner disorder that would be worse than this would be a flight to the fantasy that the university is omnicompetent to judge the issues of truth involved in all the pluralisms of contemporary society.

The New Problematic

If pluralism in the sense explained is the characteristic fact of contemporary society, it is also the original root of certain problems that are no less characteristic. An increasing preoccupation with the problematic aspects of pluralism is indeed one of the most interesting phenomena of the present time, which distinguishes it from the heyday of classical liberalism, when man's faith in the assumptions, spoken and unspoken, of an extreme individualism was still unshaken. For instance, it used to be assumed, as a cardinal merit of a pluralist society, that the truth would always be assured of conquest if only it were subjected to the unbridled competition of the market place of ideas. But it is now no longer possible to cherish this naïveté. For further instance, it used to be assumed that an ever-expanding variety of conflicting religious and philosophical views was per se an index of richness, a pledge of vitality, a proof of the values of individualism, a guarantee against stagnation, and so on. But history has not left this assumption intact. In a word, it used to be assumed that pluralism represented "progress." But now the question has arisen, whether its proliferation may not be causatively related to certain observable decadences within the area of intellectual life. A few might be mentioned, but without any intention of exploring the whole subject here.

There is, for instance, the advance of solipsism, the view that my insight is mine alone and cannot be shared by another, much less by a community; this view is, of course, the destruction of the classical and Christian concept of reason. There is the dissolution of the ancient idea of the unity of truth, a unity that admits and demands distinctions and differentiations interior to itself, in consequence of which the concept of truth acquires an inner architecture whose structural elements are articulated in accord with a hierarchical principle. There is the consequent dissolution of the idea of truth itself, to the point where no assertion may claim more than the status of mere opinion, to be granted an equality of freedom with any other opinion. In further consequence there has occurred the dispersal into meaninglessness of all that Socrates meant by the "order of the soul."

There has also occurred that drastic contraction of the dimensions of reason and that severe devaluation of intelligence which usually goes by the name of "scientism," or, if you will, "positivism." This is the theory that "truth" is a univocal term, and that the single technique valid in the "search" for truth is the empirical method of science. This theory is the denial of the possibility of philosophy in the meaning that the word has had since Plato. Finally, there has taken place a decay of the political intelligence, a loss of confidence in the power of reason to fix the purposes of political life and to direct the energies of freedom in such a way as to impose a due measure of human control upon the forces of history, upon the automatisms of technology, and upon the hurrying pace of events. But perhaps the ultimate tendency of the pluralisms created by the era of modernity is felt, as I have elsewhere said, rather in the realm of affectivity than in the realm of reason as such. The fact today is not simply that we hold different views but that we have become different types of men, with different styles of interior life. We are therefore uneasy in one another's presence. We are not, in fact, present to one another at all; we are absent from one another. That is, I am not transparent to the other, nor he to me; our mutual experience is that of an opaqueness. And this reciprocal opaqueness is the root of a hostility that is overcome only with an effort, if at all.

My suggestion then is that the problem of pluralism has begun to appear in a new light. Perhaps the basic reason for this is the fact that we are entering a new era. Whether it will be a better or even a good era is another question that still remains open. In any case, we have reached the end of the era that gave itself the qualification "modern."

This observation is not original. A Catholic theologian, Romano Guardini, has written a book—*The End of the Modern World*. The thesis of this book is sustained firmly, if not so formally, by an English social scientist, Michael Polanyi. A Protestant philosopher, W. Ernest Hocking, has defined today's problem as the "passage beyond modernity." A political scientist, Eric Voegelin, has pointed to the fact that the "reduction" of man, from image of God down to a mass of biological drives, has "run its whole gamut"; and he has drawn the conclusion that this fact is "for the social scientist the most important index that 'modernity' has run its course." A historian, Geoffrey Barraclough, has done an essay with the title, "The End of European History," meaning in context the end of the history of modern Europe. A Protestant theologian, Paul Tillich, has put forward the thesis that in some identifiable sense an end has been put to what he calls the "Protestant era," which was itself an important aspect of modernity. Arnold Toynbee has gone so far as to popularize the notion that our present era is not only post-modern but also post-Christian.

If these observers, whose points of view are so diverse, may claim credence, it follows that we confront a whole new set of problems. There is, of course, the problem of salvaging those elements of truth and moral value which gave vitality to the whole movement called "modernity." But my question concerns only the manifold pluralisms, in the sense explained, which have been the special creation of modernity. With the dissolution of the age that made them, are these pluralisms somehow and to some extent to be unmade?

It would seem that the process of unmaking them is already importantly afoot. Protestantism, for instance, now feels its own inner discordant pluralisms as no longer an unqualified glory but as something of a scandal; and in the Ecumenical Movement it is in quest of its own unities. Catholicism in turn now feels that certain of its past unities were something of a scandal; we now reject, for instance, the specious unity asserted in Belloc's famous thesis that "Europe is the faith and the faith is Europe." In consequence the Church is asserting with sharper emphasis its own proper sacramental unity, altogether universal, altogether spiritual, not enfeoffed to any historical culture but transcendent to every culture at the same time that it is a leaven in all cultures. Again, the entity called "Europe" has realized that its modern pluralisms of many kinds, of which it was once boastfully jealous, are importantly the cause of its own present impotence. The "good European" has now emerged, and his quest is for some manner and measure of unity that will begin for Europe a new history and regain for it a due share of its lost significance in the realm of historical action. The Communist too, whether Soviet or Chinese, cherishes his own dream of a demonic unification of the world. And in the United States, finally, the problem of unity in its relation to the pluralisms of American society has begun to be felt with a new seriousness.

True enough, the problem is not seldom raised in a way that is false. One thinks, for instance, of the New Nativism, as represented by Mr. Paul Blanshard; or of the issue of "conformism," about which there is so much confused talk; or of the current anxieties about internal subversion, regarded as a threat to an American unity ("there are those among us who are not of us"). And so on. But even the falsities attendant upon the manner in which the issue of unity-amid-pluralism is raised bear witness to the reality of the issue itself.

The question has been asked: How much of the pluralism is bogus and unreal? And how much of the unity is likewise bogus and undesirable? The more general question has been asked: How much pluralism and what kinds of pluralism can a pluralist society stand? And conversely, how much unity and what kind of unity does a pluralist society need in order to be a society at all, effectively organized for responsible action in history, and yet a "free" society?

Similarly, certain words have now acquired a respectability that was long denied them—the word "order," for instance, which now is disjunctively coupled with the word "freedom," with the fading of the typically modern illusion that somehow "freedom" is itself the principle of order.

Finally, responsible and informed thinkers can now discourse about the "public philosophy" of America, considering it to be a valid concept which furnishes the premises for dissent, to be identified as dissent even though the public philosophy itself contains no tenets that would justify coercion of the dissenter. In the same fashion serious inquiries are now made into the American consensus —whether there be such a thing and what it is and whence it came and how it may be kept alive and operative by argument among reasonable men. Moreover, since every social consensus that supports and directs the historical action of a given political community is always to a considerable extent a legacy from an earlier age, questions have been asked about the American heritage and about the manner in which it has developed. Has the America of today been true to its own spiritual origins? Indeed, were the principles that lay at its origins ambiguous to some extent, so as to permit various lines of development, not all of them happy? Is the American man of today an "exile from his own past" (as Geoffrey Brunn said of European man)?

The central point here is that the quest for unity-amid-pluralism has assumed a new urgency in the mind of post-modern man.

In this connection it might be well to advert to the fact that, since St. Augustine's description of the "two cities," it has been realized that societal unity may, broadly speaking, be of two orders—the divine or the demonic. It is of the divine order when it is the product of faith, reason, freedom, justice, law, and love. Within the social unity created by these forces, which are instinct with all the divinity that resides in man, the human personality itself grows to its destined stature of dignity at the same time that the community achieves its unity. Societal unity is of the demonic order when it is the product of force, whether the force be violent or subtle. There are, for instance, all the kinds of force that operate in the industrial society created by modernity (irrational political propaganda, commercial advertising, all the assaults upon reason and taste that are launched by mass amusements, and the like). These forces operate under the device of "freedom," but unto the disintegration of the human personality, and unto the more or less forcible unification of social life on a level lower than that established, forever, by Aristotle's "reasonable man" and by his Christian completion. The quest for unity-amid-pluralism must therefore be critical of its own impulses. Its stimulus must not be passion, whether the passion be imperialist (the will to power) or craven (fear and anxiety).

The Problem for the University

What then might be the functions of the university in the face of the problem of pluralism as newly presented at the outset of the post-modern era? The premise of the question is the fact that the basic issues have come to matter to men in a new way. Does this fact matter to the university? Many of the commitments of modernity—shared by the university, because it too has been modern— have dissolved in disenchantment. Does their dissolution make any difference to the university? The positivistic universe (if the phrase be not a contradiction *in adiecto*) has come to seem a wilderness of disorder to the soul of man, which cannot be content to live in chaos, since it is always aware, however dimly, that it is natively committed to the discovery of an order in reality or, alternatively, to the imposition of an order on reality, perhaps at high cost both to reality and to itself. Is post-modern man's new commitment to order of any interest to the university?

I know, of course, that the word "commitment" used in regard of a university raises specters. I am not myself fond of the word; it is more distinctively part of the Protestant vocabulary, which is not mine. (Moreover the dictionary adds to its definition: ". . . esp. to prison"!) In any case, some nice questions center around the word. Is the university, as a matter of fact, uncommitted? And in what senses or in what directions? Is "non-committalism" an intellectual virtue or is it a vice of the whole personality? Is a commitment to "freedom," understanding "freedom" to be a purely formal category, any more a valid premise of the intellectual life than a commitment to the Kantian *Moralprinzip,* understood as a purely formal category, is a valid premise for the moral life? What, in the latter case, are the "universal norms" in accord with which the individual is to act, in such wise that the norms of his action may be made universal? And analogously, in the former case, what is this "truth" for which one is to be "free" to search?

Leaving these interesting questions aside, we might better come to more concrete matters and venture a few assertions of a practical kind. First, I venture to assert that the university is committed to the task of putting an end, as far as it can, to intellectual savagery in all its forms, including a major current form, which is the savagery of the American student (perhaps also the professor?) who in matters religious and theological is an untutored child of the intellectual wilderness. Again, the university is committed to the task of putting an end to prejudice based on ignorance, by helping to banish the ignorance. Unless indeed the university wishes to commit itself to the prejudice that religious knowledge is really ignorance.

The assertion I chiefly wish to venture, however, is that the university is committed to its students and to their freedom to learn. Its students are not abstractions. And whatever may be the university's duty (or right, or privilege, or sin) of non-committalism, the fact is that many of its students are religiously committed. To put it concretely, they believe in God. Or to put it even more concretely, they are Protestants, Catholics, Jews. The university as such has no right to judge the validity of any of these commitments. Similarly, it has no right to ignore the fact of these commitments, much less to require that for the space of four years its students should be committed to being scientific naturalists within the university, whatever else they may choose, somewhat schizophrenically, to commit themselves to be outside its walls.

The major issue here is the student's freedom to learn—to explore the full intellectual dimensions of the religious faith to which he is committed. He comes to college with the "faith of the charcoal burner," of course. And it is the right of the university to require that his quest of religious knowledge should be pursued in the high university style—under properly qualified professors, in courses of high academic content, in accordance with the best methods of theological scholarship, and so on. But this right of the university should itself conspire with the student's own freedom to learn, so as to create the academic empowerment that is presently almost wholly lacking. Your college and university student is academically empowered to grow in all the dimensions of knowledge—except the dimension of religious knowledge.

What is the formula for translating the student's freedom to learn about his religious faith into a genuine empowerment? The question would have to be argued; and it might not be possible to devise a uniformly applicable formula.

In any case, the formula of the "religious emphasis week" is hopelessly inadequate; and when it becomes simply a piece of public relations it is also unworthy of a university. Again, the formula of a "department of religion" is no good, unless the "religion" of the department includes the major historic faiths, which is rarely the case. As for a "department of religion *and* philosophy," it chiefly serves to confuse the issue. In its most destructive concrete mode of operation it blurs the clear line of distinction that traditional Christianity has drawn between the order of faith and the order of reason. (Incidentally, it is not for the university to say that this line ought to be blurred or moved from its traditional position.)

Whatever the concrete formula may be, it must reckon with the factual pluralism of American society, insofar as this pluralism is real and not illusory. There can be no question of any bogus irenicism or of the submergence of religious differences in a vague haze of "fellowship." It is not, and cannot be, the function of the university to reduce modern pluralism to unity. However, it might be that the university could make some contribution to a quite different task—namely, the reduction of modern pluralism to intelligibility.

This is an intellectual task. It bears upon the clarification of the pluralism itself. The Protestant charcoal burner today knows well enough that he differs from the Catholic charcoal burner, and vice versa. But it is not so certain that either of them could say why, in any articulate fashion. And if one or the other should undertake to give reasons, they would probably be mistaken, or distorted, or unclear, or even irrelevant. Anyone who has attended a run-of-the mill college "bull session" will know this.

From this point of view I would specify two general academic objectives at which a college or university could legitimately aim, in the field of religious knowledge, as its contribution to a clarification of the problem of pluralism.

The first is a genuine understanding of the epistemology of religious truth—or, if you will, an understanding of the nature of religious faith. It is precisely here that modern pluralism has its roots. Karl Barth was making the point when he said, in effect, that it is no use discussing the question, whether we believe in common certain articles of the creed, when we are in radical disagreement on the more crucial question, what is the meaning of the word with which the creed begins, "Credo." It is in consequence of this radical disagreement that Catholicism and Protestantism appear as, and are, systems of belief that bear to each other only an analogical relationship. That is to say, they are somewhat the same, and totally different. One would expect the mature Catholic and Protestant mind to understand this fact, which takes a bit of understanding.

The second understanding—and academic objectives can be stated only in terms of understanding—would be of the various systems of belief, precisely as systems, in their inner organic consistency (whatever it may be), and in their relation to other areas of human knowledge (insofar as these relations are intellectually discernible).

These two objectives are not unworthy of an institution of higher learning. They also coincide with the objectives that the student should be made free to reach. If he did reach them, he would be on emergence from college less a rustic than when he entered. And would not his college gently rejoice? The preservation of rusticities can hardly rank high among the preoccupations of the college dean.

When considered in terms of these two objectives, the practical difficulties appear less formidable than they are sometimes thought to be. There may indeed be some three hundred religious bodies in America. But there are not that many "styles" of religious belief. In fact, there are generically only three—the Protestant, the Catholic, and the Jewish. They are radically different "styles" and no one of them is reducible, or perhaps even comparable, to any of the others. And in each case the style of the epistemology of faith is related to the structure of the theology (or possibly to the absence of a theology).

The academic content of possible courses would be no great problem, except as it involves selection from a wealth of materials. The Catholic theological tradition is a treasury that even lifelong study cannot exhaust. Judaism has its learning, rich and venerable. And today the Protestant has the task of assimilating the already great, and still growing, body of ecumenical theology. No college or university should have to worry about its academic standards if it were to turn its students loose, under expert guidance, into these three great storehouses of thought.

Under expert guidance—that might be the greatest practical problem. Specially trained men would be needed. One could only hope that they would become available as opportunities opened before them. For the rest, I should only insist on one principle. It was stated by John Stuart Mill when he said, in effect, that every position should be explained and defended by a man who holds it, and who therefore is able to make the case for it most competently. This is, in a special way, a restatement of the principle upon which St. Augustine tirelessly dwelt: "*Nisi credideritis, non intelligetis.*" Unless you believe, you will not understand. The communication of understanding supposes its possession. I do not myself accept the pedagogical canon, seemingly popular in university circles, that every position ought to be explained by one who is sympathetic with it but who personally rejects it. It has never seemed to me that this is a canon of "objectivity" at all. Nor does it ensure the communication of a critical understanding of the position in question, given the principle that only an immanent critique, as it is called, can lead to this desirable type of understanding. In any case, my own view is that the only path to genuine understanding of a religious faith lies through the faith itself. The possession of the faith is therefore the proper qualification of the professor who would wish to communicate a critical understanding of it.

These are but a few practical suggestions toward a definition of the role of the university in the face of the problem of pluralism today. In conclusion, it should go without saying that the function of the university is not at all messianic. It is entirely minimal. The basic issues, deeply considered, do in the end raise in the mind of man the issue of "salvation." But if post-modern man hopes for salvation, he must set his hope elsewhere than on the university. Henry Adams's gratitude to Harvard for its contribution to his intellectual development is the highest gratitude that the university can merit from man in search of salvation. Harvard, said Adams in effect, did not get in my way. But this is no small cause for gratitude when the issue at stake is salvation.

PART II

~

FOUR UNFINISHED ARGUMENTS

CHAPTER SIX

~

Is It Justice?
The School Question Today

It is a commonplace that the Founding Fathers lived in, and legislated for, a far simpler age than ours. For instance, they completed their work long before the advent of what Alexander Meiklejohn has called the great "revolution" of modern times, that is, the transfer of education from the church to the state. Hence, when they framed the First Amendment, they had before them a comparatively simple problem. It was no more than the problem of religion in its relation to the public order of society and therefore to the (still uncomplicated) institutions of the state. Among these institutions the school had not yet found a place. Then came the revolution. In consequence, the School Question has become an integral part of our historical legacy of problems. The argument about it is still far from finished. Or, from another point of view, the real argument has hardly begun.

I shall omit all discussion of the historical genesis of the problem, in its two related aspects, that is, the relation of religion to public education, and the relation of the religious school to public authority and law. Moreover, I shall not elaborate the contention that this twofold problem is altogether real today, indeed, never more real than today. This contention will be readily granted by anyone who has followed and understood the changes that have been operated within our pluralist society over the past two generations.

The Old Solution in the New Situation

Changes in educational theory have taken place, with the result that the question today among informed educators is not the outdated one, whether there should be an "ideological" element present in the schooling of the young. The only question now is, what should this ideological element be? Moreover, people of perception today see quite clearly that the legal denial of all manner of public aid to religious schools does not fit with the present social affirmation of the value of what these schools are doing, precisely inasmuch as they are giving solid religious instruction and formation.

Again, changes have occurred in the religio-social structure of America that have profoundly altered the understanding which nineteenth-century America had of itself. From a socio-religious point of view, American society has assumed a new pluralist structure, notably different from the structure it exhibited a century ago when the public school system had its beginnings.

America's new self-understanding—its understanding of the new structure of its religious pluralism—has invalidated four concepts of the public school that have been entertained. I mean the concept of the public school as (a) vaguely Protestant or (b) purely secular in its atmosphere. I also mean the concept of the public school as the vehicle (a) for the inculcation of "democracy" as a quasi-religious ideology, or (b) for the transmission of spiritual and moral values in some non-sectarian sense. None of these four concepts fit with the present facts of American life. American society is neither vaguely Protestant nor purely secular. The religion of America is not "democracy," nor is it some generalized faith in "values." Religion in America has a form, a precisely defined form, a pluralistically structured form. This is the fact.

This fact has consequences. It has consequences with regard to the present desire and effort to relate public education more vitally to religion. It also has consequences with regard to the dual pattern assumed by the American educational system in the nineteenth century—that is, the public school as the single publicly supported school, and the church-school as barred from public support. This historical pattern is outdated. It is an anomaly in our present pluralist society. It is a relic of the past, surviving in the present on the momentum of ideas and social facts that time itself has left behind.

Obviously, I am not implying that there is an easy or rapid solution for the presently unsolved problem of the segregationist pattern of American public education—the segregation of religion, in the concrete pluralist sense, from public school premises, and the segregation of the religious school from public aid. The solution, like the creation of the problem itself, will be the work of generations. And nobody knows in this moment what the solution will be, save that it will be reached, as I shall say, by a balance of all the relevant principles.

In any event, the dynamism of change will be the familiar one that continually operates in American life. I mean a growth in moral insight, assisted by a realistic grasp of socio-religious reality. Perhaps an analogy will illustrate the workings of this dynamism.

The Supreme Court has ruled that the doctrine of "separate but equal" educational facilities for Negroes is incompatible with the present-day American constitutional concept of civic equality within the unity of the body politic. The decision is a good example of the way in which sociological alterations sharpen moral judgments and thus lead to legal changes.

From the moral point of view the "separate but equal" doctrine was always unjust; racial discrimination cannot be defended on moral grounds. Nonetheless, the doctrine could once have been defended from a sociological point of view as necessary in the circumstances—in view of the unenlightened state of the public conscience, the temporarily inferior cultural status of the Negro, etc. However, circumstances have changed and the level of the public conscience has risen above ancient irrational prejudices. The sociological defense of the doctrine is no longer admissible. Therefore, the moral judgment must prevail. And the law should conform itself to this moral judgment. The doctrine of separate but equal facilities, which never had any status in morals, no longer has any status in law.

The analogy is easily constructed. The doctrine that public aid should be denied by law to certain schools simply on the grounds that they teach a particular religion was never in conformity with the moral canon of distributive justice. This moral norm requires that government, in distributing burdens and benefits within the community, should have in view the needs, merits, and capacities of the various groups of citizens and of society in general. The operation of this norm is visible in many fields—income tax laws, selective service, social security, labor laws, etc. It ought likewise to control the action of government in support of schools. The principle of distributive justice would require that a proportionately just measure of public support should be available to such schools as serve the public cause of popular education, whether these schools be specifically religious in their affiliation and orientation, or not.

Admittedly, the application of this moral principle within the special conditions of American society would be extremely difficult. But I am here citing the principle itself; I leave aside such concrete problems of application as, for instance, the question, what would concretely be a "proportionately just" measure of support for any existent institutionalized system of religious schools. My point is that the nineteenth-century pattern of popular education—the dual pattern described above—has always fallen under adverse moral judgment, and the principle of judgment has always been the moral norm of distributive justice.

Nonetheless, this dual pattern, with its legal denial of public support to church-affiliated schools, which never could have been defended by any manner of abstract argument, might once have been defended by a manner of sociological argument. The grounds would be that it sufficiently reflected the realities of American society; that it fitted with the community's understanding of itself as somehow vaguely Protestant or secular; that it was in accord with the nineteenth-century concept of American religious pluralism; that it was a necessary concession to popular religious prejudices; that, in general, it approved itself to the public conscience as being necessary in the circumstances. None of these sociological arguments is presently valid. They have been basically invalidated by the alteration in the pluralist structure of American society.

The public school system still, of course, merits strong defense, the more so as it gradually succeeds in relating itself realistically to the religious realities of the United States. But the old dual pattern is out of touch with contemporary socio-religious reality. The notion of "public education" as meaning a unitary and monolithic school system which singly and alone is entitled to public support has been rightly called (by Mr. Robert E. Rodes, Jr.) "an aberration in the general picture of our society, which is pluralistic."

One would expect that, as the pattern of society has altered and assumed a new pluralistic structure, so too would the pattern of the school system. The religious school would still remain "private" in a sense; it is a special kind of school which serves the religious and educational needs of a particular community—the Catholic community, for instance. However, the change in the sociological status of this particular community within the one American community would require some manner of corresponding change in the status of the school system that serves its needs.

We have not to do here with a small eccentric group, existing on the periphery of American society, whose needs might possibly be overlooked in the interests of some greater good. On the contrary, we have to do with a segment of our society, fully integrated into its pluralist structure, which has now become so large that its educational needs and interests have become public needs and interests, at the same time that they remain special to the particular community. It must be remembered that the good of a pluralist society has to be defined in pluralist terms. The needs and interests of the three communities which make up American society are not all the same. But the social equality of these three communities entitles each of them to require that the public service should accommodate itself to its particular needs, in accordance with a good American principle to which I shall later refer. This accommodation would, in turn, require an alteration in the present status of the school system which serves the needs of a particular religious community in America. The denial of all manner of public aid to this kind of school system is an anomaly today. It represents a failure or a refusal to deal with the facts, with the altered realities of American life.

Here again, a true appreciation of sociological change serves to clarify a moral principle. The denial of aid to the religious school does not square with the fact of our pluralist social structure. One who sees this will likewise see that this denial does not square with the principle of distributive justice. American government today is not reckoning fairly with the diverse educational needs of the pluralist community which it is supposed to be serving. There is something wrong here. And the realization that something is wrong is forcing itself upon an increasing number of American citizens who understand both the nature of our society and the principles of our government. There is an increasing disposition to recognize that the state laws which forbid all manner of public aid to church-affiliated schools are both out of date and at variance with justice. I do not believe that anyone really sees the solution to this problem; it is much too complicated. But I do believe that a decisive number of people see the problem itself. And they realize that nineteenth-century legislation does not solve the problem as it appears in mid-twentieth century.

The Old Principles and the New Solution

From the restricted legal point of view the general problem is to validate in law an interpretation of the First Amendment in its application to the school experience of religion that will rightly command the rational consent of the governed. This is not impossible. Our whole constitutional history has been guided by what is now an explicit theory—the theory of the dynamic development of judicially enforced constitutions. Our constitutional law is a living law. It has, therefore, two characteristics. First, it must remain true to the inner spirit that animates all its provisions; I mean the idea that the American is a free man under a limited government whose actions are themselves subject to a higher law which derives from the Eternal Reason of the Creator of all things and is embodied in the very nature of man as God's creature and image. Second, remaining true to this inner idea and spirit, our constitutional law must reckon with the changing realities of American life—whether they be social or economic or religious realities. A constitutional development is truly dynamic when it reveals both of these characteristics.

I venture to say that the *McCollum* rule, taken in all its naked absoluteness, reveals neither of them. It is false to the spirit of the Constitution in consequence of the limitations it places on the religious freedom of American citizens. It is reactionary in consequence of its failure to take account of today's educational, social, and religious realities. It is the very opposite of a dynamic development in the true American tradition.

Such a development can be set afoot only if we renew the wisdom of the past in the light of the realities of the present; if, that is, we repossess the full American tradition and then apply it for what it inherently is— a tradition of progress.

An initial question concerns the mind of the Founding Fathers as expressed in the legislative history and intent of the First Amendment. There are those who say that the "no establishment" clause, thus historically interpreted, simply forbids preferential aid to one religion and consequently permits non-preferential aid to all religions. There are those who further say that the whole problem of government aid to religion in the school ought to be solved by a return to this historical understanding of the First Amendment. This point of view has a certain currency. It is sometimes asserted that it represents the official position of the Catholic Church in America—an assertion that is erroneous.

Without pausing to analyze the merits of this view, which are considerable, I shall simply say that it does not furnish us with all the premises necessary for the constitutional development that is needed today. The historical canon of original legislative intent is important, but it is hardly decisive in this present matter. What will be decisive is the full American tradition itself. The problem is to assemble all the relevant principles, bring them into harmony, and give them whatever rightful development they may need in the light of today's realities.

One constitutional principle, of course, is "no establishment of religion"; it is otherwise called the principle of "separation of church and state," or in more recent language, the principle of "no aid to religion." These three concepts are equivalent. But their concrete meaning is not self-evident. They are, in the words of Mr. Justice Frankfurter, "spacious concepts." Their content and implications require continuing reexamination and revision as new problems of application arise. And the tradition itself gives us three imperative norms to guide us in this matter of interpretation and application.

The first norm is the traditional concern to keep inviolate, in changing circumstances, the right to the free exercise of religion. This right is guaranteed by the same Amendment which legislates the separation of church and state. It is the more lofty provision, to which separation of church and state is instrumental. Therefore, it must be a primary judicial and popular concern to view the two clauses of the First Amendment in their right relation to each other. It is contrary to the American tradition to view separation of church and state as a categorical absolute, to be rigidly enforced, no matter what may be the effects on free exercise of religion.

Second, it is not permissible to read into the concept of separation of church and state a philosophy of hostility to religion. This principle was explicitly recognized by the Supreme Court in the *Zorach* case. The whole intent of the First Amendment was to protect, not to injure, the interests of religion in American society. Here there enters with its full force the fact also adverted to by the Court in the *Zorach* case: "We are a religious people whose institutions presuppose a Supreme Being." Lincoln put it more briefly in his famous phrase, "This nation under God." In America the separation of government and religion (to use Madison's favorite phrase, which is more exact than "separation of church and state") does not mean that government is hostile or even indifferent to the things of God. On the contrary, the tradition in America has been (again to use the words of the *Zorach* decision) that government "respects the religious nature of the people and accommodates the public service to their spiritual needs."

Here, in the concept of "accommodation" we have the third legal principle inherent in our tradition. It is simply an extension of the more general principle of the service-character of American government. In Lincoln's more concrete formula, ours is a government "for the people," for the service of their felt needs, for the promotion of their common good. It has never been the tradition in America for government in any of its agencies to regard the spiritual and religious needs of the people as being entirely outside the scope of its active concern. On the contrary, instances of government accommodating its public service to these needs are deeply imbedded in our constitutional history.

The two outstanding examples are, first, chaplaincies in the armed forces and the use of government funds for the construction of chapels for use by the military; and, second, the grant of tax exemption to properties of religious institutions. These are certainly instances of governmental aid to religion. They serve to illustrate the fact that the constitutional principle of "no aid to religion" cannot be regarded as an absolute.

It cannot be contended, as some writers wish to contend, that these and other instances of governmental aid to religion represent departures from tradition, violations of constitutional principle, survivals from the past that future "progress" will do away with. This is a wrong view. These examples are living reminders of what the tradition really is. They are entirely in accord with the full body of American principle in this matter of the relation of government and religion. In particular they illustrate the principle that governmental aid to religion is not unconstitutional when it represents a legitimate accommodation of the public service to the religious and spiritual needs of the people.

Such accommodation—or, if you will, such cooperation between church and state—has traditionally been regarded as permissible under conditions that are not difficult to define. One condition is that such cooperation should not infringe, but rather support, the right to the free exercise of religion. Another condition is that government responsibility for action in the particular matter should be well defined. These two conditions are particularly clear in the case of military chaplaincies. The men and women in the armed forces are clearly the objects of special governmental responsibility, not least in what regards their spiritual welfare. Hence, it devolves upon government to fortify the right to the free exercise of religion in the circumstances of military life.

This principle of accommodation served as a guide in the decision of the *Zorach* case. It appears in this statement of the Court: "When the state encourages religious instruction or cooperates with religious authorities by adjusting the schedule of public events to sectarian needs, it follows the best of our traditions."

It is this, the best of our traditions, that now needs development to meet the problem which educational and religio-social changes have made acute. The principle of the accommodation of the public service to the spiritual needs of our religious people is itself a spacious concept. Its development will afford the proper counterbalance to the presently overdeveloped doctrine of "no aid to religion." What it implies in the way of cooperation between church and state will bring into truer focus the presently exaggerated doctrine of separation of church and state. The result will be a more harmonious statement of the full American tradition of the right relations between government and religion.

The appropriateness of developing this doctrine of accommodation in the matter of government aid to religion in education can hardly be denied. We, as a people, are agreed that government should not undertake responsibility for the care of the sacred order of religious life; governmental responsibility is limited to a care for the freedom of religion. No other course is practicable or just, given our social situation of religious division. However, the special area of the school experience presents a different case. Government has assumed responsibility in this area; it has undertaken to promote, aid and support education. Moreover, it is precisely in this area of education that the spiritual needs of a religious people are today being sharply felt. Government cannot ignore these needs, on peril of a certain danger to itself; for the fortunes of free government are intimately linked to the fact of a religiously informed and virtuous citizenry. There is, therefore, every reason for applying in the area of education the fully developed principle of accommodation of the public service to the genuine spiritual needs of our religious people.

No one will deny that the problem of applying this principle will be difficult. It will not be easy to draw the line between constitutional accommodation of the public service in aid of religion in education, and unconstitutional aid to religion itself. Just as it will not be easy to determine where legitimate governmental support of religious freedom ends and where illegitimate governmental establishment of religion begins. But this is precisely the type of constitutional adventure to which we are committed by the very nature of the American commonwealth. The jurisprudence for making the adventure successful lies to hand. It is a matter of having the intelligence and courage to make harmonious use of the principles available. The American tradition is a treasury. It is our responsibility to bring forth from it new things and old.

Under present circumstances this dynamic constitutional development must take place, step by step, on an *ad hoc* basis, through the process of litigation. There is the problem of declaring the public law. But there is also, as I intimated above, the problem of clarifying the public conscience. In an atmosphere of reasonable and factual argument unclouded by passion or prejudice, it must be brought to the attention of the American public that a massive problem still awaits solution. The most fatal thing would be the complacency of supposing that the problem of religion in education was finally settled by the *McCollum* doctrine of absolute and complete separation of church and state. So far from solving the problem, this doctrine has made it more acute. Until the problem is solved with all justice and realism the American ideal of ordered freedom, for which the Bill of Rights stands, will not have been achieved.

CHAPTER SEVEN

~

Should There Be a Law?
The Question of Censorship

In foregoing chapters I have had occasion to emphasize the providential good fortune that befell the American Republic in that its constitutional structure was defined and its major institutions established within the context of the liberal tradition of politics. Within this wider civilizational current of ideas—Greek, Roman, Germanic, and Christian—the tradition of law has held a place of primacy. It is not too much to say that there has been a virtue in the Western tradition of law which warrants us in calling it redemptive, at least in a terrestrial sense. Western man has sought in the idea of law a manifold redemption—from the arbitrary despotisms of uncontrolled power; from the threat or fact of injustice to his person and to his property; from dispossession of his human and civil rights; from the degradation that ensues upon social inequalities destructive of his personal significance and worth; from the oppressive evils of an inequitable distribution of wealth; from the multiple rapacities that seem to lurk in the human enterprises of commerce and trade; from the disruption of life by the irrational forces of passion, caprice, and chance that militate against the "life of expectability," to use Sir Ernest Barker's phrase for the high human good that is guaranteed by the rule of law.

In America the force of law has been used for all these worthy purposes. They are visibly the purposes of justice in society. On the whole, the record in this area of justice reveals both wisdom and effectiveness in the use of civilization's most indispensable instrument. There are, however, other pages in the record. The force of law has also been used in other areas of moral concern; and in them the results, when not disastrous, have been dubious. There seems to be sufficient reason for thinking that the American mind has never been clear about the relation between morals and law. These two orders of reality are frequently confused, in either one of two ways.

First, there is a failure to understand the true meaning of the medieval adage: "Whatever is right ought to be law." The medieval man was not thinking of coercive statutes, backed by the state and its police, that would compel the people to do whatever is right. He was merely saying that whatever is right ought to be a matter of custom; that is, the moral order ought to be reflected in the habitual order of everyday life and action. He could also, as he did, turn the adage around and say: "Whatever is law (custom) ought to be right." That is, the sanction of the mores, as we call them, is not in the sheer fact that they prevail, but in their rightness. In both cases the medieval man was expressing, quite exactly, a right concept of the distinction and relation that obtains between the order of moral law and the order of human law or custom. In American history, however, a perverted sense of the adage has been frequent. It chiefly appears in the reformer's constant shout: "There ought to be a law!" That is, whenever it appears that some good thing needs doing, or some evil thing needs to be done away with, the immediate cry is for the arm of the law. And there has often been no pause to ask, whether this is the sort of good or evil that law can, or ought to, cope with. The reformer's adage has been: "Whatever is moral ought to be legislated." The simplism of the adage reveals the failure to grasp the difference in order between moral precepts and civil statutes.

This confusion breeds another. If what is moral ought by that fact to be legal, it follows that what is legal is by that fact also moral. In common speech, if it's not against the law, it's all right; stay within the law and you can't go wrong. Here the chaos is complete. Law is deprived of all true sanction from the order of morals. Morality is invoked to sanction any sort of law. And as a result both law and morality lose all meaning.

Perhaps the heyday of reformist confusion of law and morals was the notorious "Comstock Era," the 1870's. And doubtless the most famous relic of the era is the Connecticut birth-control statute. It was passed in 1879 under Protestant pressure. Originally Chapter 78, Public Acts of Connecticut (1879), it is now Section 8568 of the General Statutes, Revision of 1949. Since most people have never seen the text, it ought to be cited:

"*Use of drugs or instruments to prevent conception*. Any person who shall use any drug, medical article or instrument for the purpose of preventing conception shall be fined not less than fifty dollars or imprisoned not less than sixty days nor more than one year or be both fined and imprisoned."

The text reveals a characteristic Comstockian-Protestant ignorance of the rules of traditional jurisprudence. In general, the "free churches," so called, have never given attention to this subtle discipline, at once a science and an art, that mediates between the imperatives of the moral order and the commands or prohibitions of civil law. In fact, so far from understanding jurisprudence, these sects have never really understood law but only power, whether they wield the latter in the form of majority rule or of minority protest. In any case, the Connecticut statute confuses the moral and legal, in that it transposes without further ado a private sin into a public crime. The criminal act here is the private use of contraceptives. The real area where the coercions of law might, and ought to, be applied, at least to control an evil—namely, the contraceptive industry—is quite overlooked. As it stands, the statute is, of course, unenforceable without police invasion of the bedroom, and is therefore indefensible as a piece of legal draughtmanship. (The two decisions handed down by the Connecticut Supreme Court of Errors were in actions brought, not under the statute itself but under the general accessory statute, Section 8875, Revision of 1949.)

But what matters here is the mentality exhibited, and the menace in it. Protestant moral theory, as I shall later suggest, seems never to have been able to grasp the distinction between private and public morality. But unless this distinction, like that between morality and law, is grasped, the result is a fiasco of all morality. From the foolish position that all sins ought to be made crimes, it is only a step to the knavish position that, since certain acts (like the private use of contraceptives) are obviously not crimes, they are not even sins. Upon a foolish disregard of the distinction between private and public morality there ensues a knavish denial that there is any such thing as public morality.

From this point of view—the relation between law and morality—it might be interesting to explore the issue of censorship. The issue itself is not of major importance in American society. What is important is that so much bad argument gets into the discussion of it. It presents itself therefore as an issue in right thinking. This is the sort of issue with which this book is concerned.

In the difficult matter of censorship the casuistry could be endless. I shall therefore simply attempt to define certain central issues and to state some of the principles that bear upon their solution. We shall not be concerned with the problem of censorship in the area of news or opinion, or of public morality in general, but only as it arises in the fields of literature and the arts. Here the perennial issue of obscenity has recently come to the fore.

The discipline of the Catholic Church in this matter is stated in canon 1399 of the Code of Canon Law. Among the eleven categories of books whose reading is *ipso iure* prohibited to Catholics the ninth is this: "Books which have for their principal purpose the description, narration, or teaching of matter lascivious or obscene." However, this canonical discipline is outside our present subject, which deals with the issue of censorship as it arises in the civil order.

An argument is sometimes set afoot about whether "the state," abstractly conceived, has or has not some right of censorship over the media of communications. And there is the complementary argument whether the individual writer or artist has or has not a right to absolute freedom of expression. These arguments I leave aside. We can start from a fact of political history, that every government has always claimed what is called police power, as an attribute of government.

This power in itself is simply the principle of self-preservation and self-protection transferred to the body politic. It extends to the requirements of public morals, public health, public safety, public order, and the general comfort of society. The only question is, how far and in what circumstances does it extend to all these social values?

In virtue of the police power, society, acting through the agency of government, is entitled to impose restraints on property rights and on personal freedoms. The question is, what manner of restraints, under what conditions, is government thus empowered to impose, in restriction of rights and in restraint of freedom? These are the concrete questions that are relevant to censorship, which is, I take it, an exercise of the police power. It might, if you wish, be an exercise of what is called *patria potestas*, the emergency power which government is entitled to use, on occasion, to protect children and those who are *ad instar puerorum*, legally to be reckoned as children by reason of their helplessness. But the same concrete questions return: when and for what reasons and under what limitations is government empowered thus to act *in loco parentis?*

In addition to the problem of governmental or legal censorship there is the problem of censorship (at least in some wide sense of the word) as exercised by non-governmental bodies—by civic committees or voluntary associations of one sort or another. We shall also have to consider this aspect of the problem.

The Central Issue

The issue that is central in the whole problem is the issue of social freedom. More exactly, it is the issue of striking a right balance between freedom and restraint in society. This is the most difficult problem of social science, to such an extent that all other difficulties are reducible to this one. No complete discussion is possible here; I shall simply make certain assertions, general in themselves, but relevant to our special problem.

First, in society constraint must be for the sake of freedom. It seems a paradox to assert that the imposition of a constraint must be justified by an increase in freedom, since every constraint is a decrease of freedom. What I mean, however, is that the constraint must create a freedom in another respect. Traffic regulations, for instance, are a constraint on freedom of movement on the streets; but they are justified because they create a freedom to move—at least, nowadays, in some minimal sense! Tax laws are a constraint on your freedom to do what you want with your money; but they create other freedoms —to live in security behind a national defense establishment, for instance. The whole texture of civilization is a web of restraints, which deliver man from a host of slaveries—to darkness, cold, and hunger; to ignorance and illness and wearisome labors. Delivered from these base slaveries man is free to be a man, to live the inner life of reason and love, the classic life of wisdom, the Christian life of faith.

The problem of constraint for the sake of freedom is difficult enough when it is only a question of organizing the material conditions of life. But it becomes even more inextricable when it is a question of organizing communications within society; for in this field religious and moral, intellectual and emotional values come into play. It is easy enough to see that the "press" (understood to mean all the media of communication) can be the vehicle both of corruptive and of beneficial influences. It is easy enough to say that corruptive influences ought to be put under reasonable restraints. And it is easy enough to define what you mean by a corruptive influence; it is that which destroys or diminishes the rational freedom of man, either by damaging his power of personal reflection or by exciting his passions to the point where they interfere with his rational control of his thoughts and action. On these grounds you can certainly make a case against sexual propaganda of certain kinds as corruptive of human freedom. The influence of inordinate and unregulated sexual passion on the life of reason in man is a commonplace of human and historical experience. The susceptibility of youth to dominance by carnal desires, to the detriment of rational freedom, is particularly well documented—and hardly in need of documentation.

However, when you have made your case against these influences as socially corruptive, you have only reached the threshold of the problem of social freedom. Many questions remain. For instance, when and under what circumstances do these influences become so corruptive that they require animadvertence by organized society itself? (It is presumed that the first solicitations of corruptive influences are resisted by the special resources of the family and the Church.) Again, what agencies are to be enlisted against these influences—the public agencies of government and law, or the private agencies known as voluntary associations? Either or both? And to what extent each? Above all, what is the norm whose requirements are to be enforced, in one way or another, against influences that are corruptive? It is, of course, the norm of public order. But what requirements of public order can be made valid against the claims of freedom?

Even supposing these questions to have been satisfactorily answered, a further complicating consideration remains. The fact is that the imposition of constraints, the limitation of freedom, has consequences. They are numerous; but two require special notice.

First, if you impose a constraint on freedom in one domain, in order to increase freedom in another, you may take the risk of damaging freedom in a third domain, with consequences more dangerous to the community. Social freedom is a complex, whose constituent elements are closely interlocked. You may, for instance, wish to "clean up" political campaigns by limiting the freedom of the contestants to attack each other's personal integrity; but the means you take to this end may damage the freedom of the electoral process itself. Every constraint has multiple effects; it may impose restraints on a freedom which you would wish to see untouched.

There is, secondly, a consequent consideration. Because social freedoms interlock so tightly, it is not possible to know antecedently what the multiple effects of a regulation will be. At best, the effect you want can only be foreseen with probability, not certainty. And unforeseen effects may follow, with the result that a regulation, in itself sensible, may in the end do more harm than good.

For this reason, the social reformer whose only strength is a sense of logic may well be a menace. For instance, if drunkenness and alcoholism are social vices whose effect is to diminish and impair the free will of men (as indeed they are), the logical thing is to ban alcohol. Here in America we learned by experience the disastrous effects of that type of mad logic. In contrast, the illogicality of the liquor law in Belgium commends itself. The retail sale of liquor in public bars is forbidden, but you can get liquor if you go to a store and buy two quarts at once. When you unravel its seeming lack of logic, you find that the Belgian liquor law protects the citizen against his own reckless impulses, but permits him the freedom to act deliberately. This, of course, is his essential human freedom.

I should call attention here to the somewhat unique difficulties presented by the problem of the public enforcement of standards of sexual morality. Jacques Leclercq, of the Catholic University of Louvain, who is no slight authority, concludes a brief advertence to this subject with this remark: "In short, it may be said that no government has ever succeeded in finding a balanced policy of combating unhealthy sexual propaganda without injuring legitimate freedom or provoking other equally grave or worse disorders."

Everybody agrees that debauchery of the sexual faculty is morally wrong, and that incitement to such debauchery should be legally forbidden. On the other hand, in the case of incitement as open as houses of debauchery, a view that goes back to St. Augustine's treatise, *De ordine*, warns against the dangers of attempting a total coercive repression of this particular incitement.

The strictness of traditional Catholic doctrine in regard to sexual lust appalls the libertarian; the laxness of the many Catholic governments in the same regard equally appalls the Puritan. In 1517 the number of prostitutes in the city of Rome considerably surpassed the number of married women. And in 1592, under a Pope of formidable strictness, Sixtus V, there were more than 9,000 prostitutes amid a population of 70,000. This was in the capital of the papal states. The figures are not indeed edifying; but perhaps they are interesting, not least when one considers that during the same era the newly constituted Index of Forbidden Books was being used with extreme severity by successive Pontiffs (Paul IV, Pius IV, Pius V) against heretical propaganda. To this day the Italian who is merely amused by the obscene *pasquinata* is deeply offended by the earnest heresies of a Baptist minister from Texas.

To the proper Bostonian all this is profoundly shocking. Just as to the Continental European, especially if he is a Latin, the spectacle of the U.S.A. is infinitely puzzling. A man is free to call error truth, and truth error, if he likes; but he is not free to use the notorious four-letter word which, in direct French monosyllabic translation, has achieved literary dignity in Larousse as *le mot de Cambronne*. Again, the Supreme Court declares that the category of the sacrilegious is altogether indefinable, while the Post Office rules that Aristophanes' *Lysistrata* is an obscene book. This is indeed puzzling.

Considerations such as these would seem to indicate that the problem of social freedom is insoluble, if by solution is meant a simple formula that is applicable to all cases and similar for all countries. However, a community can do one important thing; it can decide on the general orientation it wishes to give to its particular solution. We have done this in the United States. We have constitutionally decided that the presumption is in favor of freedom, and that the advocate of constraint must make a convincing argument for its necessity or utility in the particular case.

I would only add that the presumption in favor of freedom does not rest on doctrinaire grounds. Its basis was not the philosophic rationalism that called itself Enlightenment, but only a political pragmatism more enlightened than the Enlightenment ever was, because it looked to the light of experience to illuminate the prudential norms necessary to guide it in handling a concrete social reality that is vastly complicated. In this light the option was made for the civil freedom of the citizen under a government whose powers are limited, and under a rule of the law whose reach is likewise limited, chiefly by the axiom that the constraints of law must serve the cause of essential social freedom.

In our case, the consequence of this fundamental option, which gives a basic orientation to our constitutional law, is that freedom of expression is the rule, and censorship the exception. A more particular further consequence is the ban laid by the First Amendment (exceptional cases apart) on all prior restraint of communications, at the same time that the government reserves the right to punish, subsequently, communications that offend against law. The freedom toward which the American people are fundamentally orientated is a freedom under God, a freedom that knows itself to be bound by the imperatives of the moral law. Antecedently it is presumed that a man will make morally and socially responsible use of his freedom of expression; hence there is to be no prior restraint on it. However, if his use of freedom is irresponsible, he is summoned after the fact to responsibility before the judgment of the law. There are indeed other reasons why prior restraint on communications is outlawed; but none are more fundamental than this.

After this brief discussion of the central issue involved in censorship I come to my proposition. It may be briefly stated thus: censorship in the civil order ought to be a juridical process. In using the word "juridical" I mean that the premises and objectives of the process should be defined in accord with the norms of good jurisprudence; that the forms of procedure should be properly judicial; and that the structure and workings of the process should be sustained by the consent of the community. I should maintain that this concept of a juridical process should be verified, *mutatis mutandis*, in every form of censorship, whether governmental or non-governmental.

Governmental or Legal Censorship

Censorship exercised by public authority is obliged to be literally juridical, in the sense described. As a legal process this censorship is controlled by the canons of necessity or utility for the common good. That some degree of punitive censorship is necessary is sufficiently evident. Pornography, for instance, the kind of obscenity that is a perverse and vicious profanation of the sacredness of sex, seems to hold a permanent attraction for a portion of humanity. That it is a corruptive social influence is not to be denied; consequently, few would deny that its repression is necessary. Beyond this, how much more censorship is useful, and how useful is it? That seems to be the central question.

A preliminary answer is furnished by the principle, basic to jurisprudence, that morals and law are differentiated in character, and not coextensive in their functions. It is not the function of the legislator to forbid everything that the moral law forbids, or to enjoin everything that the moral law enjoins. The moral law governs the entire order of human conduct, personal and social; it extends even to motivations and interior acts. Law, on the other hand, looks only to the public order of human society; it touches only external acts, and regards only values that are formally social. For this reason the scope of law is limited. Moreover, though law is indeed a moral force, directive of human society to the common good, it relies ultimately for its observance on coercion. And men can be coerced only into a minimal amount of moral action. Again from this point of view the scope of law is limited.

Therefore the moral aspirations of law are minimal. Law seeks to establish and maintain only that minimum of actualized morality that is necessary for the healthy functioning of the social order. It does not look to what is morally desirable, or attempt to remove every moral taint from the atmosphere of society. It enforces only what is minimally acceptable, and in this sense socially necessary. Beyond this, society must look to other institutions for the elevation and maintenance of its moral standards—that is, to the church, the home, the school, and the whole network of voluntary associations that concern themselves with public morality in one or other aspect.

Law and morality are indeed related, even though differentiated. That is, the premises of law are ultimately found in the moral law. And human legislation does look to the moralization of society. But, mindful of its own nature and mode of action, it must not moralize excessively; otherwise it tends to defeat even its own more modest aims, by bringing itself into contempt.

Therefore the law, mindful of its nature, is required to be tolerant of many evils that morality condemns. A moral condemnation regards only the evil itself, in itself. A legal ban on an evil must consider what St. Thomas calls its own "possibility." That is, will the ban be obeyed, at least by the generality? Is it enforceable against the disobedient? Is it prudent to undertake the enforcement of this or that ban, in view of the possibility of harmful effects in other areas of social life? Is the instrumentality of coercive law a good means for the eradication of this or that social vice?

And, since a means is not a good means if it fails to work in most cases, what are the lessons of experience in the matter? What is the prudent view of results—the long view or the short view? These are the questions that jurisprudence must answer, in order that legislation may be drawn with requisite craftsmanship.

It is, in fact, the differentiated character of law and morals that justifies the lawyer or judge when he insists that punitive censorship statutes should be clearly drawn, with the margin of uncertainty as narrow as possible.

The net of all this is that no society should expect very much in the way of moral uplift from its censorship statutes. Indeed the whole criminal code is only a minimal moral force. Particularly in the field of sexual morality the expectations are small; as I have suggested, they are smaller here than anywhere else. It is a sort of paradox, though an understandable one, that the greater the social evil, the less effective against it is the instrument of coercive law. Philip Wylie may have been right in saying that American society "is technically insane in the matter of sex." If so, it cannot be coerced into sanity by the force of law. In proportion as literary obscenity is a major social evil, the power of the police against it is severely limited.

This brings up the matter of consent. Law is indeed a coercive force; it compels obedience by the fear of penalty. However, a human society is inhumanly ruled when it is ruled only, or mostly, by fear. Good laws are obeyed by the generality because they are good laws; they merit and receive the consent of the community, as valid legal expressions of the community's own convictions as to what is just or unjust, good or evil. In the absence of this consent law either withers away or becomes tyrannical.

The problem of popular consent to the order of law and to its manifold coercions becomes critical in a pluralist society, such as ours. Basic religious divisions lead to conflict of moral views; certain asserted "rights" clash with other "rights" no less strongly asserted. And the divergences are often irreducible. Nevertheless, despite all the pluralism, some manner of consensus must support the order of law to which the whole community and all its groups are commonly subject. This consensus must include, in addition to other agreements, an agreement on certain rules which regulate the relations of the divergent groups among one another, and their common relation to the order of law. In what concerns our present subject of censorship, I suggest that there are four such rules. Before stating them I would note that in the United States at present all the religious groups are—from the sociological, even if not from the statistical, point of view—minority groups.

First, within the larger pluralist society each minority group has the right to censor for its own members, if it so chooses, the content of the various media of communication, and to protect them, by means of its own choosing, from materials considered harmful according to its own standards.

Second, in a pluralist society no minority group has the right to demand that government should impose a general censorship, affecting all the citizenry, upon any medium of communication, with a view to punishing the communication of materials that are judged to be harmful according to the special standards held within one group.

Third, any minority group has the right to work toward the elevation of standards of public morality in the pluralist society, through the use of the methods of persuasion and pacific argument.

Fourth, in a pluralist society no minority group has the right to impose its own religious or moral views on other groups, through the use of the methods of force, coercion, or violence.

I cannot pause here to demonstrate the reasonableness and justice of these four rules. I would only note that they are not put forth as rules that were made in heaven, necessarily inherent in the constitution of an "ideal" society. On the contrary, they are to be considered as rules made on earth, by the practical reason of man, for application in the conditions—by no means "ideal"—of a religiously and morally divided society. Agreement on them would seem to be necessary in the common interests of social peace. Their supposition is the jurisprudential proposition that what is commonly imposed by law on all our citizens must be supported by general public opinion, by a reasonable consensus of the whole community. At the same time they suppose that within a pluralist society the minority groups have certain definite, if limited, rights to influence the standards and content of public morality. The statement of these rules leads to the next subject.

Non-governmental Censorship

In the United States there are a multitude of voluntary agencies which exercise some measure of surveillance, judgment, and even control of various media of communication. For the most part they shy away from the idea of being called "censoring" agencies. We need not quibble over the word; the frequent fact is that many of them achieve the results of censorship, even when they refuse the name. With regard to these agencies I should maintain the general proposition stated above—that their censoring should also be a juridical process, if not literally, certainly in spirit.

The juridical premise of their action is not in doubt. In the United States it is generally acknowledged that the voluntary association is entitled to concern itself actively with matters that relate to the public welfare. It is invidious to stigmatize all such associations as "pressure-groups," pursuing "private interests." The fact is that, in their own way, they can perform a public function.

The more difficult question concerns the methods used by these associations or committees. There can be no slightest quarrel when they use simply the methods of persuasion; that is, when they appeal for voluntary cooperation on the grounds of a common moral and social responsibility. Thus, for instance, many associations interested in decent literature and movies (surely a public interest) seek the responsible cooperation of producers and theater-owners, and publishers and distributors, with a view at least to diminishing the volume of obscenity, or other objectionable features, in these media. Surely here all is entirely rightful and prudent.

Other methods—at the other end of the spectrum, so to speak—seem to have at least the appearance of coercion. As an example one might take the organized boycott, against a merchant, a theater, etc. It is a sort of "consumers' strike"; it is sometimes accompanied by picketing; it normally involves some form of economic sanctions invoked against the offending party. What is to be thought of such methods?

It will be agreed that the use of formal coercion in society is reserved to public authority and its agencies of law. Coercion of a more informal kind—through economic pressure, etc.—is also employed by various associations that do not hesitate to identify themselves as "power-groups." Such, for instance, is a trade union. It does indeed seem a bit incongruous that other types of voluntary association, concerned with values that are spiritual and moral, aesthetic and cultural, should pursue their ends by what appear to be the methods of power rather than of persuasion. On the other hand, it is not possible to prove the position, taken by some, that an action like the boycott of a moving-picture is somehow "unrightful," or "unconstitutional," or "undemocratic." No one can show that such an action lies beyond the limits of a primeval American right to protest and object. The action may indeed be strenuous; but the American right to protest and object is permitted to run to some pretty strenuous extremes.

This said, against the doctrinaire, it remains true that methods of action which verge upon the coercive exhibit some incongruity when used by citizen-groups in the interests of morality in literature or on the screen. Even if they raise no issue of abstract right, they do raise the concrete issue of prudence, which, equally with justice, is one of the cardinal virtues. The issue rises most sharply in the case of Catholic associations. The chief danger is lest the Church itself be identified in the public mind as a power-association. The identification is injurious; it turns unto a hatred of the faith. And it has the disastrous effect of obscuring from the public view the true visage of the Church as God's kingdom of truth and freedom, justice and love. Our purpose is to stand before the world as men and women of faith, and therefore of reason too, whose reliance is on the methods of reason and not of force. We would wish always to be men and women of courage, ready to face any issue; but also men and women of prudence, who understand the art of procedure, and understand too that we are morally bound, by the virtue of prudence, to a concrete rightness of method in the pursuit of moral aims.

It should be noted too that prudence is an intellectual virtue, a refinement of intelligence. It may therefore properly be asked, how intelligent is it to have recourse to methods that approach coercion in this delicate field of censorship? Few things are worse than to make oneself ridiculous. And when an effort to coerce is made at the dictates of stupidity, the result arouses ridicule as well as resentment.

This brings up the question, who is competent to censor, even in some extralegal fashion? To say that all censorship should be a juridical process is to say by implication that it ought to be intelligently done. This means close attention to the qualifications of the censor. Here the example of the Church is instructive. In his reform of the discipline of censorship Benedict XIV laid great stress on the rule that the censor is to possess professional competence in the particular field in which he is called upon to pass judgment. Censorship is no job for the amateur. Like stress is placed on the censor's obligation to perform his task impartially, in the fullness of the judicial spirit that forbids the intrusion of any private likes or dislikes. In the process of censorship there is no room for the personal, the arbitrary, the passionate. The censor is not called upon for a display of moral indignation; he is asked only for a judgment, calm and cool, objective and unemotional. So too in the civil sphere, the less we have of moral indignation, and the more we have of professional competence and an unclouded faculty of judgment, the better it will be for the juridical nature of the censorship process.

In what concerns the problem of obscenity I would not discount the value of what is called the "common estimation" of men. People in general have a fairly clear notion of what obscenity is. And people in general can make, for themselves, a pretty good judgment on whether a particular work is obscene. Certainly the Code of Canon Law seems to suppose that the ordinary Catholic can make this concrete judgment for himself. I repeat, for himself. The question is, who can make it for others, i.e., as a censor?

Here a distinction is in order. Certainly the ordinary father and mother ought to be qualified to act as censors within the family and to decide what their children may or may not be prudently exposed to, in the way of reading, movies, etc. But I should not think that the ordinary father or mother, *qua* such, is qualified to act as censor within society at large, or to decide what literature and movies may be displayed before the general public. Society has an interest in the artist's freedom of expression which is not necessarily shared by the family. If adult standards of literature would be dangerous for children, a child's standard of literature is rather appalling to an adult. If therefore any censorship is to be administered in the interest of society, the professional competence of the literary critic must play a role in the process.

Here perhaps the characteristic Catholic care for the welfare of children (often coupled with the typically American cult of the child-centered home) ought to be aware of a danger. The contemporary argument about censorship is sometimes described as a "battle between the literati and the philistines." The description is snobbish, if you will. But it would be lamentable if Catholics were to go over to the camp of the philistines. After all, we do stand, not only within the oldest religious tradition of the Western world, but also within its most venerable tradition of intellect, literature, and art. The tradition has produced great achievements in writing, painting, and the plastic arts. Not all of them are fit for children indeed— not even the Bible in all its parts. But that is no justification for any form of philistinism.

In one further and final respect the process of extralegal censorship ought to be juridical, pursued in the spirit of law—that is, in its adoption of minimal aims. Fussiness is out of order. There ought to be a few, only a few, areas of concentration, in which a little bit (if not much) can be done. I suggest that the chief area is the "pornography of violence," as it has been called. Mischief enough is done by the obscenities that occur in the portrayal of illicit love (by literary hacks who never learned what the genuine artist knows instinctively—that, though art may "say all," there are certain things it is never allowed to say explicitly). But here sex is at least rescued from full profanation by its tenuous connection with love, as love is still resident in lust. However, when sex is associated with, and becomes symbolic of, the hatreds and hostilities, the angers and cruelties, that lie deep in men and women, the profanation of the most sacred thing in sex—its relation to love and to the hope of human life—is almost complete. It could move perhaps only one step deeper into the diabolical—in that association of sex and blasphemy that pervades the Black Mass.

The image of the truly evil thing in the obscenities of our day is seen on the typical cover of the "tough" kind of pocket-book—the seminude woman, with a smoking gun in her hand. The scene is one of impurity, but that is its lesser evil. The real evil is the violence in the impure scene. There is the perversion. If some restraint could be imposed upon this pornography of violence—so damning in its revelation of a vice in our culture—it would indeed be a moral achievement.

Conclusion

It is a good thing to keep our problems in perspective. Our chief problem, of course, is not literary censorship, but literary creation. This is true in the Church. She has no trouble in finding censors; but she prays continually that God may give her men of learning who can write the works that need to be written. The American Catholic community particularly needs to attend seriously to this problem of literary creation. Leo XIII is indeed remembered for his revision of the Index of Forbidden Books. But he was not the first Pope to point to the dangers of reading bad books. It is his greater glory that he was the first Pope to say, in substance and effect, in a multitude of discourses, that today there is great danger in not reading good books.

~

CHAPTER EIGHT

Is It Basket Weaving?
The Question of
Christianity and Human Values

If it be a question here of touching on some unfinished arguments, there is one that can hardly be overlooked. In 1948 M. Francis Hermans published a four-volume work entitled, *Histoire doctrinale de l'humanisme chrétien*. It is the story of an argument that has been going on, in a variety of fields and with varying degrees of intensity, for long centuries. Perhaps it was Clement of Alexandria who started it. Certainly it was given a mighty impulse by Origen, that towering genius of the third century, who first seriously raised and persistently explored the issue, never to be laid aside or finally settled, of the stature of human intelligence within the ambit of Christian faith. The whole patristic period was full of the argument, in Antioch and especially in Alexandria, which was then the "capital of the creative half of the Empire." None of the great Fathers could, or even attempted to, avoid the issue posed by the collision of the Church with the classical culture of antiquity. "Look, Master! What wonderful stones and buildings!" Variants of this Gospel exclamation (Mark 13:1) were heard, as Christian men surveyed the impressive edifice of Hellenism. But was the answer to be that of the Gospel: "Not one stone shall be left here upon another that shall not be torn down"? If Christian men shrank from this answer, as in general they did, what then was to be the disposition of these pagan "stones and buildings" within what they called the new "economy," the new order of salvation, whose roots were in

Judaism and not in Hellenism; in the events of a salvation-history and not in the achievements of the human mind.

The essential question has been restated in many forms, in many contexts, as the Christian era ran on. It arose sharply in each of the three Renaissances (we all hold now, I think, that there were three, not one). Erasmus raised it again just before the outset of the baroque era, through all of which it ran, despite Luther's efforts to damn and down it. And—to telescope the history—it is here with us today.

On February 28, 1951, in his reply to the address of the new Minister Plenipotentiary of the Republic of Liberia, Pius XII thus stated it:

> The profession of Christian truth and fidelity to the fundamental tenets of the Catholic faith are indissolubly bound up with the sincere and constant assertion of human nature's most authentic and exalted values. . . . True religion and profound humaneness are not rivals. They are sisters. They have nothing to fear from one another, but everything to gain. Let each remain loyal to the law of its being, while it respects the vital needs and varied outward manifestations of the other, and the resultant harmonizing of two forces will endow any people engaged in the fulfillment of its appointed tasks with the most valuable incentives to real prosperity and solid progress.

This statement touches firmly, confidently, though in general terms, upon the perennial problem of Christian humanism. The problem itself is transtemporal because it is doctrinal, based upon the principles of being, in the present order of nature and of grace. At the same time, the precise manner in which the problem appears must vary from age to age, because the virtualities in it cannot become explicit in any one historical context.

After World War I the problem came to the fore in Europe, as the last vestiges of Jansenism lost their tenacious hold on the Catholic conscience and as men of the Church undertook to define a more positive Catholic attitude towards what is called modern culture, after the lines of battle, as drawn in the nineteenth century, had ceased to mark real areas of conflict. The great crisis of World War II and the compelling necessity of some vision of a "new Christian order" gave further urgency to the problem. And it has been widely discussed in its various aspects, notably that of the theology of history and of "terrestrial realities," the concept of progress, the general significance of the dimension of time in its relation to the concept of nature and to the life of grace, the relation of science and the mastery it has achieved over the material world to the coming of the Kingdom.

The Problem in America

The problem, as it exists in the United States, would seem to be the more acute in proportion as it is unrecognized. Obviously, the type of humanism called "classical" has had little influence on American culture. With us the problem has other roots. America represents a human achievement of a unique kind, not paralleled in history. In a quite different sense from France, America has been revolutionary, the home of a revolution that at least claims to be permanent. The dynamism of this revolution has been an emphasis put by Americans on the assertion, which must be considered sincere and surely has been constant, of certain human values. The sheer constancy of the assertion of these values gives challenging point to the claim that they are authentically human. And a certain greatness that invests the achievement which America has spread across the pages of history is proof that the values upon which the achievement drew for inspiration are exalted.

There is undoubtedly an impurity about the American achievement. Is it altogether a human achievement? Or does it reveal traits of the inhuman, perhaps even the demonic? The questions are valid, but they are in a sense peripheral to the central question which the achievement itself, in its present reality and in its promise of continuity, presents to the Christian conscience.

If the problem of Christian humanism be the dual problem of acceptance of the human, as the human stands revealed in each particular historical juncture, and its transformation by the powers of faith and grace, then the question rises, whether, and in what sense, and to what degree this total *res humana* which America represents can and ought to be accepted, can and ought to be transformed? Is this *res humana* simply a rival to the *res sacra* which is Christianity? Or can they be made "sisters," in Pius XII's metaphor? Can the forces which lie behind each be so harmonized as to endow our people "with the most valuable incentives to real prosperity and solid progress"? Has America any significance in regard to the Christian man's quest of an earthly culture at once human and Christian? Or do the colossal structures of temporal life erected by this national giant simply encumber the ground, as sheer obstacles to a progress that could merit the qualification, "solid"? What are we to do with this staggeringly enormous thing—reduce it all to ashes and lay other foundations for a different structure? Or can a program of acceptance and transformation be justified in the light of Christian faith?

It is not the purpose of this chapter to answer these questions. The purpose is more modest. It is simply to indicate the problem, and then to present, as relevant to its solution, the two lines or tendencies which the Christian intelligence has taken as it has reflected on the problem in its more general manner of presentation.

The American problem can only be indicated, not constructed in its full detail. But the general architecture of it can be seen well enough if one looks for a moment at two things, the American economy and the American political system. Together they have powerfully determined the ethos of American culture, formed the *homo Americanus* and shaped a special kind of institutionalized *res humana*.

The American Economy

By "economy" here I mean that most intricate and powerful combination of science, technology and business which is perhaps the dominant and most characteristic aspect of the national life. (With business one should join advertising, as tail to the kite—though it would be hard to know which is tail and which is kite.) In the context of the problematic of Christian humanism, the American economy demands attention perhaps chiefly by its unique historical claim to have abolished the problem of poverty. Not that poverty itself has yet been fully abolished. There are still "depressed areas" and underprivileged groups; and many people whose income lies below the 1958 per capita median ($2,057) know what poverty is. But, the claim of some goes, poverty as a problem has been abolished, in the sense that the means for its solution exist and are known. A general freedom from want is not a politician's promise but an economic certainty.

This is, if you will, an accomplishment of the material order; but its moral implications are extensive. It means, in the first place, that the American people as a whole possesses, or has within reach, that minimum of material abundance which is necessary for the practice of virtue. Here is a greatly human goal. The shackles of a secular fear, that has weighed heavily on mankind throughout its history, have been struck off, or loosened, in one vast quarter of the globe. How far want and the fear of want have been destructive of the human soul, and how far they have been sanctifying, would be a nice, and likewise an impossible, judgment. In any event, judgment on the validity of freedom from want as a human goal must be clear and affirmative. Christian thought does not consider poverty as a good in itself.

This raises the question, what is to be the Christian judgment upon that great *res humana,* that sprawling product of human energies, the American economy, which has wrought this human achievement and reached this human goal? In itself it appears as a force for humanism against a force that is in itself dehumanizing. Does one accept this *res humana* or not? Or, if this disjunction is too violent, what is the Christian attitude? Even if the acceptance is reserved, what is the program of transformation? In the form of the American economy, nature confronts grace. It is in the milieu generated by this thing of nature that grace must work. Must it here work against nature? Or is this thing of nature something that grace can perfect?

In sheer point of fact, the Church in America has accepted this thing which is the American economy. Her life, the life of grace, is tied to it in multiple respects. It is, in fact, the thing that has given peculiarity both to certain institutions of the American Catholic Church and to certain forms of Catholic life. The major instance is the whole system of Catholic education, supported by the voluntary contributions of the faithful, who have found in it a means of professing their faith and expressing their spirit of charity and sacrifice. Catholic education in its present many-storied structure would be impossible apart from the American economy, the wealth it has created, and the wide distribution of this wealth that it has operated. Important alterations in the economy (not to speak of changes in the tax structure) could deal a serious blow to the *res sacra* which is Catholic education. Other institutions of the Church's apostolate would be similarly affected; the involvement of any large diocese in the workings of the American economy is fairly deep.

Is there then some manner of "sisterhood" here, to be frankly recognized? Has grace struck an accord with nature? Certainly the Christian and the human are here entangled; but how are they related? And what duties toward the furtherance of this thing of nature, which itself furthers the work of grace, are engendered? The problem, as thus put, is indeed on the institutional level; but thence it goes to the depths of the Christian conscience.

It might also be noted that here is an aspect of the Church's alliance with, and to that extent dependence on, the people and their energies, which is a unique characteristic of American Catholicism. In this it stands in contrast to its European ancestor, whose tradition has been one of alliance with, and to that extent dependence on, government and its favors, for the material support which the Church (as an institution that occupies ground in this world) inevitably needs. Again, important alterations in the structure of the economy, in the direction of "state socialism" (using the term only descriptively), could subtly alter the relation of the Christian people to the institutions of the Church. And this change would in turn subtly qualify in new fashion the life of the Church in America—whether desirably or not, that is the question.

The American Polity

A problem similarly appears when one considers the American political system. The essential peculiarity of the system has not been the assertion that in the words of John Locke, "the people shall be judge" of "the prince and the legislative act," nor in the determination that government shall be by the people. The Middle Ages knew this meaning of the sovereignty of the people and acknowledged that a sense of justice presumed to be resident in the people empowers them to judge the prince and the legislative act. The genius of the American system lies rather in the bold answer given to the urgent nineteenth-century question, "Who are the people?" After some initial hesitation America replied forthrightly, "Everybody, on a footing of equality." This is a greatly humanist statement, pregnant with an acceptance of the human that was unique in history. This answer denied that the people are the great beast of aristocratic theory. It also denied that the people are immature children, as in the theories of the enlightened despot, who reserved to himself, as Father and King of the nation-family, the total *ius politiae* and the right of spiritual and political tutelage over his subject-children. The American proposition asserted that the people can live a life of reason, exercise their birthright of freedom, and assume responsibility for the judgment, direction, and correction of the course of public affairs. It implied that there is an authentic and exalted human value in this commission to the people of the right of self-government.

On this premise the American system made government simply an instrumental function of the body politic for a set of limited purposes. Its competence was confined to the political as such and to the promotion of the public welfare of the community as a political, i.e., lay, community. In particular, its power of censoring or inhibiting utterance was cut to a minimum, and it was forbidden to be the secular arm of any church. In matters spiritual the people were committed to their freedom, and religion was guaranteed full freedom to achieve its own task of effecting the spiritual liberation of man. To this task the contribution of the state would be simply that of rendering assistance in the creation of those conditions of freedom, peace, and public prosperity in which the spiritual task might go forward.

Within the problematic of a Christian humanism the question here is whether this concept of the people in their relation to the temporal power can and ought to be accepted. Can the human value in the statement that the people shall judge the prince and the legislative act—as well as elect him, limit his powers, and direct the manner of their exercise—be affirmed? Can all its implications be loyally accepted? Nature has made the statement. Is the work of grace one of contradiction, or of transformation?

Heretofore the Catholic answer has been somewhat ambivalent. The American political idea and the institutions through which it works have been accepted in practice, rather completely and perhaps naively. At the same time there seems to exist an implied condemnation of the system in theory. The condemnation appeals to the stand taken by the Church against Jacobin democracy, the type of government based on radically rationalist principles that emerged from the French Revolution. A condemnation of the American idea is implied only because there has been an official failure to take explicit account of the fact that the American political system and its institutions are not of Revolutionary and Jacobin inspiration. The question now is, whether this ambivalent attitude is any longer either intellectually or morally respectable, whether it takes proper account of the realities in the situation and of the special affirmation of the human that America has historically made.

The Mastery of Nature

One further area of the problem may be noted with a brevity not commensurate with its importance. America illustrates in uniquely striking fashion the commonplace that there has been a constantly ascending progress in man's knowledge and control of nature. The human creature has followed a steady upward curve in the development of his scientific creativeness. The "Cartesian dream" of men "commes maîtres et posseseurs de la nature" has steadily assumed real substance. The contrast in the matter of man's spiritual and moral progress is a commonplace, but the fact of material progress remains. And it is visible in America almost to the point of shockingness. What then is the value of all this in terms of the coming of the Kingdom? Nature is making resounding assertions and writing a record of enormous scientific and industrial achievement. What is the answer of grace to these assertions? What is the judgment of faith upon these achievements?

All this has been said simply to show that sufficient evidence confronts us to make us realize that the problem of a Christian humanism is really in our midst in an indigenous form, not elsewhere paralleled. A practical consideration gives the problem added urgency. Lengthy and deliberate cultivation of a *mystique de la terre* has tended to paralyze the action of any specifically Christian mystique. Affirmation of the *res humana*, once made in the context of belief in God and an all-ruling moral order, has gone over into exclusive affirmation of the *res huius saeculi*, under ignorance or even denial of the transcendent. Belief in man has proved, with some groups, to be an enemy of belief in God. The cultivation of human values by human energies, under no appeal to higher sanction or assistance, has found as its counterpart the theory that all values are simply immanent in man and have no transcendent reference. A mentality has been created to which the idea of the absolute is a horror.

Two Tendencies

In the face of these aberrations and the present corruption of the intellectual and moral climate that they have induced, the temptation has been felt to utter prophetic condemnation of the total *res humana* which America represents. The sequel to this condemnation, some may feel, can only be withdrawal from the doomed city—a spiritual withdrawal, made as completely as it is possible to make it. Nature as well as history is to be refused and denied. And the energies of the spiritually withdrawn are to be spent solely in the search for the Kingdom of God, whose coming is not upon this earth.

This temptation, I say, is felt. There are among us signs of an integrist movement which looks upon nature and history only as sources of corruption. And there are the beginnings of an American Catholic Right, with a historically unique and curious mentality. The Old French Catholic Right, for instance, firmly believed that the spiritual fortunes of the Church were wedded to the earthly fortunes of monarchy. The new American Catholic Right believes that the fortunes of the Church—and of the individual soul—are completely divorced from all manner of earthly fortunes.

The former attitude had its roots in history, in the long alliance of the Church with monarchy. It erred against the transcendence of the Church to political forms. At least, the error was clear and the reasons for it understandable. The latter attitude also has its roots in history, in the secular separation of Catholics from the main currents of national life, which has helped to induce a certain abstractionism of thought. How this attitude is to be reconciled with the immanence of the Church in history does not appear. The attitude is not yet clear and the reasons for it are difficult to understand.

An observer may therefore say that there are discernible in the United States certain signs of the two orientations that Catholic thought has taken, as it has faced the problem of a Christian humanism. But neither of the orientations—participation vs. withdrawal—is clearly defined or fully reasoned. Each of them ought to be, and it might help in this direction to look briefly at these two orientations. One looks towards what may be called an eschatological humanism; the other, towards an incarnational humanism.

Contempt of the World

The first orientation makes its dominant appeal to Scripture, and its emphases coincide with certain scriptural emphases upon fundamental aspects of the *res christiana*. The first emphasis is upon the fact that in the present order the end of man is transcendent to any end that man himself might envisage. The human purpose, as set by grace, not only extends beyond time and earth; it also looks to fulfillment in a manner of perfection that, properly speaking, is not worked out but received as a gift. This perfection will lie in seeing God as He is in Himself, in knowing and loving Him by grace as He knows and loves Himself by nature. This perfection will be indeed a perfection of the human, but it is discontinuous with all purely human effort. By the same token, heaven, the state of this perfection, is radically discontinuous with history, the arena of human effort and achievement. And even history has a Master who causes all things within it to work together towards a good that is not of this world and that lies beyond human desire and striving. The meaning of history lies in the Pauline "mystery," the hidden divine action, the ever-renewed act of divine power whereby the Kingdom of God comes. The Kingdom is not built from below, nor does it repose upon any cornerstone laid by human hands. It is a divine act; it is an irruption from above.

And this City of God is the proper city of man. Within the earthly City man is an alien; it is not his home, he does not find his family there, he is no longer even native to it, he has been reborn. At best, he is a pilgrim in its streets, a man in passage, restless to be on the way toward the Holy City that is his goal. While he lingers, almost literally overnight, his attitude is one of waiting and expectancy. He can strike no roots; for the soil is not such as could nourish the life he cherishes. Ever before his eyes is the *dies Domini,* the day of the Great Catastrophe, when all the laborious magnificence of this man-built City will suddenly vanish, as the ground beneath its seemingly solid substance is withdrawn. Abruptly, there will be an end; this City will no longer be. And that which is will be only He Who Is, with those who are in Him. In these perspectives, only those human values are worth affirming which grace itself evokes; all others will end in insubstantial ashes. All true humanism is therefore eschatological; the only true human values are those which are supernatural and eternal.

The works of earth, the objects upon which human energies may be poured out, the multiplicity of tasks which make up the whole human cultural enterprise—upon these the judgment of the early hermits is still fundamentally valid. They are the works of time, only valuable because they fill in the time of waiting. The old monk wove a basket one day; the next day he unwove it. The basket itself did not matter; but the weaving and unweaving of it served as a means of spending an interval, necessary to the frail human spirit, between periods of performance of the only task that did matter, the contemplation of heavenly things. Only the making of a soul was the true human value. For the rest, what did it matter whether one wove baskets or wrought whole civilizations?

Again, the eschatological view lays emphasis upon sin as a permanent human fact that casts a shadow over all human achievements, whatever the purity of their conception. If sin be not overcome by grace, and a new principle of life imparted to man by God, even the highest human virtues are but *splendida vitia*. Even when sin is overcome and man is healed by the grace of redemption, he is not made whole, made fully "continent" in the Augustinian sense—with all his energies permanently unified upon the good. Still (so runs the theme of St. Augustine upon which all Christian writers have played their variations) man does not fully know himself, nor is he master of circumstances. He has dominion over his acts, not over their consequences, which can run on inexorably out to the limits of that solidary unit which is humanity. How then shall man know that this *res humana*, over which he sincerely and laboriously works, will retain the humanity of his intention and not be unrecognizably disfigured, once it has escaped his control and is loose in a world of shaping circumstances?

Sin is a constant. Matter is resistant to human purposes, cursed in man's work. And there is a Principle of Evil abroad, an enemy of human nature, who can organize even the good that men do into a pattern of evil, sow tares among their wheat and send fish of poisoned flesh into the nets which they let down to gather food for mankind. All the works of sinful man stand under the judgment of God. The divine promise is not of peace but of the sword. And the thrust of the punishing sword is into the very marrow of the human—into the mysterious place of division between flesh and spirit, whence sin takes its origin.

How then shall man promise himself that he will create the human, only the human? The very promise is prideful. Humanism is a goal that only pride can conceive. At the very moment when the structure of it is complete, its very weight would bring it down.

Finally, the eschatological view lays emphasis on the central truth that Christianity is the Cross. And the Cross represents the inversion of all human values. The human is put to death; and out of death comes life.

Darkness overtakes the light; and in that moment the light disperses the darkness. The truth goes down to defeat; and that is its hour of victory. The Kingdom is refused; and thus it comes. Earthly hopes find their definitive disappointment; and out of their wreckage there rises by the sole power of God a new hope, glorious, immortal, the creation of the Spirit.

Moreover, the crucifixion was not only an act in history; it was also the utterance of a judgment and the promulgation of a law. The law says that he who would save his life must lose it; the things of this life have their value in that they provide the material for renouncement. Only through this renouncement, this acceptance of a similitude of Christ's death, is there resurrection to the true life. The judgment permanently shatters the illusion that is nonetheless a permanent temptation of the human spirit—to want salvation to come here on earth in some manner of new or renewed "Kingdom of Israel," a realm of peace and plenty, ruled by the elect of God. In these perspectives the true man appears as the *homo coelestis*, who has eaten his Pasch, accomplished his *transitus*, gone over through a death into the life that is really life.

These, briefly, are the dominant accents in the doctrine of eschatological humanism. Pushed to the extreme, the conclusion would be that man not only may in fact neglect, but even should by right neglect, what is called the cultural enterprise—the cultivation of science and the arts, the pursuit of human values by human energies, the work of civilization—in order to give undivided energies to the invisible things of the spirit. No Christian of course draws this extreme conclusion and makes it a law for humanity, though individuals may hear it, in one or other form, as the word of God to them, and hearken to it, and be God's witnesses to the oneness of the one thing necessary, by the completeness of their contempt for the world.

Affirmation of the Worldly

The tendency towards an incarnational humanism is founded on accents laid on other, and no less Christian, principles. The end of man, it asserts, is indeed transcendent, supernatural; but it is an end of *man* and in its achievement man truly finds the perfection of his nature. Grace perfects nature, does not destroy it—this is the central point of emphasis. There is indeed a radical discontinuity between nature and grace, but nature does not therefore become irrelevant to grace. There must be no Lutheranism, which would fix a great gulf of separation between orders that are only distinct. Again, the perfect man of St. Paul will achieve the fullness of his age and stature only in heaven and not in history; nonetheless he grows in history. The Body of Christ is really a-building here in time. And its growth is that of a Body, not simply of a soul. There must be no Platonism, which would make man only a soul. The *res sacra* which grace would achieve is likewise a *res humana* in the full sense.

In the stage of growth proper to its earthly pilgrimage the Body of Christ finds organic place for developed human values. It carries on the mission of Christ: "to save that which perished." And that which perished was not only a soul, but man in his composite unity, and the material universe too, in that its relation of subjection to man was shattered and it fell into a mysterious slavery of disobedience to human purposes, from which it longs for deliverance.

The Church then is catholic in her redemptive scope; all men are to be saved, all that is human is to be saved. There is indeed to be a war upon the flesh, but in order that the body may be dignified. The Christian heart must cultivate a contempt for the world, but diligently cherish its reverence for the work of the Creator, who is Creator not only of heaven but of the earth, of the visible as well as the invisible. In order to protect the true meaning of the doctrine of sacrifice, its premises must be strongly affirmed—that the life which one loses, gives up, renounces, is a good life. Otherwise the losing of it would not be a saving loss but a sheer loss, a destruction and not a redemption (one would not and could not "buy back" that which was destroyed as of no value).

Therefore in the perspectives of an incarnational humanism there is a place for all that is natural, human, terrestrial. The heavens and the earth are not destined for an eternal dust-heap, but for a transformation. There will be a new heaven and a new earth; and those who knew them once will recognize them, for all their newness.

Again, this view emphasizes the Christian doctrine of merit and its implications. *Gratiam non propter merita dari*, grace is unmerited—the Augustinian adage is still a battle-cry against permanent Pelagian naturalism. Nonetheless there is such a thing as merit. And if the doctrine be transposed out of a purely juridical universe of discourse, it means that human effort remains real and really valuable, integrally itself, though now necessarily situated at the interior of a larger unity of action wherein the divine motion retains the primacy. The doctrine asserts the essential soundness of human nature, which is sinful but not corrupt. And it carries the heart-lifting implication which Irenaeus enforced against Gnostic Manichaeism: "the material is susceptible of salvation."

There is the further implication that all that is good in the order of nature and of human and terrestrial values "merits" doing, and that the doing of it can be meritorious, salvific of the doer, incorporative of the thing done into the one overarching Christian endeavor, the bringing of all things under the headship of Christ. The Christian takes the Pauline phrase in its full universality. For him the development of the natural and the human is not an effort apart from the intention of grace; it is a part of this intention. The two efforts of nature and of grace are not indeed continuous and of the same order; but they are in themselves related and they can be related in the one intention of the Christian man.

Though nature stands in no relation of proper causality to grace, it is both dispositive and disponible in regard of grace. The supernatural is not the same as the miraculous. It does not follow upon nature, but it does not go against nature. There must be disposition of the subject, whether the subject is an individual to be interiorly justified, or a civilization to be rectified in its manner of organization. The concept of the *praeparatio evangelica* is a valid one; it implies the value and the providential character of human cultural effort. God, the Father of all, does indeed fix by His own authority the times and the seasons; but their advent is not wholly unrelated to the strivings of men.

Furthermore, this incarnational humanism stresses the fact that He who entered the stream of history as its Redeemer is the Logos, Eternal Reason. Through His Spirit He is still immanent in history, there to do a work of reason—that work of reason which is justice, and that work of pacification which is in turn the work of justice. Hence all efforts, by whomsoever put forth, toward the rationalization of human society, its "justification" and its pacification, are put forth in the line of action of the Logos Himself. He is in mysterious alliance with them. That kingdoms should be *magna latrocinia* is not inevitable; nor is the civil power an institution simply for the punishment of sin—a divine instrument to whose actions, even when unjust, man must attribute justice. What we know as "the state," the order of law and justice, is in its own sphere ministerial to the action of the Logos. It does not, and may not attempt to, lead men to the eternal life of grace; only Christ, as Son and Head of the Church, has that power. But it does and must lead men to the life of reason; and in this sense its humanizing action is participative in the action of Christ, as Logos and King of kings.

Finally, an incarnational humanism appeals to history and sees in history a manner of law. The fact is that Christianity did give rise to a culture, to an enormous explosion of human effort that altered the face even of this earth. This was not its primal mission, of course. But, as Leo XIII loved to repeat, Christianity could not have operated more beneficial effects upon the whole process and order of human living-together, if it had been instituted precisely for this purpose. Christianity freed man from nature by teaching him that he has an immortal soul, which is related to matter but not immersed in it or enslaved to its laws. Christianity released man from a Greek bondage to history and its eternal cyclic returns. It taught him his own uniqueness, his own individual worth, the dignity of his own person, the equality of all men, the unity of the human race.

On the impulse of these lessons he set about building himself a world in which he might live as a man and a Christian, in the enjoyment of his birthright of freedom and in the discharge of the responsibility this birthright imposed upon him. He assumed in fact the post that is his by right—that of being lord of the world, endowed with the intelligence to understand its laws and processes and harness its energies to his own purposes.

History shows that the whole cultural enterprise was not unrelated to Christianity in its origins. And history proves too that it was not unrelated to Christianity in its finality. The faith was once supported by a civilization. It does not, if you will, absolutely need this support—at least the individual Christian does not. He can live the Christian life amid the barren horror of a concentration camp. But the Church, the community of the faithful, not all of whom are heroes, does need this manner of support. And therefore the creation of a temporal order of justice and civic fraternity has been a humanistic aspiration connatural to the Christian heart. The aspiration is never Utopian. The Christian knows how intertwined are the human and the sinful; how "the Christian world" is not "the Church" and cannot be. Achievements in this order are never ideal; but they are human achievements. Their value is real, if limited, and is not to be undermined by any exaggerations of the Christian contempt for the world. In their humanism they are Christian achievements.

Prudence and Confidence

Here then, in very brief compass, are the two general orientations which Christian thought has taken as it has meditated on the problem of a Christian humanism. It is obvious that the doctrines upon which the tendencies respectively rest are not mutually exclusive; these doctrines are integral to the Gospel and complementary to each other. However, the emphases made in the eschatological view are exclusive of those made in the incarnational view; and each set of emphases, when really lived, results in a distinct style of life. The choice of emphasis is one of the privileges of Christian freedom. Every Christian must make the effort to live out of the whole Gospel. However, each Christian is limited as a man, and the lines of the structure which grace erects must somehow be obedient to the contours of individual human nature. Each Christian has his gift from God, Who would have each man wholly His witness but not necessarily a witness to the whole of Him. Only the Church herself as the community of the faithful, in her many-splendored variety, is witness to the whole counsel of God. And even she, while still *in via,* is this manner of witness only imperfectly. There can therefore be no question of dissolving either one of these two tendencies and the style of life it creates.

Finally, there are risks inherent in each tendency. An eschatological humanism runs the risk of entrusting the fortunes of this world and the forms of all its institutions to the dubious wisdom of the unregenerate. And this would condemn the faithful to live in conditions of barbarism—perhaps the highly civilized barbarism which the wisdom of the flesh, making use of the instrumentalities of science, is capable of creating. The Egyptians can indeed accumulate great spoils; but as long as they remain only in Egyptian hands they can only help make Egypt a land of bondage. On the other hand, he who would seek to make his way toward the Kingdom of God and His grace through a search for the common good of the earthly City and an affirmation of the goods of nature is taking a long and difficult road. The effort to despoil the Egyptians can result in inner self-despoilment.

All this and much more must be borne in mind when one approaches the problem of Christian humanism in its American position. Actually, there are two problems. First, is there a place in good theology for the human values which America has historically emphasized? More practically, is a terrestrial, incarnational humanism possible within the conditions of society which the American emphasis tends to create? More important, can this manner of humanism be useful to the Christian in his specially Christian quest, the quest for sanctity? Are conditions of freedom and great material prosperity valuable only because they enlarge the opportunities for Christian renouncement? Or are they simply analogous to that Ciceronian period in which the patrons of "devout humanism" preached? They preached in these cadences not because they are particularly "good in themselves," but merely in order to be heard and heeded in an age whose ear was attuned to the Ciceronian period. In application, have these conditions of freedom and prosperity simply an "apostolic value," such that one should simply "use" them as means to an end no more related to them than a Ciceronian period is related to the Gospel message? On this hypothesis these social conditions, institutions, and ideals might well have only the character of a necessary evil.

Or is this whole American situation and the humanism to which it tends and the style of life to which it leads capable of being affirmed as a human good, an end-in-itself—an intermediate end indeed, but not solely a means? (The question here obviously concerns only what is good and of human value in the total dynamism which creates what is called "the American situation.") Concretely, is the ideal of a "free people" and a "prosperous nation" a genuine value, a legitimate end to be striven for as good in itself? Or is it simply a means to an entirely disproportionate end, in the sense that a free people can protect the freedom of the Church and a wealthy nation can support her institutions?

The second problem is analogous but wider. What is the relation between terrestrial and eschatological humanism? In other words, does the cultivation of human values by human energies deployed in an effort that is not directly aroused by grace but is open to its direction, once aroused—does this manner of humanism contribute to the coming of the Kingdom of God? Or is it fundamentally irrelevant—a form of basket weaving? To ask this, of course, is to raise the question of the relation between history and the Church—the relation between the great human effort at unification, which is the basic cultural enterprise, and the divine effort of the Spirit, which is to "gather into one the scattered children of

God." This is indeed a mighty question. And to raise it is to invite to a journey down avenues of mystery, which, for all that, are legitimate avenues of reverent Christian inquiry.

It remains only to indicate the spirit of the inquiry, as set by the Church herself. In her doctrinal affirmations the Church is confident, even optimistic. True religion and profound humaneness, she says, are not rivals but sisters, who have nothing to fear from each other but everything to gain. This is a very firm assertion. On the other hand, the Church is prudent, even cautious, in the area of practice. Her concrete counsels to her children have not the same confidence as her doctrinal statements; they are touched with an accent of warning, even of fear. She boldly urges the truth; she carefully guides action.

The reason for this difference in attitude is clear. The wound of nature, which is our heritage from the original sin, makes itself felt in two lines— in the line of intelligence in its relation to the true, and in the line of the will in its relation to the good. But in the latter line the wound is more profound, mysterious, crippling. The will deviates from the good more easily and radically than the intelligence deviates from the true. Hence the Church stoutly defends reason and its powers of knowing and of harmonizing its knowledge with its Christian beliefs. She is less certain of man himself in his total being and less confident of his power to harmonize his whole human effort with his Christian faith, in that ever precarious synthesis known as a Christian humanism. It is in this same spirit of both confidence and prudence that the problem is to be approached.

CHAPTER NINE

~

Are There Two or One?
The Question of the
Future of Freedom

In a previous chapter I took note of the contemporary currency of the phrase, the "end of modern times." Whether modern times began with the fall of Constantinople in the fifteenth century (the conventional view) or with the rise of Gnosticism in the second century (the more convincing view) is a matter of dispute. In any case, though the adjective "modern" will continue to be used in advertising copy as synonymous with "up to date," it will from now on be increasingly used in scholarly circles as synonymous with "out of date." A new era has begun. Whatever its characteristics, they will not be those of "modernity." It is a journalistic certainty that it will be an era of unprecedented dangers, unlike any that modernity confronted. The danger of violent destruction threatens the very physical fabric of civilization. And more insidious corruptions menace the spiritual nature of man himself. One does not have to believe that downfall is our inevitable civilizational fate. But one does have to recognize that confusion is the present civilizational fact.

For the rest, I venture the prediction that the post-modern era will see the revival of one (and the most basic) of the unfinished arguments of the Christian era. The state of the question is put in the title of this chapter, which will not be enigmatic to anyone who knows the intellectual and political history of what is called "the West," a concept that has no meaning apart from Christianity. I should like to spin an argument on this question, as thus stated.

The Question and the Method of Inquiry

Is the Problem today rightly identified in one word, "freedom"? The point might be argued. In any case, the Problem is not "freedom" in the sense in which modernity has understood the term. So rapidly have the generations slipped beneath our feet that the prophets of modernity and its "freedom"—the Miltons and the Millses, the Madisons and the Jeffersons—have already begun to seem slightly neolithic figures to our backward glance. Certain of their insights retain validity. But the adequacy of their systems can no longer be upheld. The broad question has arisen, whether the problem of freedom in the post-modern era can be satisfactorily dealt with in terms of philosophies (and theologies) which bear too heavily the stamp of modernity.

The problem does not center on some minor malfunctions of the mechanisms of freedom. Our "free institutions," in their procedural aspects, are working today as well as they ever have worked or ever will work. Some tinkering with them may be needed. But tinkering is not our full task. It is characteristic of the present moment that all the serious talk is about Basic Issues.

The initial difficulty is that these Basic Issues are not easily located and defined. Perhaps rather abruptly, I shall venture a twofold formulation.

First the Basic Issues of our time concern the spiritual substance of a free society, as it has historically derived from the central Christian concept, *res sacra homo*, man is sacredness (only the abstract noun can render the Latin rightly). Second, the Basic Issues concern the fundamental structure of a free society. I do not mean its legal structure, as constitutionally established. Few of the real problems today are susceptible of solution, or even of statement, in legal language. I mean rather the ontological structure of society, of which the constitutional order should be only the reflection. This underlying social structure is a matter of theory, that is, it is to be conceived in terms of a theorem with regard to the relation between the sacredness inherent in man and the manifold secularities amid which human life is lived.

This twofold formulation is very general. I set it down thus to make clear my conviction that the Basic Issues today can only be conceived in metaphysical and theological terms. They are issues of truth. They concern the nature and structure of reality itself—meaning by reality the order of nature as accessible to human reason, and the economy of salvation as disclosed by the Christian revelation.

But these general formulas may not be useful for purposes of argument. And argument, I take it, is our immediate need. Therefore a more pragmatic approach to our problem is indicated. Professor Hocking has stated its premise in his book, *The Coming World Civilization:* "For whatever is real in the universe is no idle object of speculation; it is a working factor in experience or it is nothing. Consciously or subconsciously we are always dealing with it; to entertain false notions about it, or simply to neglect it, will bring about maladjustments which thrust this neglect forward into consciousness. A false metaphysic, engendering empirical malaise, calls for a new work of thought, begetting an altered premise."[1]

The statement suggests a method of inquiry. What are our malaises today? That is, what are the discomforts and uneasinesses that trouble not the surface of mind and soul, but their very depths? Are these distresses somehow traceable to falsities in the philosophy that has inspired the political experiment of modernity? If so, what new work of thought is needed? And what alterations in the premises of the modern experiment are called for?

A process of questioning, more or less inspired by this method, has been going on of late; and in the course of it many ideas dear to a later modernity have found their way into Trotsky's famous "dustbin of history."

For instance, we no longer cherish the bright and brittle eighteenth-century concept of "reason"; we do not believe in the principle of automatic harmony nor in the inevitability of progress. We have rejected that doctrine of modernity which asserted that government is the only enemy of freedom. We see that the modern concept of freedom itself was dangerously inadequate because it neglected the corporate dimension of freedom. We see too that modernity was wrong in isolating the problem of freedom from its polar terms—responsibility, justice, order, law. We have realized that the modern experiment, originally conceived only as an experiment in freedom, had to become also an experiment in justice. We know that the myopic individualism of modernity led it into other errors, even into a false conception of the problem of the state in terms of the unreal dichotomy, individualism vs. collectivism. We have come to disbelieve the cardinal tenet of modernity which regarded every advance in man's domination over nature—that is, every new accumulation of power—as necessarily liberating. We have begun to understand the polyvalence of power. In fact, we know that we are post-modern men, living in a new age, chiefly because we have begun to see what modernity never saw—that the central problem is not the realization of the Cartesian dream. This dream today is largely reality; man is the master and possessor of nature. Our problem now is the dissolution of a nightmare that never visited Descartes—the horrid vision of man, master of nature but not of himself, the possessor of nature who has lost his own identity.

It may be useful here to carry this process of questioning further, and to an altogether basic level. This can best be done, I think, by viewing the modern political experiment in its continuity with the longer liberal tradition of the West. My generalization will be that the political experiment of modernity has essentially consisted in an effort to find and install in the world a secular substitute for all that the Christian tradition has meant by the pregnant phrase, the "freedom of the Church."

My first assertion will be that this freedom, though not a freedom of the political order, was Christianity's basic contribution to freedom in the political order. Some brief articulation of the concept will initially be necessary.

Second, I shall say that modernity dropped the phrase out of its political vocabulary, and eliminated the thing from its political edifice and installed in its place a secular surrogate, with results that we now begin to see. Thirdly I shall attempt to identify some of the more acute stresses and distresses now being experienced at our present stage, the term of the modern experiment. Finally, I shall attempt to state some of the spiritual issues which lie, I think, at the origin of our empirical malaises. It will be sufficient for my purpose simply to present these issues for argument.

The Freedom of the Church

In his book, *Libertas: Kirche und Weltordnung im Zeitalter des Investiturstreites* (a broad study of the basic issues involved in that great medieval struggle between opposed conceptions of the nature and order of Christian society, which centered around Gregory VII), Gerd Tellenbach writes: "In moments of considered solemnity, when their tone was passionate and their religious feeling at its deepest, Gregory VII and his contemporaries called the

object towards which they were striving the 'freedom' of the Church."
More than six centuries earlier the same idea had inspired Ambrose in his
conflicts with Gratian and Theodosius. And eight centuries later, Leo XIII
used the same phrase to define the goal of his striving in a more radical conflict between the Church and modernity, now fully developed, not only as
a spirit but also as a polity. In more than sixty Leonine documents the
phrase, the "freedom of the Church," appears some eighty-one times.

On any showing, even merely historical, we are here in the presence of
a Great Idea, whose entrance into history marked the beginning of a new
civilizational era.

It is a historical commonplace to say that the essential political effect
of Christianity was to destroy the classical view of society as a single ho-
mogenous structure, within which the political power stood forth as the
representative of society both in its religious and in its political aspects.
Augustus was both *Summus Imperator* and *Pontifex Maximus*; the *ius div-
inum* was simply part of the *ius civile*; and outside the empire there was no
civil society, but only barbarism. The new Christian view was based on a
radical distinction between the order of the sacred and the order of the
secular: "Two there are, august Emperor, by which this world is ruled on
title of original and sovereign right—the consecrated authority of the
priesthood and the royal power." In this celebrated sentence of Gelasius
I, written to the Byzantine Emperor Anastasius I in 494 A.D., the emphasis laid on the word "two" bespoke the revolutionary character of the
Christian dispensation.

In his book, *Sacrum Imperium*, Alois Dempf called this Gelasian text
the "Magna Charta of the whole 'freedom of the Church' in medieval
times." It was the charter of a new freedom, such as the world had never
known. Moreover, it was a freedom with which man could not enfran-
chise himself, since it was the effect of God's own "magnificent dispensation," in Gelasius's phrase. The whole patristic and medieval tradition,
which Leo XIII reiterated to the modern world, asserts the freedom of the
Church to be a participation in the freedom of the Incarnate Son of God,
the God-Man, Christ Jesus. For our purposes here we can consider this
new freedom to be twofold.

First, there is the freedom of the Church as a spiritual authority. To the
Church is entrusted the *cura animarum*; and this divine commission endows
her with the freedom to teach, to rule, and to sanctify, with all that these

empowerments imply as necessary for their free exercise. This positive freedom has a negative aspect—the immunity of the Church, as the suprapolitical sacredness (*res sacra*), from all manner of politicization, through subordination to the state or enclosure within the state as *instrumentum regni*.

Second, there is the freedom of the Church as the Christian people—their freedom to have access to the teaching of the Church, to obey her laws, to receive at her hands the sacramental ministry of grace, and to live within her fold an integral supernatural life. In turn, the inherent suprapolitical dignity of this life itself claims "for the faithful the enjoyment of the right to live in civil society according to the precepts of reason and conscience" (Pius XI). And this comprehensive right, asserted within the political community, requires as its complement that all the intrapolitical sacrednesses (*res sacra in temporalibus*) be assured of their proper immunity from politicization.

This concept, the *res sacra in temporalibus*, had all the newness of Christianity itself. It embraces all those things which are part of the temporal life of man, at the same time that, by reason of their Christian mode of existence, or by reason of their finality, they transcend the limited purposes of the political order and are thus invested with a certain sacredness. The chief example is the institution of the family—the marriage contract itself, and the relationships of husband and wife, parent and child. Included also are other human relationships in so far as they involve a moral element and require regulation in the interests of the personal dignity of man. Such, for instance, are the employer-employee relationship and the reciprocal relationships established by the political obligation. Sacred too is the intellectual patrimony of the human race, the heritage of basic truths about the nature of man, amassed by secular experience and reflection, that form the essential content of the social consensus and furnish the basic guarantee that within society conditions of freedom and justice, prosperity and order will prevail, at least to some essential human degree.

Instinctively and by natural inclination the common man knows that he cannot be free if his basic human things are not sacredly immune from profanation by the power of the state and by other secular powers. The question has always been that of identifying the limiting norm that will check the encroachments of secular power and preserve these sacred immunities. Western civilization first found this norm in the pregnant principle, the freedom of the Church.

I should perhaps emphasize that the phrase must be given its full meaning. As a matter of history, the liberal tradition of Western politics did not begin its lengthy, slow, and halting evolution because something like Harnack's wraith-like *Wesen des Christentums* began to pervade the dominions of imperial Rome. This pale phantom would have been altogether unequal to the task of inaugurating a new political history. What appeared within history was not an "idea" or an "essence" but an existence, a Thing, a visible institution that occupied ground in this world at the same time that it asserted an astounding new freedom on a title not of this world. Through the centuries a new tradition of politics was wrought out very largely in the course of the wrestlings between the new freedom of the Church and the pretensions of an older power which kept discovering, to its frequent chagrin, that it was not the one unchallengeable ruler of the world and that its rule was not unlimitedly free.

In regard of the temporal order and its powers and processes this complex Existent Thing, the "freedom of the Church," performed a twofold function.

First, the freedom of the Church as the spiritual authority served as the limiting principle of the power of government. It furnished, as it were, a corporate or social armature to the sacred order, within which *res sacra homo* would be secure in all the freedoms that his sacredness demands. Men found their freedom where they found their faith—within the Church. As it was her corporate faith that they professed, so it was her corporate freedom that they claimed, in the face of the public power and of all private powers. Within the armature of her immunities they and their human things were immune from profanation. Second, the freedom of the Church as the "people of God" furnished the ultimate directive principle of government. To put it briefly, the Church stood (in alliance with University, as I said before) between the body politic and the public power, not only limiting the reach of the power over the people, but also mobilizing the moral consensus of the people and bringing it to bear upon the power, thus to insure that the king, in the fine phrase of John of Salisbury, would "fight for justice and for the freedom of the people."

This was the new Christian theorem. I leave aside the historical question, whether and to what extent the theorem was successfully institutionalized. What matters is the theorem itself. The freedom of the Church, in its pregnant meaning, was conceived to be the key to the

Christian order of society. What further matters is the historical fact that the whole equilibrium of social forces which under the guidance of this theory made (however imperfectly) for freedom and justice within society was destroyed by the rise of the national monarchies and by the course of their political evolution in the era of royal absolutism.

Political Modernity

The basic effort of modern politics, as I have suggested, looked to a re-establishment of the equilibrium. In a much too rapid description of it, the process was simple. The early Christian dualism of Church and state (or better, the dyarchy of Gelasius's "Two there are") was in a sense retained. That is, it endured in a secular political form, namely, in the distinction between state and society which had been the secular political outgrowth of the Christian distinction between Church and state. However, the freedom of the Church, again in its pregnant sense, was discarded as the mediating principle between society and state, between the people and the public power. Instead, a secular substitute was adopted in the form of free political institutions. Through these secular institutions the people would limit the power of government. They would also direct the power of government to its proper ends, which are perennially those of John of Salisbury—the fight for justice and for the freedom of the people.

The key to the whole new political edifice was the freedom of the individual conscience. Here precisely lies the newness of the modern experiment. A great act of trust was made. The trust was that the free individual conscience would effectively mediate the moral imperatives of the transcendental order of justice (whose existence was not doubted in the earlier phases of the modern experiment). Then, through the workings of free political institutions these imperatives would be transmitted to the public power as binding norms upon its action. The only sovereign spiritual authority would be the conscience of the free man. The freedom of the individual conscience, constitutionally guaranteed, would supply the armature of immunity to the sacred order, which now became, by modern definition, precisely the order of the private conscience. And through free political institutions, again constitutionally guaranteed, the moral consensus of the community would be mobilized in favor of justice and freedom in the secular order. This, I take it, has been in essence the political experiment of modernity. It has been an attempt to carry on the liberal tradition of Western politics, whose roots were in the Christian revolution, but now on a new revolutionary basis—a rejection of the Gelasian thesis, "Two there are," which had been the dynamic of the Christian revolution.

The rejection of the Gelasian thesis has been common to all the prophets of modernity, from Marsilius of Padua onwards. All of them have been united in viewing the freedom of the Church, in the sense explained, as a trespass upon, and a danger to, their one supreme value—the "integrity of the political order," as the phrase goes. Two citations may be given as illustrative. Rousseau complains: "Jesus came to establish on earth a spiritual kingdom. By separating the theological system from the political system he brought it about that the State ceased to be one, and caused internal divisions which have never ceased to agitate Christian peoples. From this twofold power there has resulted a perpetual conflict of jurisdiction which has rendered all good politics impossible in Christian states. No one has ever been able to know which one to obey, priest or political ruler." Thomas Hobbes put the same issue with characteristic bluntness and clarity: "Temporal and spiritual government are but words brought into the world to make men see double and mistake their sovereign," which is Leviathan, the Mortal God.

In this indictment of Christianity for having made the state "cease to be one," and in this protest against men who "see double," one hears the authentic voice of the secular power as modern history has known it.

It would not be difficult to demonstrate that this monistic tendency is somehow inherent in the state, in both of its aspects—both as an expression of reason and also as a vehicle of power. Nor would it be difficult to show how this monistic tendency has been visible in practically all the states that have paraded across the stage of history, even in states that bore the name of Christian. In any case, the tendency has achieved its most striking success in the modern era. It is the most salient aspect of political modernity. Over the whole of modern politics there has hung the monist concept of the indivisibility of sovereignty: "One there is." This has been true even in those states in which the sovereignty, remaining indivisible, has been institutionalized according to the principle of the separation of powers.

The dynamism behind the assertion, "One there is," has, of course, varied. In the seventeenth and eighteenth centuries it was royal absolutism, whose theorists—Widdrington, Barclay, James I—proclaimed a social and juridical monism in the name of the divine right of kings. In the nineteenth century the dynamism was the Revolution, that whole complex of forces which created Jacobin democracy and proclaimed the *république indivisible* in the name of the sovereignty of the people understood as the social projection of the absolutely autonomous sovereignty of individual reason. In the twentieth century the most successful dynamism has been Soviet Communism, which makes the assertion, "One there is," in the name of the unitary class which is destined for world sovereignty, and in the name of its organ, the Party, whose function is to be the servant and ally of the materialist forces of history.

In the twentieth century too, as the modern era runs out, the ancient monistic drive to a oneness of society, law, and authority has also appeared in the totalitarianizing tendency inherent in the contemporary idolatry of the democratic process. This democratic monism is urged in the name of something less clear than the *république indivisible*. What is urged is a monism, not so much of the political order itself, as of a political technique. The proposition is that all the issues of human life—intellectual, religious, and moral issues as well as formally political issues—are to be regarded as, or resolved into, political issues and are to be settled by the single omnicompetent political technique of majority vote. On the surface the monism is one of process; Madison's "republican principle" affords the Final Grounds for the Last Say on All Human Questions. But the underlying idea is a monism of power: "One there is whereby this world is ruled—the power in the people, expressing itself in the preference of a majority; and beyond or beside or above this power there is no other."

The inspiration of democratic monism is partly a sentimentalist mystique—the belief that the power in the people, in distinction from all other powers, is somehow ultimately and inevitably beneficent in its exercise. But the more radical inspiration is the new idea, unknown to medieval times, which modern rationalism thrust into political history. Christianity has always regarded the state as a limited order of action for limited purposes, to be chosen and pursued under the direction and correction of the organized moral conscience of society, whose judgments are formed and mobilized by the Church, an independent and autonomous community, qualified to be the interpreter of man's nature and destiny. It has been specific of modernity to regard the state as a moral end in itself, a self-justifying entity with its own self-determined spiritual substance. It is within the secular state, and by appeal to secular sources, that man is to find the interpretation of his own nature and the means to his own destiny. The state itself creates the ethos of society, embodies it, imparts it to its citizens, and sanctions its observance with rewards and punishments. Outside the tradition of Jacobin or Communist dogmatism, the modern democratic secular state does not indeed pretend to be the Universe or to speak infallibly. But it does assert itself to be the embodiment of whatever fallible human wisdom may be available to man, because it is the highest school of human experience, beyond which man can find no other School and no other Teacher.

Professor Hocking has put the matter thus: "Outside the Marxist orbit the prevalent disposition of the secular state in recent years has been less to combat the church than to carry on a slow empirical demonstration of the state's full equivalence in picturing the attainable good life, and its superior pertinence to actual issues. As this demonstration gains force the expectation grows that it will be the church, not the state, that will wither away. Where the fields of church and state impinge on each other, as in education and correction, the church will in time appear superfluous. Where they are different, the church will be quietly ignored and dropped as irrelevant." This, says Hocking, is the "secular hypothesis." It is, he adds, the premise of the "experiment we call 'modernity.'" In the language I have been using, the hypothesis asserts: "One there is by which the world is ruled."

The "one" here (sc., outside the Marxist orbit) is the self-conscious free individual, armed with his subjective rights, whose ultimate origins he may have forgotten but whose status as legal certitudes he cherishes. This individual, the product of modernity, has been taught by modernity to stand against any external and corporate authority, except it be mediated to him by democratic processes; to stand against any law in whose making he had no voice; to stand finally against any society which asserts itself to be an independent community of thought, superior to the common opinion created by the common mind of secular democratic society, and empowered to pass judgment, in the name of higher criteria, on this common mind and on the majority views it assembles.

Outside the Jacobin and Communist tradition this "one ruler," the modern man, does not object to religion, provided that religion be regarded as a private matter which concerns only the conscience and feelings of the individual. In his more expansive moments he will not object even to organized religion—the "churches"—provided they accept the status of voluntary associations for limited purposes which do not impinge upon the public order. But he will not tolerate any marring of his image of the world as modernity conceives it—the image of democratic society as the universal community whose ends are coextensive with the ends of man himself. It is the One Society, with One Law, and with One Sovereign, the politically equal people. Modernity has declared the Gelasian doctrine to be heretical and has outlawed it, in the name of modern orthodoxy, which is a naturalist rationalism.

This dominant image of democratic society as ultimately monist in its structure (whatever may be its constituent and subordinate pluralisms), and as ultimately secular in its substance (whatever historical tribute it may have levied on religious spiritualities), represents the refined essence of political modernity. Its significance lies in the fact that it confronts us with an experiment in human freedom which has consciously or unconsciously been based on a denial or a disregard of the essential Christian contribution to human freedom, which is the theorem of the freedom of the Church.

Troubles Today

We come now to the uneasinesses stirring in the world of post-modern man, and in his soul too. The first may be quickly run over, although it is most profoundly serious. I mean all the uneasiness aroused by our confrontation with international Communism. Communism is, of course, political modernity carried to its logical conclusion. All that is implicit and unintentional in modernity as a phenomenon in what is called the West has become explicit and deliberate in the Communist system. The "secular hypothesis," in Hocking's phrase, has been lifted to the status of a dogma. And Hobbes's prohibition has seen most vicious enforcement; man is not allowed to "see double and mistake his lawful sovereign." The operations of the Communist system would seem to offer an empirical demonstration of the fact that there can be no freedom or justice where God is denied and where everything meant by the freedom of the Church is deliberately excised from the theorem on which the life of the community is based.

The measure of human malaise within the Communist orbit cannot be estimated accurately. In any case, the malaise cannot be geographically contained. Stress and distress are the condition of the whole world. And we ourselves feel them, or at least should feel them, most sharply in the form of the question, whether we are spiritually and intellectually equipped to meet the Communist threat at its deepest level.

Communism in theory and in practice has reversed the revolution which Christianity initiated by the Gelasian doctrine: "Two there are by which this world is ruled." This new system has proposed with all logic an alternative to the basic structure of society, and a surrogate of society's spiritual substance, as these are defined in the Christian theorem. And the question is, whether there are in the spirit of modernity as such the resources whereby the Christian revolution, with all its hopes of freedom and justice, can be reinstated in its course, and the reactionary counter-revolution halted. The issue is clear enough; two contrary views of the structure of reality are in conflict. And the issue is certainly basic—too basic to be solved either by military measures or by political techniques. Free elections, for instance, have their value. But of themselves they leave untouched the basic issue, which is joined between the clashing assertions: "Two there are," and "One there is."

The second post-modern uneasiness derives from the current experience of the "impotence of the state." Here I adopt Hocking's phrase and the thesis it states, as developed in the first part of his book, already cited. (With certain of his subsequent analyses and theses, and with their Gnostic overtones, I have serious difficulties.) The net of it is that the modern state has, as a matter of empirical fact, proved impotent to do all the things it has undertaken to do. Crime and civic virtue, education, the stimulus and control of economic processes, public morality, justice in the order and processes of law—over all these things the modern state assumed an unshared competence. But it has proved itself incompetent in a fundamental sense. The reason is that "the state depends for its vitality upon a motivation which it cannot by itself command." As long as this motivation can be assumed to be existent in the body politic, the order of politics (in the broadest sense) moves with some security to its proper ends. But if the motivation fails, there is no power in the state itself to evoke it.

We confront again the dilemma which modernity resolved in its own sense. Is the life of man to be organized in one society, or in two? Modernity chose the unitary hypothesis, that the state itself is the highest form of human association, self-ruled, and self-contained, and self-motivating. But the unitary hypothesis has not been able to sustain itself under the test of experience. Post-modern man has become most uneasily aware of the limitations of the state even in the discharge of its own functions.

The challenge here is to the validity of the suprapolitical tenet upon which modernity staked the whole success of its political experiment. This tenet, I said, was that the individual conscience is the sole ultimate interpreter of the moral order (and of the religious order too), and therefore the sole authentic mediator of moral imperatives to the political order. But the truth of this tenet, confidently assumed by modernity, is now under attack from a battery of questions.

Is the failure of motivation within the state somehow due to the falsity of this tenet? Is the pragmatic law in operation—that whatever is not true will somewhere fail to work? Or again, is the individual conscience, in modernity's conception of it, equal to the burden that has been thrust upon it—the burden of being the keystone of the modern experiment in freedom? Is it disintegrating under the burden? If so, what of the free society which it undertook to sustain? Will it perhaps disintegrate in one or other of the two ways in which a political structure can disintegrate—into a formless chaos or into a false order? Will the modern experiment then prove to be simply an interlude between despotisms—between the known and limited despotisms of the past, and the unknown despotisms of the future, which may well be illimitable? In a word, in consequence of having been enthroned as the One Ruler of this world, has the *conscientia exlex* of modernity succumbed to *hubris*, and is it therefore headed for downfall—its own downfall, the downfall of the concept of the moral order amid the bits and pieces of a purely "situational" ethics, and the downfall of the political order projected by the spirit of modernity?

From another point of view the same questions return. It was an essential part of modernity's hope that the moral consensus upon which every society depends for its stability and progress could be sustained and mobilized simply in terms of a fortunate coincidence of individual private judgments, apart from all reference to a visibly constituted spiritual and moral authority. Has this hope proved valid? Is it perhaps possible that the profound intellectual confusions in the mind of post-modern man are somehow witness to the fact that modernity's hope has proved to be hollow? If there be no consensus with regard to what freedom is, and whence it comes, and what it means within the very soul of man, how shall freedom hope to live within society and in its institutions?

There is a final malaise upon which I should touch. It is, I think, related to the fundamental ambiguity of modern times.

Modernity, I said, rejected the freedom of the Church, in the twofold sense explained, as the armature of man's spiritual freedom and as a structural principle of a free society. Initially the rejection was addressed only to a truth of divine revelation. The whole system of moral values, both individual and social, which had been elaborated under the influence of the Christian revelation was not rejected. I mean here all the values which form a constellation about the central concept, *res sacra homo*. As a matter of fact, these values were adopted as the very basis for the modern political experiment. Modernity, however, has maintained that these values are now known to be simply immanent in man; that man has become conscious of them in the course of their emergence in historical experience; that, whatever may have been the influence of the Christian revelation on the earlier phases of this experience, these values are now simply a human possession, a conquest and an achievement of humanity by man himself. Now that I have arrived, said modernity, Christianity may disappear. Whatever aesthetic appeal it may still retain as a myth, it is not needed as a dynamic of freedom and justice in this world. *Res sacra homo* is now under a new patronage—singly his own.

This is what Romano Guardini has expressively called the "interior disloyalty of modern times." He means, I think, that there has occurred not only a falsification of history but a basic betrayal of the existential structure of reality itself. If this be true, we are confronted by the gravest issue presented by the whole experiment of modernity. The issue again is one of truth. Upon this issue hangs the whole fate of freedom and justice, if only for the pragmatic reason that the structure of reality cannot with impunity be disregarded, even less by society than by the individual.

Tomorrow's Alternatives

It will perhaps be sufficient if I simply present the issue as I see it, without undertaking to argue it. Here are its terms. On the one hand, modernity has denied (or ignored, or forgotten, or neglected) the Christian revelation that man is a sacredness, and that his primatial *res sacra*, his freedom, is sought and found ultimately within the freedom of the Church. On the other hand, modernity has pretended to lay claim to the effects of this doctrine on the order of human culture—the essential effect, for our purposes here, being the imperative laid on John of Salisbury's "king" (say, if you will, the state in all its range of action) to fight for justice and for the freedom of the people. In terms of this denial (or ignorance) and of this pretension (or hypothesis) modernity has conceived its image of political man. Justice is his due, and his function too; but not on the title of his sacredness as revealed by Christ. Freedom is his endowment, and likewise his duty; but not on the title of the freedom of the Church. A fully human life is his destiny; but its fulfillment lies within the horizons of time and space.

The question is, whether this modern image of political man be a reflection of reality (historical, philosophical, theological), or a mirage projected by prideful human reason into the *terra aliena* of a greatly ignorant illusion. Undoubtedly, this question will be answered by history, in which the pragmatic law operates. But it would be well, if possible, to anticipate the operation of this law by embarking upon a "new work of thought, begetting an altered premise."

The sheerly historical alternatives are clear enough. I shall state them in their extremity, using the method of assertion, not of interrogation.

On the one hand, post-modern man can continue to pursue the mirage which bemused modern man. As he does so, a spiritual vacuum will increasingly be created at the heart of human existence. But this vacuum cannot remain uninhabited. It will be like the house in the Gospel, swept and garnished, its vacancy an invitation to what the Gospel expressively calls the "worthless spirit" (*spiritus nequam*). He then will enter in with seven spirits more worthless than himself, and there set about the work that befits his character. He is the Son of Chaos and Old Night; his work is to turn vacuity into chaos.

Less figuratively, if post-modern man, like modern man, rejects the Christian mode of existence, the result will be that an explicitly non-Christian mode of existence will progressively come into being at the heart of human life. It will have its own structure and its own substance. And since it exists, it must manifest its existence and its dynamism. And it will do so—in violence, in all the violence of the chaotic. Violence is the mark of the Architect of Chaos, the Evil One, whose presence in the world is part of the structure of the world. It is not by chance that the mark of violence should have been impressed so deeply on these closing decades of the modern era, and that the threat of violence should hang so heavily over post-modern man as he takes his first uncertain steps into the new era. It was Nietzsche, I think, who said that the non-Christian man of modern times had not yet fully realized what it means to be non-Christian. But in these last decades the realization has been dawning, as we have watched the frightening emergence and multiplication of that "senseless, faithless, heartless, ruthless" man whom Paul met on the streets of non-Christian Corinth and described in his Letter to the Romans.

This development, into a dreadful chaos of violence in which justice and freedom alike would vanish, is not inevitable. An alternative is possible. The way to it lies through a renunciation by post-modern man of the "interior disloyalty of modern times." Thus the new era would have a new premise on which to pursue the experiment in freedom and justice which political society perennially is. However, I must quickly add that this renunciation is not a political act. If one accepts the doctrine of the Second Council of Orange (A.D. 529), it is the work of the Holy Spirit, who "corrects the will of man from infidelity unto faith."

Nevertheless, the "new work of thought" to which post-modern man is impelled as he reflects on the increasing fragility of the "secular hypothesis" will not be irrelevant to the fortunes of the future. If only we do not deny our malaises or seek to drown them, the experience of them can be turned to rational account. It is, after all, not beyond the power of reason to recognize illusion when the results of illusion are encountered in experience. Hence reason itself, and its high exercise in argument, could lead us to the recognition of a law, even more basic than the pragmatic law, which our forebears of the modern era most seriously failed to reckon with. It is the law of reality itself: "Only that ought not to be which cannot be." This perhaps would be the altered premise—a rational premise—that a new work of thought might beget.

Note

1. New York: Harper and Brothers, 1956.

PART III

~

THE USES OF DOCTRINE

~

CHAPTER TEN

Doctrine and Policy in Communist Imperialism: The Problem of Security and Risk

As one observes the courses of American action in the world today, the doubt arises whether we at all "hold these truths" or any truths as determinative of our purposes and directive of our policies. This doubt has more than once arisen in the preceding pages. It has also been a stimulus in the recent efforts to define our National Purpose, or at least to launch a public debate about the National Purpose. A new situation seems to have come to pass. History attests that the Founding Fathers—practical men, all of them—were well aware of the uses of doctrine. Today there is evidence that we have no use for doctrine—or perhaps even no doctrines to use.

If now there is a vacuum where once there was substance, the fact is serious. It is particularly serious in view of our present confrontation with the Soviet Union. Coexistence with the Communist empire is the present fact. There are those who wish to transform the fact into a policy by adding various adjectives to the word "coexistence." There is talk, for instance, of "peaceful" coexistence, or of "competitive" coexistence. But, before coexistence, however qualified adjectivally, can become a policy, it is necessary to know just what kind of an empire we are coexisting with. This is the first difficulty. Academic and public opinion in the matter is divided. There is little common agreement, of a firmly articulated kind, with regard to the aims and motivations and scope of Communist imperialism in its action on the world scene. One could distinguish at least four or five different schools of thought. Their major differences derive from their variant estimates of the role of doctrine or ideology in Soviet behavior. There are even those who refuse to admit that ideology plays any significant role. The Soviet doctrine, they say, is pretty much the same as our doctrine—namely, that doctrine has no uses.

There are also those who are content to cite as the single characteristic of the Soviet empire that it is intent on "world domination"; and they let it go at that. But one cannot let it go at that. The intellectual tyranny of phrases, to which we have long been accustomed in domestic politics, has invaded the field of foreign policy in consequence of the impact of democracy on the conduct of war and on the making of peace. The trouble is that the stock phrases tend to become simply incantations. They are invoked as curses on the enemy or as cries of alarm to sustain a mood of fear and opposition. So it is with the phrase "world domination." It has ceased to yield any clear demonstrable meaning. It has even acquired false connotations, as if the primary Soviet aim were domination by military conquest. In consequence some would wish to discard the phrase altogether, as unreal and unhelpful. But this would be a mistake of method that would lead to substantial error in viewing the structure of the problem that confronts America today. The phrase has meaning, but it needs to be analyzed in the light of the four unique aspects of the Soviet empire.

A Fourfold Uniqueness

First, Russia is unique as a state or a power. For the first time in history it has brought under a single supreme government the 210,000,000 people scattered over the 8,600,000 square miles of the Euro-Asiatic plain, the great land-mass that stretches from the River Elbe to the Pacific Ocean. This gigantic power is a police state of new proportions and unique efficiency. Within it there is no such thing as the "rule of law"; there is only the thing called "Soviet legality." Power is used according to certain forms; but there is no concern for justice and no sense of human rights. The Soviet Union has not adopted the Western concept of law nor has it evolved a comparable concept of its own. Its theory of government is purely and simply despotism. In this respect Sir Winston Churchill was right in viewing the Russians (as Sir Isaiah Berlin reports) as a "formless, quasi-Asiatic mass beyond the walls of European civilization." These walls, that contain the Western realization of civility, were erected by men who understood the Western heritage of law—Roman, Greek, Germanic, Christian. The Soviet Union has no such understanding of law.

Moreover, through a novel set of institutions the Soviet Union has succeeded in centralizing all governmental power to a degree never before achieved. The ultimate organ of control is the Communist party, a small group of men who think and act under an all-embracing discipline that has likewise never before been achieved. Under its historically new system—a totally socialized economy—the Soviet Union has become an industrial and technological power whose single rival is the United States. In rising to this status of power it has chosen to emphasize industries and technologies that are related to war. This state is consequently a military power of the first order. It has no rival in ground forces; its air power is adequate to all the new exigencies of war; and for the first time in history the state that controls the Heartland of the World Island has become a sea power of a special kind, an underwater power. Finally, its nuclear and missile capabilities are at least equal to those of the United States, for all practical purposes and many impractical ones.

Second, Russia is unique as an empire, as a manner and method of rule, as an *imperium*. It is organized and guided in accordance with a revolutionary doctrine. For the first time in history this doctrine has consciously erected an atheistic materialism into a political and legal principle that furnishes the substance of the state and determines its procedures. Soviet doctrine is exclusive and universal in its claim to furnish, not only an account of nature and history, but also a technique of historical change. It is therefore inherently aggressive in its intent; and it considers itself destined to sole survival as an organizing force in the world of politics. The Communist doctrine of the World Revolution has indeed undergone a century of change, since the days of Marx and Engels. Substantially, however, the change has been simply development. The basic inspiration has been steady and the continuity has been organic. As Prof. Alfred G. Meyer has pointed out in his book on Leninism, "Stalinism can and must be defined as a pattern of thought and action that flows directly from Leninism."[1] Prof. Bertram D. Wolfe has documented the same thesis in *Khrushchev and Stalin's Ghost*.[2] This thesis is in possession. And there is no convincing evidence that Mr. Khrushchev represents apostasy or even heresy.

Third, Russia is unique as an imperialism. The Soviet Union is essentially an empire, not a country. Nearly half her subjects should be considered "colonial peoples." Many of the "sister republics" are no more part of Russia than India was of Great Britain. As Mr. Edward Crankshaw has reminded us, "Even if Moscow retreated to the frontiers of the Soviet Union tomorrow, Russia would still be the greatest imperial power in the world."[3] But Mr. Crankshaw's other proposition, that "Russian imperialism is at a dead end," is by no means true. It may indeed be difficult to describe the Soviet imperial design, but this is only because it is difficult to define Soviet imperialism. It is a new historical force, not to be likened to prior mysticisms of power. It is not at all based on the concept of a master-race, or on the aggrandizement of the sacred "nation," or on the fulfillment of a noble idea, such as the rule of law to be brought to the "lesser breeds." The newness of the imperialism has almost masked the fact that it is an imperialism.

It has exhibited a new mastery of older imperialistic techniques—military conquest, the enduring threat of force, political puppetry, centralized administration of minorities, economic exploitation of "colonial" regions. It has expanded the old concept of the "ally" into the new concept of the "satellite." But perhaps its newness is chiefly revealed in the creation of the historically unique imperialistic device known as "Soviet patriotism." This is not a thing of blood and soil but of mind and spirit. It is not born of the past, its deeds and sufferings, borne in common; it looks more to the future, to the deeds yet to be done and to the sufferings still to be borne. It is a "patriotism of a higher order," and of a more universal bearing, than any of the classic feelings for *das Vaterland, la patrie,* my country. It is a loyalty to the Socialist Revolution; it is also a loyalty to the homeland of the Revolution, Russia. Its roots are many—in ideology, in economic facts, and in the love of power; in a whole cluster of human resentments and idealisms; and in the endless capacities of the human spirit for ignorance, illusion, and self-deception. This higher patriotism claims priority over all mere national loyalties. It assures to the Soviet Union a form of imperialistic penetration into other states, namely, the Fifth Column, that no government in history has hitherto commanded. Soviet imperialism, unlike former imperialisms, can be content with the creation of chaos and disorder; within any given segment of time it need not seek to impose a dominion, an order. The Soviet Union may indeed lack a finished imperial design; in any case, the concept of design is too rational for a force that owes little to reason. But it has something better for its purposes, which are inherently dark. It has a revolutionary vision.

If there must be a single phrase to sum up the intentions of Soviet imperialism, it would be far better to speak of "world revolution" than of "world domination." The word "revolution" has a definite meaning that signifies a definite possibility. The world as we know it can be radically changed; it is, in fact, changing daily before our eyes. Moreover, it is possible to know the directions of change that are implicit in the Communist world revolution, as it is guided by Communist doctrine. On the other hand, "world domination" defines not a process but a term. The term may be a Communist dream. It may even be admitted that this term is a historical possibility, if one admits that anything is possible in history. However, what we are called upon to cope with is an actuality, a process that is really going on, an intention that is presently operative—the imperialism of the World Revolution.

Finally, the Soviet Union is unique as the legatee of a longer history. It is the inheritor both of Tsarist imperialism and of mystical panslavist messianism. It carries on, at the same time that it fundamentally transforms, the myth of Holy Russia, the "spiritual people," the "godbearing children of the East," whose messianic destiny is to rescue humanity from the "Promethean West." Communism, whether in theory or in practice, is not a legacy of Western history, nor is it a "Christian heresy" (the pernicious fallacy popularized by Prof. Toynbee). Essentially, it came out of the East, as a conscious apostasy from the West. It may indeed be said that Jacobinism was its forerunner; but Jacobinism was itself an apostasy from the liberal tradition of the West, as well as from Christianity, by its cardinal tenet (roundly condemned by Pope Leo XIII) that there are no bounds to the juridical omnipotence of government, since the power of the state is not under the law, much less under God. In any case, Communism has assumed the task at which Jacobinism failed— that of putting an end to the history of the West. Communism has undertaken to inaugurate a new history, the so-called Third Epoch, that will abolish and supplant what are called the two Western epochs, feudalism and capitalism.

The Primacy of Communist Dogma

My proposition is that each of these four unique aspects of the Soviet Empire has consequences for American policy. No structure of policy will be intelligent or successful that does not reckon with all of them. Indeed, all our past mistakes of policy have resulted from the American disposition to ignore, or to misunderstand, one or the other of these four unique aspects of Russia.

It would be a lengthy task, although not a difficult one, to demonstrate this proposition with a fair measure of certitude. However, I shall make only two major points.

First, if the Soviet Union be regarded simply in the first of its unique aspects, as a state or power, under precision from its other aspects, there need be no serious conflict between it and the United States. By itself, the fact that a single government rules the Euro-Asiatic plain and possesses the technical competence to exploit its natural and human resources poses no serious threat to American interests. There is no reason why the Soviet Union, regarded simply as a state or power-complex, could not live in decently cooperative harmony with the other world-power, the United States. The American locus of power lies in another hemisphere. Our geopolitical position is secure; so too is theirs. Conflicts of interests and clashes of power would arise, but they could be composed peacefully. This point needs making in order to disallow the conception that the American-Soviet confrontation is purely a power-struggle between two colossi of power, whose sheer power is reciprocally a threat, one to the other. To see the problem thus, and to base American policy on anxious conjectures as to which power is "ahead" or "behind" in the accumulation of power, is to mistake the problem completely.

Second, the many-sided conflict known, not inappropriately, as the cold war is unintelligible (and therefore must seem unreal) except in the light of the second unique aspect of the Soviet state. It is an *imperium*, a mode of rule, guided in its internal and external policy by a comprehensive systematic doctrine that contradicts at every important point the tradition of the West. Soviet theory and practice stand in organic interdependence. Only Soviet doctrine makes Soviet power a threat to the United States. Only Soviet doctrine explains the peculiar nature of Soviet imperialism and shows it to be unappeasable in its dynamism. Only

Soviet doctrine illumines the intentions of the new messianism that has come out of the East, fitted with an armature of power, and organized implacably against the West.

Here, of course, in the concept of an empire controlled by a dogma, is the sticking-point for the pragmatic American mind. Two questions arise. First, is this concept of the Soviet Empire true? Second, if it is, can the pragmatic mind take in its truth and be guided accordingly in the fashioning of policy? For my part, the answer to the first question is unhesitatingly yes. I am less sure about the answer to the second question. The American mind is consciously pragmatist. When questions can no longer be postponed, they are approached with an empirical, experimentalist attitude that focuses on contingencies of fact. The search is for compromise, for the "deal" that will be acceptable to both parties in the dispute. The notion of action being controlled by theory is alien to this mentality. The further notion of a great state submitting its purposes and action to the control of a dogmatic philosophy seems absurd. The pragmatist mind instinctively refuses to take in this notion or to study its implications.

When, therefore, this pragmatist mind reads Stalin's statement about Soviet doctrine, that "there can be no doubt that as long as we are faithful to this doctrine, as long as we possess this compass, we shall be successful in our work," it can only conclude that Stalin must have been somehow "insincere." There is the further consideration that Soviet doctrine is couched in a technical jargon that is not only alien but very boring. The practical man puts it all aside. His distrust of ideas has itself become an idea. What he wants is "the facts." And he rapidly overlooks the essential fact that the purposes and actions of the Soviet Empire are unintelligible without reference to the ideas on which its leaders act.

In his book, *The Illusion of the Epoch: Marxism-Leninism as a Philosophical Creed*,[4] Prof. H. B. Acton makes this concluding statement: "Marxism is a philosophical farrago." Other scholars, within the Academy and within the Church, after even more extensive studies have likewise stigmatized the Soviet dogma as scientific, historical, philosophical, and theological nonsense. But what matters for the statesman is not that the dogma is nonsense but that the Soviet leaders act on the dogma, nonsense though it be. The evidence for this fact may not be unambiguously demonstrable; no historical evidence ever is. But it amply suffices for a firm case that may be made the premise of sound policy. This is not the place to present all of the evidence. The record runs back to Lenin's sign-ing of the Peace of Brest-Litovsk. But the segment of history immediately succeeding World War II deserves a brief mention.

In 1945, despite her war losses, Russia was on the crest of the wave. She had territorial defense in sufficient depth on all fronts. Fellow-traveling governments controlled the new states, including the crucial salient, Czechoslovakia. In the United States, Britain, and France a mood of gen-eral, if not unbroken, goodwill towards Russia prevailed to a degree that was almost pathological. Germany, the old enemy of Czarist regimes, was in ruins, impotent, under a military government imposed by the Allies. The Western nations were disarming at breakneck speed. If Russia's own security were the goal, it had been achieved. If the goal were the fulfill-ment of an old-fashioned Czarist imperial design, looking to the consoli-dation of power, it too was substantially complete. Or, if the goal was sim-ply the extension of the new imperialism through international enlistments under the device of the "higher patriotism," looking to what Crankshaw calls the "inconsequent mischief-making of the Comintern," the way to it lay open, and eager wishful thinkers in all lands were busily engaged in enlarging the possibilities of mischief, under hardly any oppo-sition or even serious suspicion.

In any case, one would have expected subtle tactics of restraint. In-stead the "tough line" suddenly appeared—ruthless pressure for direct control of the satellites, intervention in Greece (and Persia), obstructive opposition to the Marshall Plan and the Austrian Treaty, the Berlin blockade, and the creation of the Cominform. In consequence, within three years the Kremlin had dissipated its major asset of international goodwill. It created for itself a peril that had not previously existed. A di-vided and disarmed West had begun to unite and arm itself against the menace now visible, though not yet understood.

Why did all this happen? The only satisfactory answer is that the Kremlin was guided by Communist doctrine. The capitalist powers were well disposed? They could not be; the doctrine holds that the capitalist "camp" is irreconcilably hostile. Constitutional socialist governments would protect the socialist homeland against capitalist aggression? No; the doctrine holds that Social Democracy is inherently untrustworthy and ought to be destroyed, because it only deceives the worker and con-fuses the issue by its pretension to be a Third Force. World peace is the common goal, through negotiations within the framework of the United Nations? Nonsense; the doctrine holds that the conflict between the two homeland "camps" and the two colonial "fronts" is unappeasable. It is the necessary means to the World Revolution. It will be resolved only by the World Revolution. And in its resolution the methods of force cannot be dispensed with. Finally, the doctrine held that at the end of the War the capitalist "camp" simply had to be in a state of "weakness"; its "internal contradictions" were actively at work, presaging its downfall. By the doctrine, therefore, it was the moment for the strategy of the Revolution, the strategy of forceful aggression.

All this may sound rather silly to the pragmatist. In a sense it all was rather silly. The point is that it all happened. And it only happened because Soviet doctrine decreed its happening.

Moreover, it will not do to say that this dictation of policy and events by doctrine will not happen again; that Stalin is dead; that Russia is "different"; that new men are in charge; that they are realists and opportunists, men rather like ourselves who take the pragmatic view. Russia is indeed somewhat different, but only within the limits of the doctrine. The men in charge are new, but only within the limits imposed by their thorough conditioning by the doctrine. The Soviet leadership is not subject to changes of heart. What is more important (and to the pragmatist, unintelligible), it does not even learn by experience. The doctrine is forever at hand to discount Soviet experience of how the capitalist world acts.

The doctrine casts up an image of the capitalist world that does not derive from experience and is not to be altered by experience. It is a "scientific" image, the product of a science, dialectical materialism, whose basic postulate is that determinism rules the world of human history as well as the world of nature. It is through the distorting one-way glass, as it were, of this deterministic theory of capitalism that the Soviet leaders view what we consider to be the contingencies of the historical world—only they are not seen as contingencies but as determined. So far from altering the scientific image, they are interpreted in such a way as either to confirm it or at least leave it intact. When, for instance, the capitalist world professes its desire to be friendly, just, peaceful, cooperative, etc., such professions cannot but be bogus. Historical determinism will not permit the capitalist world to be other than hostile, unjust, aggressive, and war-mongering. Mr. George F. Kennan has commented, in rather baffled, but still superior, fashion, on "the systematic Soviet distortion of the realities of our world and of the purposes to which we are dedicated" (in *Russia, the Atom and the West*[5]). Mr. Kennan too views reality through his special glass. Apparently it does not occur to him that Soviet analysts of "fact" really believe in the categories of Marxist-Leninist ideology as instruments of interpretation. Like a good American, he believes that if only the Soviet leaders could be brought to see "the facts," with complete "freedom of mind," all would be well.

It is, of course, not impossible that some basic change may take place in Soviet doctrine. But if it did the repercussions would be felt all through the edifice of power erected on the doctrine; and if they were not checked, the edifice could not long survive. The basic Soviet structure is an indivisible and interlocking whole. It cannot permit itself to be tampered with at any point, save on peril of destruction. Still less can it contemplate changes in the dogmas that sustain the edifice of imperialistic power.

The official atheism is necessary in order that the individual may claim no moral rights against the state and no freedom except within the "collective" freedom of the state. This exploitation of the individual in the service of the state is necessary as the premise of forcing further the gigantic technological development. The cult of Soviet patriotism is necessary to preserve the solidarity of the colonial empire over the more than thirty-five national minorities within the Soviet Union, and over the ring of satellite states, as well as to retain that indispensable adjunct of Soviet imperialism, the motley Fifth Column. The maintenance of the police state makes it necessary that there should be "danger from without," from irreconcilable, hostile, aggressive capitalist imperialism. This danger is also necessary to explain to the puzzled inquirer why the state is not withering away. The rejection of the possibility of entirely peaceful evolution to world socialism and the belief in force as the indispensable agent of the Revolution are necessary to sustain the burden of militarization and armament. And the whole edifice rests squarely in the basic Marxist dogma— the conflict of two opposed worlds leading dialectically and deterministically to the World Revolution. Finally, the personal security of the Soviet rulers and the continuing privileges of the "new class" are dependent on the maintenance both of the empire and of the revolutionary doctrine that sustains it. Thus self-interest buttresses belief in the doctrine.

The conclusion is that the Soviet Empire not only has been, and is, an empire controlled by doctrine, but must continue to be such, on peril of ceasing to be itself. Even to speculate about making a basic change in the established doctrine of the World Revolution would be to raise the specter of the disintegration of the empire. This specter, we may be sure, will be forbidden to rise.

Communist Dogma and American Policy

This fourfold view of the unique reality of the Soviet Empire is the only solid premise of American foreign policy in foreign affairs and military defense. It is a more intelligent premise than the concept of "world domination" in any of the current understandings or misunderstandings of that phrase. It is also a more comprehensive premise than any analysis of the relatively superficial "facts of power."

The major value of a full view of the unique character of the Soviet Union is that it creates a limited but useful set of expectations on which to base American policy. We need not be left to the resources of improvisation or even to the instinctive reactions of purely practical wisdom— the kind of wisdom that made us enter the Korean War but was never able to explain why we did enter it. The Soviet Empire is governed by the inner laws of its own nature; like any laws they create expectabilities. We may, for instance, expect Communist leadership to yield only to calculations of power and success; force and the prospect of success by its use are the determinants of Soviet action. This expectation would clarify the problem of negotiations. It would suggest that we put an end, as quietly as possible, to the Wilsonian era of diplomacy with its exaggerated trust in world assemblies and in spectacular international conferences. It would further suggest the advisability of direct negotiations with Russia. For instance, if and when any agreement on disarmament is reached, it will be reached directly between the Kremlin and the White House, without the confusing assistance of additional nations, allied or neutral.

Again, a true view of the Soviet Union, as a unique imperialism, would suggest that we cease to confuse foreign policy with diplomatic negotiations. To paraphrase a famous remark, foreign policy is when you know what you want. It supposes that you know the possibility of getting what you want, before you decide that you want it. Negotiation is simply the means of getting what you want. The Soviet Union understands this. For instance, it is a fixed Soviet foreign policy to gain public international recognition of the successes of the Communist revolution as they are racked up. This policy is pursued through "negotiations" at international conferences. These conferences negotiate nothing. Either they simply register the political and military results to date and thus fulfill Soviet policy (e.g., the 1954 Geneva "settlement" on Korea and Indo-China) or they run out in sheer futility after two million words (e.g., the prior Berlin Conference). It is time we, too, learned not to fix our policy by negotiations but to conduct negotiations in order to fulfill our policies. It is time, too, that we laid aside completely the concept of "sincerity" as a category of political morality even though it is so dear to a type of Eastern-seaboard political mind that believes in nothing else. To inquire into Soviet "sincerity" or to require "sincerity" of the Soviet Union is a complete waste of time.

The chiefly important expectability or "sincerity" is that the Soviet Union will always act on its own doctrine. As the situation dictates, it will employ either the strategy of the Revolution or the tactics of the protection of the homeland and of the Revolution's imperialist advances. In either case, since the doctrine is inherently aggressive, it permits no "disengagement." It continually probes for every vacuum of power and for every soft spot of purpose. This is why "disengagement" as an American policy could not be other than disastrous. It would surely heighten the danger of war, most probably by permitting the creation of situations that we could not possibly accept. Only the very opposite policy is safe—a policy of continuous engagement at every point, on all levels of action, by both tactical and strategic moves. At times this policy of continuous engagement might well be enforced simply by variants of the highly effective argumentative technique of the blank and silent stare. The Russians employed it well in the tent at Panmunjom. Turkey has always used it successfully; and West Berlin has learned its value. We still talk too much.

A policy of continuous engagement with the World Revolution does not mean solely a policy of hostility, contradiction, and opposition. Nor is it to be translated primarily into military terms. The engagement can be cooperative, positive, constructive in a number of ways. Here I shall mention only one, because it is so neglected.

Perhaps the most alarming pages in Wolfgang Leonhard's book, *Child of the Revolution*,[6] are those in which he reports the effect had on him by

Western newspapers, broadcasts, etc. The effect was nil. In fact, practically everything he heard or read about the West only delayed his break with Stalinism. On the intellectual or doctrinal level the disengagement between West and East seems to be almost complete. Torrents of words are poured out Eastward, of course. But they do not even engage the attention of the East. "Why do they always go on about freedom?" asked one of Leonhard's companions, as he got up, bored to death, to turn off a Western broadcast. "In the first place there is no freedom in the West, and in the second place people in the West do not even know what freedom is."

The young Communist's disgusted comment makes the necessary point. Do people of the West understand what freedom is? Can they intelligently dispute the Communist thesis, that freedom means insight into historical necessity—an insight that is based on scientific theory? (One recalls General Eisenhower and Marshal Zhukov baffling one another in Berlin over the notion of freedom.) Or is it rather the American disposition to dismiss the whole dispute as "impractical," and irrelevant to politics? Or do we think that this basic issue of theory would be settled by distributing (as has been seriously suggested) an avalanche of Sears-Roebuck catalogues in the Soviet Union?

It may be that the Illusion of our Epoch will not be overcome by argument. Certainly it cannot be overcome by force. Perhaps it will succumb only to the enemy of all illusions—time. The fact remains that Communist doctrine is an affront to the Western tradition of reason; and the manner of empire that it sustains is a further affront to the liberal tradition of politics and law that was born of the Western tradition of reason. The further fact is that the West was so late in feeling the affront and still seems largely impotent to deliver against it an effective doctrinal answer, in a moment when a doctrinal answer is of the highest practical importance, not only to the East that will hear it, but to the West that will utter it—immediately, to itself. It may, of course, be that the West has ceased to understand itself. Prof. Toynbee may, in fact, be right in saying that the West now identifies itself with technology, as its cult and its sole export. If this be true, this failure of understanding, leading to a denial, more or less explicit, of the Western tradition by the West itself, would be the fateful "internal contradiction" that might lead to downfall. Ironically, Marx never saw this form of "internal contradiction," though it is the greatest weakness in the "camp" that he opposed.

The Domestic Issue

This may be the place to comment on the basic fiasco of our engagement with Communism on the domestic scene. The subject is a bit complicated. It is, of course, not necessary to invoke Communist influence to explain the various stupidities of American wartime and postwar policies. Stupidity itself is sufficient explanation. The pattern of it was set by the American President who was "certain," he said in all good faith, "that Stalin is not an imperialist." The anti-Communist movement, centering on the issue of internal subversion, probably compounded the confusion by transforming issues of stupidity into issues of "disloyalty." The muzzy sentimentalism of the 1945 climate has indeed been altered. Reckon this, if you like, to the credit of those who raised the cry of subversion. Public opinion, in the sense of public passion (which it very largely is), has been transformed. Everybody now mortally hates and fears what is known, rather vaguely, as "the Communist menace." It was "brought home" to them amid great tumult and shouting (only in this way, it seems, can things be brought home to the American people). This was a good thing. At that, by a strange irony, those who were the loudest in bringing the menace home were or are the last ones on American earth whom one would want to see in charge of combating the menace abroad, in the field of foreign policy, where the massive menace lies. By a contrasting irony, many of those who took the sound view in matters of foreign policy were fuzzy on the issue of internal subversion.

In any case, whatever its effect on public emotion, the anti-Communist movement has been fairly spectacular in its failure to contribute to public understanding. The problem of understanding centers on three large issues. What *is* this "thing from the East"? What *is* the "Western thing" in the name of which we oppose it? What were the corrosive forces that were able to create a yawning spiritual and intellectual vacuum within the West, but were not able to fill it, with the result that the "thing from the East" found some lodgment there? Thousands of questions and answers before Congressional committees and bushels of propaganda sheets from patriotic societies have contributed almost nothing to an answer to these questions. In their turn, the forces that opposed the anti-Communist movement have rivaled it in their failure to contribute to public understanding. In considerable part they failed even to speak of the real issues, being content to retire, embattled, behind a rather porous barricade—a concept of democracy as an ensemble of procedures, a legal system of civil rights. It was not strange that in the end the public, with some instinctive feeling that the quarrel wasn't getting anywhere, and had become trivial anyway, should have grown bored with it. Imposed on a prior fiasco of understanding, this was a most lamentable result. The three basic questions still stand.

Even yet the response to Communist imperialism is largely in emotional terms—fear and hatred (or, conversely, pathetic appeals to "understand the Russians") and bursts of brief excitement over every new Communist success, and, for the rest, a last-minute rush to the resources of pragmatism in all its forms (notably including military technology) to meet particular issues as they arise.

The Uses of Force

This brings up the question that looms so large—the question of armaments and war. The underlying issue is whether a full view of the unique reality of the Soviet empire furnishes any reliable expectations in this critical area. There are several.

Soviet doctrine as a whole dictates a policy of maximum security and minimum risk. Risks can and must be minimum because the dialectic of history decrees that the capitalist world, though still powerful, is decaying and must inevitably disintegrate from within, whereas the forces of socialism are in constant ascendancy and must inevitably triumph. Security must be maximal because at every point the gains made by political or military means must be consolidated as the base for further revolutionary advance. The Soviet Union cannot be provoked into taking risks that exceed the minimum; for it does not act under external provocation but under an internal dynamism. These conclusions, already implicit in the doctrine, are confirmed by all the evidence in the historical record.

We may expect that Soviet doctrine will continue to dictate the same policy of maximal security and minimal risk. This expectation furnishes a measure by which to decide the gravest and most pervasive problem of foreign and military policy, namely, how to balance the elements of security and of risk. We may safely invert the Soviet proportions. Our policy should envisage a minimum of security and a maximum of risk. Only by such a policy can we seize and retain the initiative in world affairs. And it is highly dangerous not to have the initiative. On the premise of this balance we did, in fact, enter the Korean war, which was right. But then we retreated from the premise to a policy of minimal risk, which was a mistake.

Moreover, it would be prudent even to create situations of risk for the Soviet Union—situations in which the risk would be too great for it to take. We may be sure that the Soviet leadership will not risk the debacle of the World Revolution through a major war for the sake of anything less than the soil of the homeland of the Revolution. We may expect that it will yield tactical ground, or refrain from going after tactical ground, if the risk of holding it or going after it becomes serious. But if there is no risk, or only a minimal risk, aggressive policies will be carried through, as they were in Hungary, where nothing was done to create a risk.

At the same time, Soviet doctrine serves to warn us to be wary of the facile persuasion now being spread about that "Russia doesn't want war." There is no reason to believe that Communism has been converted to the faith of Social Democracy, which holds that the evolution to world socialism can be wholly peaceful. Any notion that the Soviet Union has tacitly entered some sort of Kellogg Pact is absurd. The use of force, as an instrument of national policy, is still an essential tenet in the Communist creed. By the whole force of Communist "insight into historical necessity" Russia still wants war—the kind of war, in the time and place, that would be necessary or useful to further the multiple ends of the World Revolution, not least perhaps by extending the colonial "liberation front."

Moreover, this same insight convinces the Soviet leadership that the capitalist world wants war. War, like imperialism and aggression in general, is inherent in capitalism. This is a matter of scientific doctrine; the Communist understands it to be so, and he cannot be persuaded otherwise. To admit that the capitalist world does not want war would be to go against the doctrine. It would also be to cancel the "danger from without" that helps to justify the police state and to explain why it cannot yet wither away. In the face of the standing Soviet conviction about the warmongering capitalist world, it would be doubly absurd to believe that the Soviet Union does not want war.

It is all a matter of the measure of risk that war would entail and of the measure of its usefulness for the World Revolution.

Precisely here, however, the present Communist insight into historical necessity—in the case, the necessity of the use of force to further the Revolution—must be less naive than once it was. It was Lenin's emphatic doctrine that "frightful collisions" must take place between East and West before capitalism is overthrown and socialism installed. Lenin was thinking not only of major wars but of other revolutionary violences. But he did believe in the inevitability of major wars. Stalin too believed that war was inevitable and that it would inevitably advance the fortunes of the Revolution. But this simple faith can no longer stand. One cannot doubt that the Leninist-Stalinist doctrine has been subjected to revision in Communist high councils in the light of the realities of nuclear war. What usefulness would attach to this manner of "frightful collision"? What risks of it should be run?

The results of this revision of doctrine may have been hinted at by Khrushchev at the 20th Party Congress in 1956. He did not refer to the new instrument of frightfulness, the H-bomb. His utterance was cautious. The Communist will not renounce his essential weapon, the threat of force. Nor will he renounce force itself. But he will carefully calculate its uses and its usefulness for his own purposes and on his own premise of policy—maximum security and minimal risk. This manner of calculation is his specialty. Moreover, he will make the conclusions of this calculation serve as the premise of his armament policies. His industry and technology are, after all, largely geared to war—not to war in general but to war as a possibly useful instrument of the World Revolution. To the Communist war is not a game, or a galvanic reaction, or an exercise in righteous anger, or a romantic adventure, or a way to develop the national character, or a sin. It is strictly and coldly a means to an end. And the end is clearly defined.

What conclusions has the Communist come to, what policies has he consequently defined for himself (he always defines his own policies, in what concerns both ends and means), in this historical moment so different from Lenin's—in this our nuclear age? The answer to this question would presumably be an important premise of American policies with regard to war and the weapons of war. Some answers should be clear.

First, all-out nuclear war is not a means of furthering the World Revolution; its only outcome would be the end of the Revolution, in the end

of the world; the risk of it therefore must be avoided in the conduct of political affairs. Second, an all-out surprise attack on the capitalist world,
with nuclear weapons, would run a maximum risk of the retaliatory destruction of the Homeland and of the Revolution itself; it is therefore excluded as a strategy of conquest. Third, on the other hand, the capitalist
world is intrinsically imperialistic, aggressive, and bent on military conquest, as its hostile "encirclement" of the Soviet Union shows. It is ready
for all-out nuclear war; and, despite its professions, it might launch a surprise attack. Therefore the Soviet Union must be ready for both contingencies. Maximum security requires maximum armament, conventional
and nuclear. Fourth, military force is still a factor in political affairs,
through its use, and especially through the sheer threat of its use. The
doctrine of the Revolution—the doctrine of "collisions"—still holds. It
will come into play whenever the risks are sufficiently minimal, and the
chances of success sufficiently solid. These conditions will be more readily verified when the use of force, including nuclear force, is on a small
scale for settling (or aggravating) local disturbances. Therefore small-
scale nuclear force must be available in quantity, together with conventional arms. But if the risk appears that the tactical action will be enlarged to the dimensions of strategic action, through the employment of
strategic nuclear weapons, it must be broken off, lest the Homeland of the
Revolution itself be endangered.

In sum, major nuclear "collisions" with the capitalist world are not inevitable; on the contrary, they must be avoided, since they cannot advance
the Communist cause. World socialism can and must be achieved without
major war, by peaceful means—political, diplomatic, economic, propagan-
distic (this, in effect, is what Khrushchev said in 1956). Adventurism is to
be rejected, since it violates the policy of minimal risk. On the other hand,
the threat of force is still a valid revolutionary weapon; so too is the use of
force itself in determined circumstances. Finally, the Homeland is in "danger from without." Therefore the armament program must be pushed
through the whole spectrum of nuclear weapons—large weapons as a deterrent for maximum security; small weapons for use with a minimum of risk.

If this diagnosis of Communist thinking is generally correct, it suggests
several conclusions with regard to American thought.

First, the danger of an all-out sneak nuclear attack on the United
States has been vastly exaggerated. We have maximal security against it

in the Soviet policy of minimal risk as long as the massive deterrent is sustained. Second, the correlative danger of an all-out nuclear war has likewise been vastly exaggerated. Many tend to make maximal a risk that is only minimal. It could only happen as the result of enormous stupidity, basically attributable to a complete misunderstanding of Soviet doctrine. This stupidity is no more inevitable than war itself. Third, the danger of limited wars has been underestimated. This maximal risk has been made minimal. It seems to be the historical American delusion that no war is worth while unless it is unlimited, waged for "ultimate" causes. There is also the special delusion proper to the nuclear age, that any use of nuclear weapons, however low in the kiloton range, must inevitably lead to world catastrophe. Hence the false dilemma: either to begin with catastrophe or to renounce all use of nuclear force.

Fourth, more generally, the whole concept of the cold war has been overmilitarized and therefore superficialized. This overmilitarization, combined with the exaggerations noted above, has affected national policy adversely in many respects. Moreover, it has tended to obscure or even discredit the validity of the very concept of the cold war. This too is lamentable, because the concept is fully valid, if it is interpreted in the light of the full reality of the Soviet empire in its fourfold uniqueness. Unfortunately, it has become too easy to say that, since the Communist threat is not primarily military (which is true), it is no threat at all and we should make disengagement our policy (which is completely false). Unfortunately too, it has become too easy to say that, since the United States is sufficiently safe from foreign military aggression (which is true), the real threat is internal Communist subversion (which is false).

Finally, all the confusions in American thinking come to a focus in the opinion that the issue of American "survival" is squarely put to the Department of Defense, supported by the Atomic Energy Commission. This opinion is entirely disastrous. We may be quite sure that the Communist mind, with its realistic and strategic habits of thought, has carefully separated the problem of the "survival" of the Communist Revolution from the problem of war. The Communist leadership has no slightest intention of making "survival" the issue to be settled by force of arms. In fact, it is prepared to abandon resort to arms, as soon as the issue of "survival" is raised. Survival is the one thing it is not willing to risk. In contrast, America is not prepared to resort to arms until the issue of "survival" is raised. Survival is the only thing it is willing to risk. Not the least irony in the current situation is the fact that the West has surrendered to the East its own traditional doctrine, that "survival" is not, and should never be allowed to become, the issue at stake in war.

The major problem put to American policy at the moment is the problem that the Soviet Union has already solved in terms of policy, namely, how to be prepared to use force on all necessary or useful occasions, and at the same time to withdraw "survival" from the issues at stake in the use of force. "The children of this world are shrewder than the children of light in their dealings with their own kind" (Luke 16:9). The children of this world understand better the uses, and the uselessnesses, of this world's darkest thing, force. They are shrewd enough to know that the institutions of this world can be advanced by force, but that their survival should not be put to the test of force.

The irony in the Gospel saying seems to be magnificently fulfilled in the American nuclear armament program. It seems to have been conceived to insure "survival" but not to fight a legitimate war for limited and justifiable ends. Perhaps one should not blame the Department of Defense or the Atomic Energy Commission. They could not get their budgets through the Congress unless they "proved" that "survival" is the issue at stake. And the Congress could not levy taxes on the people unless it "proved" that the "survival" of the people is at stake. But this is moral absurdity, not least because it is military absurdity. We have got the problem of "survival" and the problem of war so mixed up that we may finally be incapable of solving either.

Nor will it do to say that we have been forced into this position by the Communist menace. It would be almost impossible to set limits to the danger of Communism as a spiritual menace. It has induced not simply a crisis in history but perhaps the crisis of history. Its dream of the Third Epoch that will cancel Western and Christian history and the major institutions of that history (notably the rule of law and the spiritual supremacy of the Church) has gone too far toward realization over too wide a sweep of earth to be lightly dismissed as a mere dream. On the other hand, as a sheerly military menace Communism is strictly limited. It is limited in the first instance by its own doctrine. This doctrine has always assigned to military force a real role in the advancement of the World Revolution. Nevertheless, the role of force has always been ancillary, subordinate, supportive of political, economic, and ideological initiatives. Force is to be employed only when the historical moment is right and the military or political risk is minimal. Moreover, there is every reason to believe that in the nuclear age, in which all risks are enhanced most horribly, Communist doctrine has set a still more diminished value on the use of force. By a sort of perverse genius, proper to the children of darkness, it has at the same time set a higher value on the sheer threat of force.

The Soviet Union as a power-imperialism must be confronted by power, steadily and at every point. But when the question is military engagement it is quite false to say that the issue is "survival." And American persistence in thinking this could easily reduce American power to impotence. The real issue is to know how and why "survival" got to be thought of as the military issue, and then to withdraw it from the limited political and moral issues at stake in our military engagement with the Soviet Union. It is impossible to think of any other way in which our nuclear armament program can be reduced to rationality—to some sensible conformity to the canons of moral reason (which look to justice in war), and to a hardly less desirable conformity to the rules of military reason (which look to success in war).

The clue to the distortions in the present structure of American policy is deposited in a remark made by the Military Operations Subcommittee in its nineteenth report, submitted on February 20, 1958. It said: "Under present methods of operation we do not know what we are trying to accomplish through military aid." Military aid programs, it added, "are not clearly related to a strategy of defense. . . . Logistical plans have not been revised to keep step with strategic concepts and strategic concepts lag behind war technology." The general sense of this judgment, made directly with regard to military aid programs, holds with greater force of our nuclear armament program and its newer adjuncts, rockets and missiles.

The general uneasiness among the public—here at home and abroad—derives from an instinctive sense that America does not know what it is trying to do. And the uneasiness is sharpened by the general knowledge of what we are in fact doing, and have in fact been doing since the Manhattan Project. We are engaged in the exploitation of technological possibilities simply because they are possibilities, in the absence of any clearly defined strategic purposes that would be consonant with the institution of war as a valid instrument for altering the political will of an enemy—in the case, the Communist enemy, whose political will, and whose doctrine on the limited use of force in support of his will, are by no means mysterious or unknowable. The general public senses that this situation is irrational and therefore immoral. And it focuses its deeper fear and its more diffused disapproval on the relatively minor question of nuclear tests.

It is doubtless true that military concepts have always lagged behind weapons technology. The lag was tolerable when the technology was limited. This is not so today. The resources of military technology are unlimited, and there is no principle in technology itself to call a halt to their exploitation. Weapons technology has already gone so far that it has raised the issue of "survival" and thrust it into the problem of war, in defiance of every military rule and moral principle, and in defiance too of every sound calculation with regard to the enemy's will to power as supported by a will to war. It is bad enough when policy and armaments run in opposite directions; as Theodore Roosevelt said, we cannot be a nation "opulent, aggressive, and unarmed." But it is worse when policy runs after armaments, and armaments run after technology, and the pressures of budgetary considerations buttress the primacy of the technology of multimegaton weapons, because they are cheaper. An armaments race that may end in war is bad enough, since there is always an element of irrationality in war, even when it is a just war. But an armaments race that seems already to have ended in absurdity is vastly worse, because what is militarily absurd is irredeemably immoral.

It may well be that the pragmatist American mind will not hearken to discourse on the morality of war, especially since it bears beneath its pragmatism the American-Protestant taint of pacifism. However, it might listen to discourse on success in war—concretely, on the kind of success that is politically valuable in the kind of war that is possible or likely, in present circumstances, against a particular enemy, who has a fully constructed "compass" (as Stalin called it) whereby to set his intentions and to direct his action in history, and who, finally, has an articulated doctrine with regard to the limited uses of military force in support of his political will. The moralist, of course, will not object to such discourse on success in war. It forms, in fact, an essential part of his own moral discourse, as the following chapter will show.

Notes

1. *Leninism*. Cambridge: Harvard University Press, 1957.
2. New York: Praeger, 1956.
3. *Russia Without Stalin: The Emerging Pattern*. New York: Viking, 1956.
4. Boston: Beacon Press, 1957.
5. New York: Harper and Brothers, 1958.
6. Chicago: Regnery, 1958.

~

CHAPTER ELEVEN

The Uses of a Doctrine on the Uses of Force: War as a Moral Problem

There are three distinct standpoints from which it is possible to launch a discussion of the problem of war in this strange and perilous age of ours that has yet to find its name. My initial assertion will be that it is a mistake to adopt any one of them exclusively and to carry the argument on to its logical conclusions. If this is done, the argument will end in serious difficulties.

First, one might begin by considering the possibilities of destruction and ruin, both physical and human, that are afforded by existent and projected developments in weapons technology. Here the essential fact is that there are no inherent limits to the measure of chaos that war might entail, whether by the use of nuclear arms or possibly by the methods of bacteriological and chemical warfare. Carried to its logical conclusion an argument made exclusively from this standpoint leads towards the position that war has now become a moral absurdity, not to be justified in any circumstances today. In its most respectable form this position may be called relative Christian pacifism. It does not assert that war is intrinsically evil simply because it is a use of force and violence and therefore a contravention of the Christian law of love promulgated in the Sermon on the Mount. This is absolute pacifism, an unqualified embrace of the principle of non-violence; it is more characteristic of certain Protestant sects. The relative pacifists are content to affirm that war has now become an evil that may no longer be justified, given the fact that no adequate justification can be offered for the ruinous effects of today's weapons of war. Even this position, I shall say, is not to be squared with the public doctrine of the Church.

Second, one might begin the argument by considering the present historical situation of humanity as dominated by the fact of Communism. The essential fact here is that Communism, as an ideology and as a power-system, constitutes the gravest possible menace to the moral and civilizational values that form the basis of "the West," understanding the term to designate, not a geographical entity but an order of temporal life that has been the product of valid human dynamisms tempered by the spirit of the Gospel. Arguing from this standpoint alone one could well posit, in all logic, the present validity of the concept of the "holy war." Or one might come to some advocacy of "preventive" war or "pre-emptive" war. Or one might be led to assert that, since the adversary is completely unprincipled, and since our duty in face of him is success in the service of civilization itself, we must jettison the tradition of civilized warfare and be prepared to use any means that promise success. None of these conclusions is morally acceptable.

Third, one might choose as a starting point the fact that today there exists a mode of international organization that is committed by its charter to the preservation of peace by pacific settlement of international disputes. One might then argue that the validity of war even as a legal institution has now vanished, with the passing of the hypothesis under which its legal validity was once defended, namely, the absence of a juridically organized international community. But this conclusion seems, at very best, too rapid, for several reasons. The United Nations is not, properly speaking, a juridical organization with adequate legal authority to govern in the international community. It is basically a power-organization. And its decisions, like those rendered by war itself, are natively apt to sanction injustice as well as justice. It is not at all clear that the existence of the United Nations, as presently constituted, definitely destroys the hypothesis on which the validity of war as a legal institution has traditionally been predicated. It is not at all clear that the United Nations in its present stage of development will be able to cope justly and effectively with the underlying causes of international conflict today or with the particular cases of conflict that may arise.

The Basic Questions

If therefore one adopts a single standpoint of argument, and adheres to it narrowly and exclusively, one will not find one's way to an integral and morally defensible position on the problem of war. On the other hand, all of the three standpoints mentioned do derive from real aspects of the problem itself. In consequence, each of them must be exploited, if the problem is to be understood in its full scope. This is my second assertion. It is not possible here to develop it in detail. I shall merely suggest that there are three basic questions that must be explored at length and in detail. Moreover, there is an order among these questions.

The first question, with which the foregoing chapter briefly dealt, concerns the exact nature of the conflict that is the very definition of international life today. This is the first question because it sets the perspectives in which all other questions must be considered.

I would note here that Pius XII fairly steadily considered the problem of war and of the weapons of war, as well as the problem of international organization, within the perspectives of what he called "the line of rupture which divides the entire international community into opposed blocs," with the result that "coexistence in truth" is not possible, since there is no common acceptance of a "norm recognized by all as morally obligatory and therefore inviolable."

I would further note that the exact nature of the international conflict is not easily and simply defined. The line of rupture is not in the first instance geographic but spiritual and moral; and it runs through the West as well as between East and West. It cannot be a question of locating on "our" side of the rupture those who are virtuous and intelligent, and, over against "us," those who are evil and morally blind. In contrast, it cannot be a question of maintaining that both East and West are so full of moral ambiguities that the line of rupture between them either does not exist or is impossible to discern. In a word, one must avoid moral simplism and moral skepticism and a flight to moral "ambiguism" (with which the next chapter will deal) in the analysis of the international conflict.

Finally, it is most important to distinguish between the mainsprings of the conflict and its concrete manifestations; or, with Sir David Kelly (in *The Hungry Sheep*[1]), between the relatively superficial facts of change in our revolutionary world and the underlying currents of change. Moreover, it is important to relate the two levels of analysis, in so far as this can be done without artificiality.

The tendency of this whole line of analysis, bearing on the nature of the international conflict, will be to furnish an answer to a complex of questions that must be answered before it is possible to consider the more narrow problem of war. What precisely are the values, in what hierarchical scale, that today are at stake in the international conflict? What is the degree of danger in which they stand? What is the mode of the menace itself—in particular, to what extent is it military, and to what extent is it posed by forms of force that are more subtle? If these questions are not carefully answered, one will have no standard against which to match the evils of war. And terror, rather than reason, will command one's judgments on the military problem. This is the danger to which several moral theologians in Germany pointed in their statement of May 5, 1958:

> A part of the confusion among our people has its source in the fact that there is an insufficient realization of the reach of values that are endangered today, and of the hierarchical order among them, and of the degree of danger in which they stand. On the other hand, from the *Unheimlichkeit* of the technical problems [of war itself] there results a crippling of intelligence and of will.[2]

The second basic question concerns the means that are available for insuring the defense of the values that are at stake in the international conflict. This too is a large and complex question. A whole array of means is available, in correspondence with the multi-faceted character of the conflict itself. It is a matter of understanding both the usefulness and the limitations of each of them, from spectacular "summit meetings" across the gamut to the wholly unspectacular work, say, of agricultural experts engaged in increasing the food supply of underdeveloped nations. This whole complex question of the means of conflict must be fully explored antecedently to the consideration of the problem of war. The basic reason is that otherwise one can give no concrete meaning to the concept of war as *ultima ratio*. Moreover, the value of the use of force, even as *ultima ratio*, will be either overestimated or underestimated, in proportion as too much or too little value is attached to other means of sustaining and pressing the international conflict.

The third and final question concerns the *ultima ratio* itself, the arbitrament of arms as the last resort.

Here we confront the third novelty in the total problem. The present historical situation of international conflict is unique. "Never," said Pius XII in his Christmas Message of 1950, "has human history known a more gigantic disorder." The uniqueness of the disorder resides, I take it, in the unparalleled depth of its vertical dimension; it goes to the very roots of order and disorder in the world—the nature of man, his destiny, and the meaning of human history. There is a uniqueness too in the second basic question posited above, the unprecedented scope of the conflict in its horizontal dimension, given the variety of means whereby it may be, and is being, waged. A special uniqueness resides too in the existence of the United Nations, as an arena of conflict indeed, but also as an instrument of peacemaking to some degree. However, the most immediately striking uniqueness comes to view when one considers the weapons for warmaking that are now in hand or within grasp.

There are two subordinate questions under this general heading of the nature of war today. The first concerns the actual state of progress (if it be progress and not a regress to barbarism) in the technology of defensive and offensive weapons of war. The second concerns the military usefulness, for intelligible military and political purposes, of the variety of weapons developed. This latter question raises the issue of the strategic and tactical concepts that are to govern the use of these various weapons. The facts that would furnish answers to these questions are to a considerable extent hidden from the public knowledge; and, to the extent to which they are known, they have been generative of confusion in the public mind. In any case, these questions must have some reasonably satisfactory answer, if the moral problem of war is to be sensibly discussed.

Here then are three preliminary lines of inquiry to be pursued before the moral issues involved in warfare today can be dealt with, even in their generality.

The Basic Propositions

An initial, not necessarily complete, exploration of these three lines is sufficient to suggest the outlines of a general moral theory. Whether Catholic thought can be content to stop with a moral theory cast simply in the mode of abstractness that characterizes the following propositions will be a further question. In any case, it is necessary in the first instance to state the general propositions. In stating them I am undertaking to render the substance of the thought of Pius XII; but there will be only a minimum of citation, and even of explanation.

1) All wars of aggression, whether just or unjust, fall under the ban of moral proscription.

I use the term "war of aggression" because Pius XII used it. However, the concept of aggression is undoubtedly a major source of bedevilment in the whole modern discussion of the problem of war. The recent lengthy attempt to reach a satisfactory definition resulted in failure, as Julius Stone has pointed out in *Aggression and World Order*.[3] The concept, I think, is a typically modern one; older theories more characteristically spoke in terms of "injustice." I venture the opinion, merely as an opinion, that the modern prominence of the concept derives from the modern theory that there may be "justice" on both sides of a conflict. Hence the issue of "justice" is proximately decided by "aggression," *scil.*, which nation's armed forces first cross the borders of the other nation. But this military transcription of a basically moral concept is of little, if any, use in our contemporary situation, with its two unique new features. First, today's weapons systems make possible the employment of force at enormous distances without concern for the space between; the concept of "crossing borders" no longer means anything. Second, in view of the striking power of these weapons systems the nation that initiates the attack ("crosses the border") can render the opposing nation defenseless, incapable of exerting a right of self-defense. Consequently, aggression in the older military-moral sense has ceased to be a standard by which to decide the issue of justice in war; it has become simply a technique by which to decide the issue of success. The use of force can no longer be linked to the moral order merely by the concept of aggression, in the modern understanding of the concept. There is, as I have already suggested in a previous chapter, urgent need for a thorough moral re-examination of the basic American policy that "we will never shoot first." Under contemporary circumstances, viewed in their entirety, is this really a *dictamen rationis*?

Pius XII himself gives no real definition of "aggressive" war. It seems to stand simply as the contrary of a war of self-defense, whose definition, as we shall see, is more concrete and historical. Expressly, the Pope denies that recourse to force is "a legitimate solution for international controversies and a means for the realization of national aspirations." He seems therefore to be denying to individual states, in this historical moment, the *ius belli* (*compétence de guerre*) claimed in the modern era by the unlimited sovereign state, *scil.*, the right of recourse to war, on the sovereign judgment of the national state, for the vindication of legal rights and legitimate interests. The use of force is not now a moral means for the redress of violated legal rights. The justness of the cause is irrelevant; there simply is no longer a right of self-redress; no individual state may presume to take even the cause of justice into its own hands. Whatever the grievance of the state may be, and however objectionable it may find the status quo, warfare undertaken on the sovereign decision of the national state is an immoral means for settling the grievance and for altering existent conditions.

I would note here as relevant to the discussion, that modern theory distinguishes three reasons for recourse to war by the sovereign state: *ad vindicandas offensiones*, *ad repetendas res*, *ad repellendas iniurias*. Pius XII, it seems to me, outlawed the first two categories of "war-aims." The third category is proper to the concept of "defensive" war. I would further note that, if Pius XII seems relatively unconcerned to give an exact definition of aggression, it is because he seems to want to move back into the center of Catholic thought the older, broader Augustinian concept of *causa iusta*. War is not simply a problem of aggression; more fundamentally it is a problem of injustice. It is the concept of justice that links the use of force with the moral order. Would it be correct to say that Pius XII represents an effort to return Catholic thought to more traditional and more fruitful premises? If there is a way out of the present impasse created by the outworn concept of aggression in the modern sense, it can only be a return to the concept of justice. There would still remain the formidable moral and legal problem of translating *iustitia* into *tò iustum*. In politico-moral terms this is today the problem of what is called policy. As a moral problem, war is ultimately a problem of policy, and therefore a problem of social morality. Policy is made by society, especially in a democratic context; and society bears the moral responsibility for the policy made. As a problem in justice, the problem of war is put to the People, in whom, according to good medieval theory, the sense of justice resides, and from whom the moral judgment, direction, and correction of public policy must finally come. As a moral problem in the use of force, war is not simply, or even primarily, a problem for the generals, the

State Department, the technologists, the international lawyers. Here, if anywhere, "the People shall judge." This is their responsibility, to be discharged before the shooting starts, by an active concern with the moral direction of national policy. My impression is that this duty in social morality is being badly neglected in America at the moment.

The reasons why no state today can claim for itself the right of war, even in redress of injuries, derive from two of the above-mentioned lines of inquiry. First, the immeasurably increased violence of war today disqualifies it as an apt and proportionate means for the resolution of international conflicts and even for the redress of just grievances. Second, to continue to admit the right of war, as an attribute of national sovereignty, would seriously block the progress of the international community to that mode of juridical organization which Pius XII regarded as the single means for the outlawry of all war, even defensive war. In this connection, it would be well to note the observation of M. Gabriel Matagrin:

> The preoccupation of Pius XII seems to be much less to determine what might be just in the actual situation of an unorganized humanity than to promote a genuine international organization capable of eliminating war, because the juridical reason for the right of war is the unorganized state of international life.[4]

Pius XII clearly stigmatized "aggressive" war as "a sin, an offense, and an outrage against the majesty of God." Should this sin in the moral order also be transposed into a crime in the legal order? Pius expressly said that "modern total war, and ABC warfare in particular," when it is not stringently in self-defense, "constitutes a crime worthy of the most severe national and international sanctions." I should think that the same recommendation would apply to less violent forms of "aggressive" warfare. However, Pius XII did not enter the formidable technical problem, how this legal transcription of a moral principle is to be effected. The problem has hitherto been insoluble.

2) A defensive war to repress injustice is morally admissible both in principle and in fact.

In its abstractness this principle has always formed part of Catholic doctrine; by its assertion the Church finds a way between the false extremes of pacifism and bellicism. Moreover, the assertion itself, far from being a contradiction of the basic Christian will to peace, is the strongest possible affirmation of this will. There is no peace without justice, law, and order. But, said the Pope, "law and order have need at times of the powerful arm of force." And the precept of peace itself requires that peace be defended against violation:

> The precept of peace is of divine right. Its purpose is to protect the goods of humanity, inasmuch as they are the goods of the Creator. Among these goods there are some of such importance for the human community that their defense against an unjust aggression is without doubt fully justified.[5]

There is nothing new about these assertions. What is important is their reiteration by Pius XII in today's highly concrete historical context of international conflict. The reiteration of the right of defensive war derives directly from an understanding of the conflict and from a realization that nonviolent means of solution may fail. The Church is obliged to confront the dreadful alternative: "the absolute necessity of self-defense against a very grave injustice that touches the community, that cannot be impeded by other means, that nevertheless must be impeded on pain of giving free field in international relations to brutal violence and lack of conscience."

The harshness of statement in that last phrase marks a new note that came only late (in 1953) into Pius XII's utterances. I think it fair to say that the gentle Pope of Peace brought himself only with great reluctance, and under the unrelenting pressure of events, to focus on the instant possibility of war, as generated by the essential ethos of the Communist system: "brutal violence and lack of conscience." The focus becomes even sharper after the events in Hungary, and in the light of the Soviet threat to use atomic weapons in Europe if the French and English adventure in Suez were not terminated. These words from the Christmas message, 1956, need to be quoted:

> The actual situation, which has no equivalent in the past, ought nevertheless to be clear to everyone. There is no further room for doubt about the purposes and the methods that lie behind tanks when they crash resoundingly across frontiers to distribute death and to force civilized peoples to a form of life that they distinctly abhor. When all the possible stages of negotiation and mediation are bypassed, and when the threat is made to use atomic arms to obtain concrete demands, whether these are justified or not, it becomes clear that, in present circumstances, there may come into existence in a nation a situation

in which all hope of averting war becomes vain. In this situation a war of efficacious self-defense against unjust attacks, which is undertaken with hope of success, cannot be considered illicit. [6]

One can almost feel the personal agony behind the labored sentences (more tortured in the original than in the translation). The agony, and utterance itself, are born of the Pope's reluctant realization that, as he had said earlier that same year, there are rulers "who except themselves from the elementary laws of human society." The tragedy in the situation is accented by his further vision that the people over whom these rulers stand "cannot but be the first to feel the need once more to form part of the human family."

There is no indication that this reaffirmation of the traditional principle of defensive warfare, to which Pius XII was driven by the brutal facts of international life, extends only to wars conducted by so-called conventional arms. On the contrary, the Pope extended it explicitly, not only to atomic warfare but even to ABC warfare. One cannot therefore uphold the simple statement that atomic war as such, without further qualifications, is morally unjustifiable, or that all use of atomic weapons in war is, somehow in principle, evil.

There are, however, conditions. The basic condition has been stated: "One cannot, even in principle, raise the question of the liceity of ABC warfare except in the case in which it must be judged indispensable for self-defense in the conditions indicated." These further conditions are simply those found in traditional doctrine. But each of them was sharpened to a fresh stringency by Pius XII in the light of the horrors of destruction and death now possible in war.

Briefly, the war must be "imposed by an obvious and extremely grave injustice." No minor infraction of rights will suffice, much less any question of national prestige. The criterion is high, namely, that the nation should "in all truth have been unjustly attacked and menaced in its vital rights."

The second condition is the familiar principle of war as always the *ultima ratio*. Moreover, it is today the extremity of means in a unique sense, given, on the one hand, the new means of negotiation and arbitration presently available, and on the other, the depths of manifold agony into which recourse to the *ultima ratio* may now plunge humanity as a whole.

The third condition is also familiar, the principle of proportion. It invokes a twofold consideration.

First, consideration must be given to the proportion between the damage suffered in consequence of the perpetration of a grave injustice, and the damages that would be let loose by a war to repress the injustice. Pius XII laid some stress on the fact that the comparison here must be between realities of the moral order, and not sheerly between two sets of material damage and loss. The standard is not a "eudaemonism and utilitarianism of materialist origin," which would avoid war merely because it is uncomfortable, or connive at injustice simply because its repression would be costly. The question of proportion must be evaluated in more tough-minded fashion, from the viewpoint of the hierarchy of strictly moral values. It is not enough simply to consider the "sorrows and evils that flow from war." There are greater evils than the physical death and destruction wrought in war. And there are human goods of so high an order that immense sacrifices may have to be borne in their defense. By these insistences Pius XII transcended the vulgar pacifism of sentimentalist and materialist inspiration that is so common today. The tradition of reason has always maintained that the highest value in society is the inviolability of the order of rights and justice. If this order disintegrates or is successfully defied, society is injured in its most vital structure and end. Peace itself is the work of justice; and therefore peace is not compatible with impunity for the evil of injustice. It is pertinent to emphasize these truths in an age in which economic and material values have come to assume the primacy.

Second, Pius XII requires an estimate of another proportion, between the evils unleashed by war and what he calls "the solid probability of success" in the forceful repression of unjust action. The specific attention he gives to this condition was immediately prompted by his awareness of the restiveness of the peoples who are presently captive under unjust rule and who are tempted to believe, not without reason, that their rescue will require the use of force. This condition of probable success is not, of course, simply the statesman's classical political calculus of success. It is the moral calculus that is enjoined in the traditional theory of rebellion against tyranny. Furthermore, Pius XII was careful to warn that in applying this moral calculus regard must be had for the tinderbox character of our world in which a spark may set off a conflagration.

A fourth principle of traditional theory is also affirmed by Pius XII, the principle of limitation in the use of force. It may be a matter of some surprise that he gave so little emphasis and development to it, at least in comparison to the preponderant place that the problem seems to have assumed in the minds of other theorists, Catholic and non-Catholic. There is one formal text. After asserting the legitimacy of "modern total warfare," that is, ABC warfare, under the set of stringent conditions already stated, he added:

> Even then every effort must be made and every means taken to avoid it, with the aid of international covenants, or to set limits to its use precise enough so that its effects will be confined to the strict exigencies of defense. In any case, when the employment of this means entails such an extension of the evil that it entirely escapes from the control of man, its use ought to be rejected as immoral. Here it is no longer a question of defense against injustice and of the necessary safeguard of legitimate possessions, but of the annihilation, pure and simple, of all human life within its radius of action. This is not permitted on any account.[7]

This is a very general statement indeed. And it takes the issue at its extreme, where it hardly needs statement, since the moral decision cannot fail to be obvious. Who would undertake to defend on any grounds, including military grounds, the annihilation of all human life within the radius of action of an ABC war that "entirely escapes from the control of man"? We have here an affirmation, if you will, of the rights of innocence, of the distinction between combatant and noncombatant. But it is an extremely broad statement.

One finds in the earlier utterances of the Pope, when he was demonstrating the first thesis in the traditional doctrine of war (that war is an evil, the fruit of sin), much advertence to "massacres of innocent victims," the killing of "infants with their mothers, the ill and infirm and aged," etc. These tragedies stand high on the list of the evils of war. In the text cited there is no explicit return to this principle of the rights of innocence when it is formally a question of total nuclear war and the use of nuclear weapons. If there is an anomaly here, the reason for it may lie in the fact that the Pope was forcing himself to face the desperate case. And in desperate cases, in which conscience is perplexed, the wise moralist is chary of the explicit and the nice, especially when the issue, as here, is one of social and not individual morality. In such cases hardly more than a *Grenzmoral* is to be looked for or counseled. In fact, the whole Catholic doctrine of war is hardly more than a *Grenzmoral*, an effort to establish on a minimal basis of reason a form of human action, the making of war, that remains always fundamentally irrational. I am not for a moment suggesting, of course, that the principle of the rights of innocent life has become in any sense irrelevant to the contemporary problem of war. Still less am I suggesting that Pius XII modified the traditional doctrine in this respect. I am merely noting what I noted, *scil.*, that this principle receives no sharp emphasis, to say the least, in his doctrine. There may be other reasons for this than the one that I tentatively suggested in the text above.

Two further propositions in the general theory must be mentioned. The first concerns the legitimacy of defense preparations on the part of individual states. Their legitimacy is founded on two actual facts of international life. First, at the moment there does not exist what Pius XII constantly looked forward to as the solution of the problem of war, namely, a constituted international authority possessing a monopoly of the use of armed force in international affairs. Second, there does exist the threat of "brutal violence and lack of conscience." In this factual situation, "the right to be in a posture of defense cannot be denied, even today, to any state." Here again the principle is extremely general; it says nothing about the morality of this or that configuration of the defense establishment of a given nation. The statement does not morally validate everything that goes on at Cape Canaveral or at Los Alamos.

Finally, the Pope of Peace disallowed the validity of conscientious objection. The occasion was the controversy on the subject, notably in Germany, where the resonances of a sort of anticipatory *Fronterlebnis* were giving an alarming impulse to pacifist movements. Particularly in question was the deposit of nuclear weapons on German soil as part of the NATO defense establishment. The Pope's judgment was premised on the legitimacy of the government, the democratic openness of its decisions, and the extremity of the historical necessity for making such defense preparations as would be adequate in the circumstances. He concluded that such a government is "acting in a manner that is not immoral" and that "a Catholic citizen may not make appeal to his own conscience as ground for refusing to give his services and to fulfil duties fixed by law."

This duty of armed service to the state, and this right of the state to arm itself for self-defense, are, he added, the traditional doctrine of the Church, even in latter days under Leo XIII and Benedict XV, when the problem of armaments and conscription put a pressing issue to the Christian conscience.

The foregoing may do as a statement, at least in outline, of the traditional doctrine on war in the form and with the modifications given it by the authority of the Church today. It is not particularly difficult to make this sort of statement. The difficulty chiefly begins after the statement has been made. Not that objections are raised, at least not in Catholic circles, against the doctrine itself as stated. What is queried is the usefulness of the doctrine, its relevance to the concrete actualities of our historical moment. I shall conclude with some comments on this issue.

The Solution of False Dilemmas

I think that the tendency to query the uses of the Catholic doctrine on war initially rises from the fact that it has for so long not been used, even by Catholics. That is, it has not been made the basis for a sound critique of public policies and as a means for the formation of a right public opinion. The classic example, of course, was the policy of "unconditional surrender" during the last war. This policy clearly violated the requirement of the "right intention" that has always been a principle in the traditional doctrine of war. Yet no sustained criticism was made of the policy by Catholic spokesmen. Nor was any substantial effort made to clarify by moral judgment the thickening mood of savage violence that made possible the atrocities of Hiroshima and Nagasaki. I think it is true to say that the traditional doctrine was disregarded during World War II. This is no argument against the traditional doctrine. The Ten Commandments do not lose their imperative relevance by reason of the fact that they are violated. But there is place for an indictment of all of us who failed to make the tradition relevant.

The initial relevance of the traditional doctrine today lies in its value as the solvent of false dilemmas. Our fragmentized culture seems to be the native soil of this fallacious and dangerous type of thinking. There are, first of all, the two extreme positions, a soft sentimental pacifism and a cynical hard realism. Both of these views, which are also "feelings," are formative factors in the moral climate of the moment. Both of them are condemned by the traditional doctrine as false and pernicious. The problem is to refute by argument the false antinomy between war and morality that they assert in common, though in different ways. The further and more difficult problem is to purify the public climate of the miasma that emanates from each of them and tends to smother the public conscience.

A second false dilemma has threatened to dominate the argument on national defense in Germany. It sloganized itself thus: "Lieber rot als tot." It has made the same threat in England, where it has been developed in a symposium by twenty-three distinguished Englishmen entitled, *The Fearful Choice: A Debate on Nuclear Policy.* The choice, of course, is between the desperate alternatives, either universal atomic death or complete surrender to Communism. The Catholic mind, schooled in the traditional doctrine of war and peace, rejects the dangerous fallacy involved in this casting up of desperate alternatives. Hidden beneath the fallacy is an abdication of the moral reason and a craven submission to some manner of technological or historical determinism.

It is not, of course, that the traditional doctrine rejects the extreme alternatives as possibilities. Anything in history is possible. Moreover, on grounds of the moral principle of proportion the doctrine supports the grave recommendation of the greatest theorist of war in modern times, von Klausewitz: "We must therefore familiarize ourselves with the thought of an honorable defeat." Conversely, the doctrine condemns the hysteria that swept Washington when the Senate voted, eighty-two to two, to deny government funds to any person or institution who ever proposes or actually conducts any study regarding the "surrender of the government of the U.S."

When "Washington" thinks of "surrender," it apparently can think only of "unconditional" surrender. Thus does the demonic specter of the past hover over us, as a still imperious *rector harum tenebrarum.* Thus patriotism, once the last refuge of the scoundrel, now has become the first refuge of the fool. It is folly not to foresee that the United States may be laid in ruins by a nuclear attack; the folly is compounded by a decision not to spend any money on planning what to do after that not impossible event. There is no room today for the heroic romanticism of the apocryphal utterance, "The Old Guard dies but never surrenders." Even Victor Hugo did not put this line on the lips of Cambronne; he simply had him say, "Merde." For all its vulgarity, this was a far more sensible remark in the circumstances.

For my part, I am impressed by the cold rationality of Soviet military thought as described by Raymond L. Garthoff in *Soviet Strategy in the Nuclear Age*.[8] He says: "The fundamental Soviet objectives which determine political and military strategies may be concisely summarized in one: Advance the power of the Soviet Union in whatever ways are most expedient so long as the survival of the Soviet power itself is not endangered." For the Soviet Union survival is not an issue in war; for us it is the only issue. In Soviet thought military action is subordinate to political aims; with us military action creates its own aims, and there is only one, "victory," *scil.*, unconditional surrender. "The Soviet strategic concept, in the thermonuclear era as before, is founded on the belief that the primary objective of military operations is the destruction of hostile military forces, and not the annihilation of the economic and population resources of the enemy. Thus the Soviets continue to adhere to the classical military strategic concept, while contemporary American views often diverge sharply from this traditional stand." Finally, Soviet policy envisages the "long war" even after a massive exchange of thermonuclear weapons. With us, if deterrence fails, and this massive exchange occurs, that is the end. We have no policy after that, except stubbornly to maintain that it is up to the enemy, and not us, to surrender—unconditionally. There is no little irony in the fact that the Communist enemy seems to understand better than we do the traditional doctrine on the uses of force.

"Losing," said von Klausewitz, "is a function of winning," thus stating in his own military idiom the moral calculus prescribed by traditional moral doctrine. The moralist agrees with the military theorist that the essence of a military situation is uncertainty. And when he requires, with Pius XII, a solid probability of success as a moral ground for a legitimate use of arms, he must reckon with the possibility of failure and be prepared to accept it. But this is a moral decision, worthy of a man and of a civilized nation. It is a free, morally motivated, and responsible act, and therefore it inflicts no stigma of dishonor. It is not that "weary resignation," condemned by Pius XII, which is basic to the inner attitude of the theorists of the desperate alternatives, no matter which one they argue for or accept.

On the contrary, the single inner attitude which is nourished by the traditional doctrine is a will to peace, which, in the extremity, bears within itself a will to enforce the precept of peace by arms. But this will to arms is a moral will; for it is identically a will to justice. It is formed under the judgment of reason. And the first alternative contemplated by reason, as it forms the will to justice through the use of force, is not the possibility of surrender, which would mean the victory of injustice. This is the ultimate extremity, beyond even the extremity of war itself. Similarly, the contrary alternative considered by reason is not a general annihilation, even of the enemy. This would be worse than injustice; it would be sheer folly. In a word, a debate on nuclear policy that is guided by the traditional doctrine of war does not move between the desperate alternatives of surrender or annihilation. If it means simply an honorable defeat, surrender may be morally tolerable; but it is not to be tolerated save on a reasonable calculus of proportionate moral costs. In contrast, annihilation is on every count morally intolerable; it is to be averted at all costs, that is, at the cost of every effort, in every field, that the spirit of man can put forth.

Precisely here the proximate and practical value, use, and relevance of the traditional doctrine begin to appear. Its remote value may lie in its service as a standard of casuistry on various kinds of war. Its remote value certainly lies in its power to form the public conscience and to clarify the climate of moral opinion in the midst of today's international conflict. But its proximate value is felt at the crucial point where the moral and political orders meet. Primarily, its value resides in its capacity to set the right terms for rational debate on public policies bearing on the problem of war and peace in this age, characterized by international conflict and by advanced technology. This is no mean value, if you consider the damage that is being presently done by argument carried on in the wrong terms. In this connection, I am not sure that one should talk today in these categories, "war and/or peace," leaving unexamined the question just what their validity is as moral and political categories. The basic fallacy is to suppose that "war" and "peace" are two discontinuous and incommensurable worlds of existence and universes of discourse, each with its own autonomous set of rules, "peace" being the world of "morality" and "war" being the world of "evil," in such wise that there is no evil as long as there is peace and no morality as soon as there is war. This is a common American assumption. Moreover, it would help greatly to attend to the point made by Mr. Philip C. Jessup that we live today in an "intermediate state" between peace and war; he contends that, "if one were accustomed to the idea of intermediacy, it can be argued that the likelihood of 'total war' could be diminished. . . . The basic question is whether our concepts, our terminology, our law have kept pace with the evolution of international affairs."[9]

The traditional doctrine disqualifies as irrelevant and dangerous the false dilemmas of which I have spoken. It also rejects the notion that the big problem is to "abolish war" or "ban the bomb." It is true that the traditional doctrine on war looks forward to its own disappearance as a chapter in Catholic moral theology. The effort of the moral reason to fit the use of military force into the objective order of justice is paradoxical enough; but the paradox is heightened when this effort takes place at the interior of the Christian religion of love. In any case, the principles of the doctrine themselves make clear that our historical moment is not destined to see a moral doctrine of war discarded as unnecessary. War is still the possibility, not to be exorcised even by prayer and fasting. The Church does not look immediately to the abolition of war. Her doctrine still seeks to fulfil its triple traditional function: to condemn war as evil, to limit the evils it entails, and to humanize its conduct as far as possible.

The Premises of Debate

In the light of the traditional doctrine and in the no less necessary light of the facts of international life and technological development today, what are the right terms for argument on public policy? These are readily reached by a dialectical process, an alternation between principle and fact. The doctrine asserts, in principle, that force is still the *ultima ratio* in human affairs, and that its use in extreme circumstances may be morally obligatory *ad repellendam iniuriam*. The facts assert that today this *ultima ratio* takes the form of nuclear force, whose use remains possible and may prove to be necessary, lest a free field be granted to brutal violence and lack of conscience. The doctrine then asserts that the use of nuclear force must be limited, the principle of limitation being the exigencies of legitimate defense against injustice. Thus the terms of public debate are set in two words, "limited war." All other terms of argument are fanciful or fallacious. (I assume here that the argument is to be cast primarily in political terms, only secondarily in military terms; for armed force is never more than a weapon of policy, a weapon of last resort.)

I shall not attempt to construct the debate itself. But two points may be made. First, there are those who say that the limitation of nuclear war, or any war, is today impossible, for a variety of reasons—technical, political, etc. In the face of this position, the traditional doctrine simply asserts again, "The problem today is limited war." But notice that the assertion is on a higher plane than that of sheer fact. It is a moral proposition, or better, a moral imperative. In other words, since limited nuclear war may be a necessity, it must be made a possibility. Its possibility must be created. And the creation of its possibility requires a work of intelligence, and the development of manifold action, on a whole series of policy levels—political (foreign and domestic), diplomatic, military, technological, scientific, fiscal, etc., with the important inclusion of the levels of public opinion and public education. To say that the possibility of limited war cannot be created by intelligence and energy, under the direction of a moral imperative, is to succumb to some sort of determinism in human affairs.

My second point is that the problem of limited war would seem to require solution in two stages. One stage consists in the construction of a sort of "model" of the limited war. This is largely a problem in conceptual analysis. Its value consists in making clear the requirements of limited war in terms of policy on various levels. Notably it makes clear that a right order must prevail among policies. It makes clear, for instance, that the limitation of war becomes difficult or impossible if fiscal policy assumes the primacy over armament policy, or if armament policy assumes the primacy over military policy, or if military policy assumes the primacy over foreign policy in the political sense.

The second stage is even more difficult. It centers on a *quaestio facti*. The fact is that the international conflict, in its ideological as in its power dimension, comes to concrete expression in certain localized situations, each of which has its own peculiarities. The question then is, where and under what circumstances is the irruption of armed conflict possible or likely, and how is the limitation of the conflict to be effected in these circumstances, under regard of political intentions, as controlling of military necessities *in situ?* The answer to this question is what is meant by the formulation of policy. Policy is the hand of the practical reason set firmly upon the course of events. Policy is what a nation does in this or that given situation. In the concreteness of policy, therefore, the assertion of the possibility of limited war is finally made, and made good. Policy is the meeting-place of the world of power and the world of morality, in which there takes place the concrete reconciliation of the duty of success that rests upon the statesman and the duty of justice that rests upon the civilized nation that he serves.

I am thus led to one final comment on the problem of war. It may be that the classical doctrine of war needs more theoretical elaboration in order to relate it more effectively to the unique conflict that agitates the world today, in contrast with the older historical conflicts upon which the traditional doctrine sought to bear, and by which in turn it was shaped. In any case, another work of the reflective intelligence and study is even more badly needed. I shall call it a politico-moral analysis of the divergent and particular conflict situations that have arisen or are likely to arise in the international scene as problems in themselves and as manifestations of the underlying crisis of our times. It is in these particular situations that war actually becomes a problem. It is in the midst of their dense materiality that the *quaestio iuris* finally rises. To answer it is the function of the moralist, the professional or the citizen moralist. His answer will never be more than an act of prudence, a practical judgment informed by principle. But he can give no answer at all to the *quaestio iuris* until the *quaestio facti* has been answered. From the point of view of the problem of war and morality the same need appears that has been described elsewhere in what concerns the more general problem of politics and morality. I mean the need of a far more vigorous cultivation of politico-moral science, with close attention to the enormous impact of technological developments on the moral order as well as on the political order.

The whole concept of force has undergone a rapid and radical transformation, right in the midst of history's most acute political crisis. One consequence of these two related developments was emphasized by Panel Two, *International Security: The Military Aspect*,[10] of the Special Studies Project of the Rockefeller Brothers Fund: "The over-all United States strategic concept lags behind developments in technology and in the world political situation." This vacuum of military doctrine greatly troubled the members of the panel. But I know from my own association with the Special Studies Project that they were even more troubled by another vacuum in contemporary thought, *scil.*, the absence of an over-all political-moral doctrine with regard to the uses of force. This higher doctrine is needed to give moral sense and political direction to a master strategic concept. "Power without a sense of direction," they said, "may drain life of its meaning, if it does not destroy humanity altogether." This sense of direction cannot be found in technology; of itself, technology tends toward the exploitation of scientific possibilities simply because they are possibilities. Power can be invested with a sense of direction only by moral principles. It is the function of morality to command the use of power, to forbid it, to limit it, or, more in general, to define the ends for which power may or must be used and to judge the circumstances of its use. But moral principles cannot effectively impart this sense of direction to power until they have first, as it were, passed through the order of politics; that is, until they have first become incarnate in public policy. It is public policy in all its varied concretions that must be "moralized" (to use an abused word in its good sense). This is the primary need of the moment. For my part, I am not confident that it is being met. Some of the reasons will appear in the following chapter.

Notes

1. Westminster: The Newman Press, 1956.
2. *Herder-Korrespondenz* 12, no. 9 (June, 1958), 396.
3. Berkeley: University of California Press, 1958.
4. "La légitimité de la guerre d'après les textes pontificaux," *Lumière et vie* 7, no. 38 (July, 1958), 56.
5. Allocution to the visiting members of the U.S. House of Representatives' Armed Services Committee, Oct. 8, 1947, *Civiltà cattolica* 98/4 (1947), 264.
6. Acta Apostolicae Sedis, 49 (1957), 19.
7. Allocution to the World Medical Congress, 1954; AAS 46 (1954), 589.
8. New York: Praeger, 1958.
9. *American Journal of International Law* 48 (1954), 98ff.
10. New York: Doubleday and Co., 1958.

~

CHAPTER TWELVE

The Doctrine Is Dead:
The Problem of the Moral Vacuum

During the Decade of the Tentative Fifties the course of events has thrust a number of basic issues into the forum of public argument. One of them goes under the rubric, "morality and public policy." Chiefly in question is foreign policy.

My introduction to the state of the problem took place at the outset of the decade in a conversation with a distinguished journalist who is now dead. In public affairs he was immensely knowledgeable; he was also greatly puzzled over the new issue that was being raised. His first question revealed the source of his puzzlement. What, he asked, has the Sermon on the Mount got to do with foreign policy? I was not a little taken aback by this statement of the issue. What, I asked, makes you think that morality is identical with the Sermon on the Mount? Innocently and earnestly he replied: "Isn't it?" And that in effect was the end of the conversation. We floundered a while in the shallows and miseries of mutual misunderstanding, and then changed the subject to the tactics of the war going on in Korea.

Moral Theory in Transition

I have only a fragmentary acquaintance with the growing body of literature on morality and foreign policy; the subject is outside my field. But listening, as it were, on the edges of the public argument, I have come to the conclusion that my journalist friend properly introduced me to the fundamental problem. It does not lie in the concept of policy, or even in the concretenesses of actual policies, though these matters are complex enough. It lies in the concept of morality itself. Rarely does the argument get to concrete issues of policy. And even when it does, the talk quickly turns back to the root of confusion—the question: what is morality?

The reasons for this fact lie in the history of moral theory in America. But that story is long, not to be told here (I don't think it ever has been fully told). An important event, of relatively recent occurrence, has been the recognition of the shortcomings and falsities of an older American morality that dominated the nineteenth century and still held sway into the twentieth.

Its style was voluntarist; it sought the constitution of the moral order in the will of God. The good is good because God commands it; the evil is evil because God forbids it. The notion that certain acts are intrinsically evil or good, and therefore forbidden or commanded by God, was rejected. Rejected too was the older intellectualist tradition of ethics and its equation of morality with right reason. Reason is the dupe of interest and passion. And how is one to know, or dare to say, whose reason is right? In the search for moral principles and solutions reason can have no place.

In its sources the older morality was scriptural in a fundamentalist sense. In order to find the will of God for man it went directly to the Bible. There alone the divine precepts and prohibitions are stated. They are stated in so many words, and the words are to be taken at their immediate face value without further exegetical ado. When, for instance, the Gospel tells the Christian not to resist evil but to turn the other cheek, the precept is clear and absolute. The true Christian abdicates the use of force even in the face of injury.

In its mood the old morality was subjectivist. Technically it would be called a "morality of intention." It set primary and controlling value on a sincerity of interior motive; what matters is not what you do but why you do it. And it was strong on the point that an act is moral only when its motive is altruistic—concretely, when the motive is love. If any element of self-interest creeps in, the act is corrupt and sinful.

Finally, in its whole spirit the old morality was individualistic. Not only did it reject the idea of a moral authority external to the individual conscience. It also set its single focus on the individual existence and on the moral problems that arise in interpersonal relationships. As for society, it believed in a direct transference of personal values into social life; in principle it would tolerate nothing less than Christian perfection as a social standard. Its highest assertion was there would be no moral problems in society, if only all men loved their neighbor.

Within the last generation this older morality has come under severe criticism, in itself and its later historical alliance with certain trends in secular liberal thought. The attack has centered on its simplism. The discovery was made that this morality of facile absolutes was ill-suited to cope with the growing complexity of an industrial society, domestically and in its foreign relations.

It did not go beyond the false notion that society is simply the sum of the individuals living in it, and that public morality is no more than the sum of private moralities. It did not understand the special moral problems raised by the institutionalization of human action. It did not grasp the nature of politics, the due autonomy of the political, the limiting factors of political action, or the standing of success as a political value. It had no sense of the differential character of morality and legality, no theory of jurisprudence, no idea of the distinction between private sin and public crime.

In consequence of all these shortcomings, the older morality possessed no resources for discriminating moral judgment. It tended to thrust its simple yeas and nays upon political, social, and economic reality without any careful prior analysis of the realities in question. It disregarded the duly autonomous character of their lines and life.

It distorted the meaning of Plato's famous dictum and understood it to say that society is the individual (not "man") writ large. In a word, what the older morality failed to understand was the nature of man himself.

The critique of the older American morality seems to have been not only just but also successful. The older morality, though still around, is no longer dominant. This is good. It is perhaps particularly good that the older morality is still around. Doubtless it is useless against the demons that inhabit the organized structures of society and exert their sway over history from these seats of institutionalized power. On the other hand, it had a certain virtue of exorcism against the demons that dwell in the life of the individual. And it is always good that at least some demons are cast out from among us, even though their departure still leaves us in combat with the "rulers of this world of darkness," whose dominion will endure until the Day of the Lord.

The avowed purpose of the newer American morality is to reckon with the full complexity of man's nature and of human affairs. Hence against the absolutism of the old morality, in which the contingent facts got lost under insistence on the absolute precept, the new morality moves towards a situationalism, in which the absoluteness of principle tends to get lost amid the contingencies of fact. Against the abstract fundamentalist literalism of the old morality the new system is consciously pragmatist; not the wording of the precept but a calculus of the consequences of the act is the decisive moral norm. Whereas the old morality saw things as so simple that moral judgment was always easy, the new morality sees things as so complicated that moral judgment becomes practically impossible. The final category of moral judgment is not "right" or "wrong" but "ambiguous."

Finally, against the self-righteous tendency of the old morality, the new theory teaches that to act is to sin, to accept responsibility is to incur guilt, to live at all is to stand under the judgment of God, which is uniformly adverse, since every act of moral judgment is vitiated by some hidden fallacy, and every use of human freedom is inevitably an exercise in pride.

The current argument about morality and foreign policy goes on within the climate of moral opinion created at once by the older American morality, and by the newer morality, and by the conflict between them—a conflict which does not rule out certain similarities, notably their common rejection of the whole style and structure of natural-law morality. Three basic problems, each related to the others, furnish the focus of concern.

The Three Problems

The first is the gulf between individual and collective morality. Since the day of Roger Williams and his separation of the "garden" (the Christian community) and the "wilderness" (society or "the world"), prevalent American moral theory has never found a way to bridge the chasm between the order of private life and the order of law, public policy, and institutional action, especially when the question concerns the nation-state. The private life is governed by the will of God as stated in the Scriptures. It is to bear the stamp of the Christian values canonized by the Scriptures—patience, gentleness, sacrifice, forbearance, trust, compassion, humility, forgiveness of injuries, and, supremely and inclusively, love. On the other hand, it is the plainest of historical facts that the public life of the nation-state is not governed by these values. Hardly less plain is the fact that it cannot be. What, asked my journalist friend quite sensibly, has the Sermon on the Mount got to do with foreign policy? Pacifism, for instance, may be a dictate of the individual conscience, but it cannot be a public policy. What then is the will of God for the nation-state? How and where is it to be discovered? There is no charter of political morality in the Scriptures. Must one, therefore, admit that all politics is simply *Realpolitik*—the selfish pursuit of national interest in a nicely calculated play of power to which ethical norms are irrelevant?

The other two questions are consequent. First, is it not the historical fact that the nation-state acknowledges only one imperative, the dictate of national interest? And is not the fact itself also normative? Is it not right that the nation should so act? Would it not be wrong for the nation to act apart from the national interest, short of it, or beyond it? But if you hold this, do you not come into open conflict with the basic tenet of both the older and the new American morality, which is that self-concern is the primal sin; that the pursuit of self-interest is the pursuit of evil; that the whole function of Christian morality is to call self-interest into question, deny it all theoretical justification, and condemn it in practice? This is the moral theory. Strictly applied, it must assert that the nation is sinful and guilty in all its actions, since they are never free of the taint of interest.

Faithfully held, this theory requires that the nation should be called upon to transcend self-interest, resist its dictates, and act beyond them in a spirit of disinterested altruism. Or, since this moral call would have the ring of nonsense in the field of politics, and since morality is not supposed to sound like nonsense, one could choose not to hold and apply the theory strictly. One could fall back on the position that self-interest is a legitimate motive for the nation, even though it is an illegitimate motive for the individual. Then the question is, in the name of what theory do you make this distinction? Is this to bridge the gulf between private and collective morality, or simply to fall headlong into it?

The final issue is perhaps the most basic. It certainly is the most in-
clusive, since it spans all the prominent issues of the day—armaments,
the politics of the cold war, the economics and politics of the revolution
of rising expectations. It is the issue of power. As far as the sheer fact goes,
most Americans seem to have finally awakened to the central relationship between foreign policy and force. But the awakening was to a state
of moral bafflement and anxiety, insofar as it took place in the climate of
moral opinion described above.

In the climate of this moral opinion a cold breath of evil more than
faintly emanates from the very words "power" and "force." It seems to
have been part of the American dream that this nation could go through
history with clean hands by the simple Kantian expedient described in
Péguy's genial phrase: "Kantianism has clean hands, because it has no
hands." Concretely, a nation's "hands," wherewith it shapes the stuff of
history, are its instruments of power—military, economic, and diplomatic
power, together with the power of sheer presence and prestige. We have
never wanted to have such hands, much less to get them dirty by handling any history save our own. Our historic declaration was that power-
struggles were for the "barbarous" nations of Europe, not for us. Now we
have become suddenly conscious of our hands—that they are sinewy beyond comparison; that they are sunk in the affairs of the world; that they
are getting dirty beyond the wrists.

At least we feel them to be dirty, and the feeling is one of guilt. The
United States today is an imperialism, like it or not. And we like it so little that we are even unwilling to admit the fact. The cause of our anxiety
is not that there has been little in our past political experience to teach
us wisely to wield the instrument of empire, which is power. It is rather
that there is nothing in current American moral theories to teach us the
moral quality of power itself. The prevalent teaching is simply that power
is evil. The teaching, in fact, is that the evil in human nature is precisely
a will to power. The will is activated as the hand closes on the thing; at
that moment innocence is lost, never to be regained. To be human is bad
enough; but to be powerful is to be corrupt, with a corruption that in-
creases with each increment of power.

In what moral terms, therefore, is America to justify itself in its possession
of power? And in what terms is America to justify itself to the world for its

uses of its power? Can these hands be cleansed? Or must the scriptural phrase be inverted to read: Let him who is unjustified become still more unjust? The national straits are even more narrowed when one considers that the teaching says one further devastating thing. It says that to refuse to use power is to be "irresponsible," and therefore to be more guilty yet.

The Basic Issue

These seem to be the basic issues involved in the current controversy about morality and foreign policy. I have found myself in a fog as I have listened intermittently, while cynics dispute with moralists, and political realists dispute with ethical idealists, and fundamentalists dispute with "ambiguists" (I apologize for the barbarism, but I must have a descriptive term for this school of thought, whose favorite word is "ambiguity").

Only one thing is clear. The real issue does not concern the moral quality of this or that element of American foreign policy. The real issue concerns the nature of morality itself, the determinants of moral action (whether individual or collective), the structure of the moral act, and the general style of moral argument. One cannot argue moral issues until they are stated; but what are the terms of statement of the moral issues involved in foreign policy? One cannot come to practical solutions until one has first formulated the relevant principles and also analyzed the factual situation in which the principled solution is to be practiced; but by what methods do you arrive at your principles and establish their relevance, and what is your analysis of the factual situation? As these issues are touched, or as they are avoided, the whole argument flies off in all directions.

The proper bafflers are the ambiguists. Their flashes of insight are frequent enough; but in the end the fog closes down. They are great ones for the facts, against the fundamentalists, and great ones for "conscience," against the cynics. They insist on the values of pragmatism against the absolutists; but they resent the suggestion that they push pragmatism to the point of a relativism of moral values. My main difficulty, however, is that I never know what, in their argument, is fact and what is moral category (surely there is a difference), or where the process of history ends and the moral order begins (surely there must be such a point).

When they undertake to describe the historical-political situation for which policy is to be framed, one has the same feeling that comes on seeing a play by Sartre. No human characters are on the stage, only Sartre's philosophical categories. So, in the ambiguist descriptions, the factual situation always appears as a "predicament," full of "ironies," sown with "dilemmas," to be stated only in "paradox," and to be dealt with only at one's "hazard," because in the situation "creative and destructive possibilities" are inextricably mixed, and therefore policy and action of whatever kind can only be "morally ambiguous."

The Tyranny of Categories

But this is to filter the facts through categories. So far as one can see by an independent look "out there," the dilemmas and ironies and paradoxes are, like the beauty of the beloved, in the eye of the ambiguist beholder. They represent a doctrinaire construction of the facts in terms of an antecedent moral theory. And every set of facts is constructed in such a way as to make the moral verdict "ambiguous" a foregone conclusion.

The ambiguist rightly puts emphasis on the complexity of the situations with which foreign policy has to deal; no one could exaggerate the complexity hidden under the phrase, "the cold war." But does the fact of complexity justify the vocabulary of description or the monotonous moral verdict? It is as if a surgeon in the midst of a gastroenterostomy were to say that the highly complex situation in front of him is so full of paradox ("The patient is at once receiving blood and losing it") and irony ("Half a stomach will be better than a whole one") and dilemmas ("Not too much, nor too little, anesthesia") that all surgical solutions are necessarily ambiguous. Complicated situations, surgical or moral, are merely complicated. It is for the statesman, as for the surgeon, to master the complications and minister as best he can to the health of the body, politic or physical. The work may be done deftly or clumsily, intelligently or stupidly, with variant degrees of success or failure; but why call it in either case "ambiguous"? The philosophers of moral ambiguity will, of course, say that the ambiguity, properly speaking, is not in the political situation but in political man, who carries into politics the paradox, irony, and ambiguous amalgam of virtue and corruption that reside in his own nature (or in the human "self," as the ambiguists prefer to say, since they have a peculiar meaning all their own for the word "nature"). There you have it.

In point of sheer method there is no reason why the ambiguist should not make use of a conceptual scheme to guide his analysis of political fact, and to furnish the terms for his statement of moral issues, and to determine the style of his argument in favor of his solutions. Every moralist does this. Every moralist has his concept of the moral order. All practical moral inquiry has theoretical presuppositions. Each moral theory has its own categories of statement and its own style of argument. And in the end every structure of moral doctrine and decision rests on a concept of the nature of man.

To this concept of man's nature the critical argument comes back. The ambiguist indicts the fundamentalist and the secular liberal for their one-dimensional views of man. But he does not recognize that the same in-dictment recoils on his own head. He easily disposes of all the utopi-anisms, both "hard" and "soft," that result from the one-dimensional fundamentalist and secular liberal views. He then spins an enormously complex analysis of the "real" nature of man in personal and political life. And at the end of it (this is the real paradox) he has again compressed the moral life of man into one dimension. Inescapably, beyond all help of divine grace—and even further beyond all help from human reason and freedom—the life of man, personally and politically, is lived in the single moral dimension of ambiguity. He who relishes irony should relish this—that the whole complicated argument against simplistic theories should result in the creation of a theory that is itself simplistic; that the smash-ing attack on the bright and brittle illusion of utopianism should win its victory under the banner of an opposite illusion that is marshy and murky but no less an illusion.

I have outlined the argument about morality and foreign policy in a way to suggest that it is an intramural argument within the Protestant community. So it is.

The question I have asked myself is, whether and on what terms it might be possible for me to enter the argument. The answer is not easy.

Three Pseudo-problems

My own terms of moral definition, argument, and judgment are, of course, those of the tradition of reason in moral affairs—the ancient tradition that has been sustained and developed in the Catholic Church. Consequently, listening to the public argument on morality and foreign policy, I have found it difficult to discover just what all the shouting is about. Three major issues have come to the fore. The trouble is that all three seem to me factitious. From where I sit, so to speak, in the moral universe, they are all pseudo-problems. Were I to enter the argument, this is the first point I should have to make.

The Protestant moralist is disturbed by the gulf between the morality of individual and collective man. He is forever trying somehow to close the gap. Forever he fails, not only in doing this but even in seeing how it could possibly be done. Thus he is driven back upon the simplist category of "ambiguity." Or he sadly admits an unresolvable dichotomy between moral man and immoral society.

I am obliged to say that the whole practical problem is falsely conceived in consequence of a defective theory. No such pseudo-problem arises within the tradition of reason—or, if you will, in the ethic of natural law. Society and the state are understood to be natural institutions with their relatively autonomous ends or purposes, which are predesigned in broad outline in the social and political nature of man, as understood in its concrete completeness through reflection and historical experience. These purposes are public, not private. They are therefore strictly limited. They do not transcend the temporal and terrestrial order, within which the political and social life of man is confined; and even within this order they are not coextensive with the ends of the human person as such. The obligatory public purposes of society and the state impose on these institutions a special set of obligations which, again by nature, are not coextensive with the wider and higher range of obligations that rest upon the human person (not to speak of the Christian). In a word, the imperatives of political and social morality derive from the inherent order of political and social reality itself, as the architectonic moral reason conceives this necessary order in the light of the fivefold structure of obligatory political ends—justice, freedom, security, the general welfare, and civil unity or peace (so the Preamble to the American Constitution states these ends).

It follows, then, that the morality proper to the life and action of society and the state is not univocally the morality of personal life, or even of familial life. Therefore the effort to bring the organized action of politics and the practical art of statecraft directly under the control of the Christian values that govern personal and familial life is inherently fallacious. It makes wreckage not only of public policy but also of morality itself.

Again, the Protestant moralist is deeply troubled by the fact that nations and states have the incorrigible habit of acting in their own self-interest, and thus violating the fundamental canon of morality which sees in self-concern the basic sin. Here again is a pseudo-problem. I am, of course, much troubled by the question of the national interest, but chiefly lest it be falsely identified in the concrete, thus giving rise to politically stupid policies. But since I do not subscribe to a Kantian "morality of intention," I am not at all troubled by the centrality of self-interest as the motive of national action. From the point of view of political morality, as determined by the purposes inherent in the state, this motive is both legitimate and necessary.

There is, however, one reservation. I do not want self-interest interpreted in the sense of the classic theory of *raison d'état*, which was linked to the modern concept of the absolute sovereignty of the nation-state. This latter concept imparted to the notion of national self-interest an absoluteness that was always as illegitimate as it is presently outworn. The tradition of reason requires, with particular stringency today, that national interest, remaining always valid and omnipresent as a *motive*, be given only a relative and proximate status as an *end* of national action. Political action stands always under the imperative to realize, at least in some minimal human measure, the fivefold structure of obligatory political ends. Political action by the nation-state projected in the form of foreign policy today stands with historical clarity (as it always stood with theoretical clarity in the tradition of reason) under the imperative to realize this structure of political ends in the international community, within the limits—narrow but real—of the possible. Today, in fact as in theory, the national interest must be related to this international realization, which stands higher and more ultimate in political value than itself.

No false theoretical dichotomy may be thrust in here. The national interest, rightly understood, is successfully achieved only at the interior, as it were, of the growing international order to which the pursuit of national interest can and must contribute. There is, of course, the practical problem of defining the concrete policies that will be successful at once in the national interest and in the higher interest of international order. The casuistry is endlessly difficult. In any case, one ought to spare oneself unnecessary theoretical agonies, whose roots are often in sentimentalism; as, for instance, the effort to justify foreign aid in terms of pure disinterested Christian charity. To erect some sort of inevitable opposition between the pursuit of national interest and the true imperatives of political morality is to create a pseudo-problem.

The third source of Protestant moral anxiety is the problem of power. The practical problem, as put to policy, is enormously complicated in the nuclear age, in the midst of a profound historical crisis of civilization, and over against an ideology of force that is also a spreading political imperialism. This, however, is surely no reason for distorting the problem by thrusting into it a set of theoretically false dilemmas—by saying, for instance, that to use power is prideful and therefore bad, and not to use it is irresponsible and therefore worse. The tradition of reason declines all such reckless simplism. It rejects the cynical dictum of Lenin that "the state is a club." On the other hand, it does not attempt to fashion the state in the image of an Eastern-seaboard "liberal" who at once abhors power and adores it (since by him, emergent from the matrix of American Protestant culture, power is unconsciously regarded as satanic). The traditional ethic starts with the assumption that, as there is no law without force to vindicate it, so there is no politics without power to promote it. All politics is power politics—up to a point.

The point is set by multiple criteria. To be drastically brief, the essential criterion is the distinction between force and violence. Force is the measure of power necessary and sufficient to uphold the valid purposes both of law and of politics. What exceeds this measure is violence, which destroys the order both of law and of politics. The distinction is teleological, in the customary style of the tradition of reason. As an instrument, force is morally neutral in itself. The standard of its use is aptitude or ineptitude for the achievement of the obligatory public purposes. Here again the casuistry is endlessly difficult, especially when the moralist's refusal to sanction too much force clashes with the soldier's classic reluctance to use too little force. In any case, the theory is clear enough. The same criterion which governs the state in its use of coercive law for the public purposes also governs the state in its use of force, again for the public purposes. The function of law, said the Jurist (this is the title that Aquinas regularly gives to Ulpian), is to be useful to the community; this too is the function of force.

The community, as the Jurist knew, is neither a choir of angels nor a pack of wolves. It is simply the human community which, in proportion as it is civilized, strives to maintain itself in some small margin of safe distance from the chaos of barbarism. For this effort the only resources directly available to the community are those which first rescued it from barbarism, namely, the resources of reason, made operative chiefly through the processes of reasonable law, prudent public policies, and a discriminatingly apt use of force.

(Note here that Christianity, as I have already said, profoundly altered the structure of politics by introducing the revolutionary idea of the two communities, two orders of law and two authorities. But it did not change the nature of politics, law, and government, which still remain rational processes. To the quality of these processes Christian faith and grace contribute only indirectly, by their inner effect upon man himself, which is in part the correction and clarification of the processes of reason.)

The necessary defense against barbarism is, therefore, an apparatus of state that embodies both reason and force in a measure that is at least decently conformable with what man has learned, by rational reflection and historical experience, to be necessary and useful to sustain his striving towards the life of civility. The historical success of the civilized community in this continuing effort of the forces of reason to hold at bay the counterforces of barbarism is no more than marginal. The traditional ethic, which asserts the doctrine of the rule of reason in public affairs, does not expect that man's historical success in installing reason in its rightful rule will be much more than marginal. But the margin makes the difference.

Again the Basic Issue

All this is the sort of thing that the theorist of natural law would have first to say were he to enter on the ground floor, so to speak, of the controversy about morality and public policy. He could not possibly argue concrete problems of policy in the moral terms of the ambiguist. Insofar as these terms are intelligible to him at all, they seem to him questionable in themselves and creative of pseudo-problems in the field of policy. In turn, the Protestant moralist, whatever his school, cannot possibly argue questions of policy in the moral terms of the tradition of reason. The tradition is alien to him at every point—in its intellectualism, its theological emphasis on the Reason of God, its insistence on the analogical character of the structures of life (personal, familial, political, social), its assignment of primacy to the objective end of the act over the subjective intention of the agent, and its casuistical niceties. At best, the whole theory is unintelligible; at worst it is an idolatry of reason and an evacuation of the Gospel.

It has also become customary to point out that, whatever the merits of the tradition, it is dead, in the sense of Nietzsche's dictum, "God is dead." So I was told recently. It happened that I wrote a little piece on the traditional moral doctrine on the limitations of warfare, as fashioned by the tradition of reason. (It stands as the previous chapter in this book.) A friendly critic, Professor Julian Hartt of the Yale Divinity School, had this to say: "Father Murray has not, I believe, clearly enough come to terms with the question behind every serious consideration of limited war as a moral option, i.e., where are the ethical principles to fix the appropriate limits? *Where*, not *what*: can we make out the lineaments of the community which is the living repository (as it were) of the ethical principles relevant and efficacious to the moral determinations of the limits of warfare?" This is a fair question.

After a look around the national lot, Professor Hartt comes to the conclusion that the American community does not qualify; it is not the living repository of what the tradition of reason has said on warfare. I am compelled regretfully to agree that he is right. Such is the fact. It may even be that the American community, especially in its "clerks," who are the custodians of the public philosophy, is not the repository of the tradition of reason on any moral issue you would like to name. This ancient tradition lives, if you will, within the Catholic community; but this community fails to bring it into vital relation with the problems of foreign policy. There seems, in fact, to be some reason for saying that the Catholic community is not much interested in foreign affairs, beyond its contribution in sustaining the domestic mood of anti-Communism.

But if it be the fact that the tradition of natural law, once vigorous in America, is now dead, a serious question arises. What then is the moral doctrine on which America is to base its national action, especially its foreign policy?

One could put the question in the first instance to the government. It is clear that the Department of Defense and its allied agencies find sufficient moral warrant for their policies in their loyalty to the good old

Western-story maxim: "Don't shoot first." With the moral issue thus summarily disposed of, they set policy under the primatial control of that powerful dyarchy, technology and the budget, which conspire to accumulate weapons of mass annihilation that are morally unshootable, no matter who shoots first. Those who are disquieted by this situation—which is not ambiguous but simply wrong—are invited to find comfort in the emanations of crypto-pacifism from the White House, which seems to hold that we shall never shoot at all. The moral argument for this unambiguous position, whose simplism rivals that of the ambiguists, is never made clear. The inquiry into the moral bases of policy would probably produce other weird and wonderful answers, if elsewhere pursued—within the Department of State, for instance, with regard to disarmament, foreign aid, and diplomatic démarches among the uncommitted or emergent nations.

In any case, the question is perhaps more appropriately put to the American community at large. The theory of American government seems to be that public policies borrow, as it were, their morality from the conscience of the people. Right policies, as well as due powers, derive from the consent of the governed. Therefore, on what structured concept of the moral order does the American people undertake to fulfill its traditional public moral right and duty, which is to judge, direct, correct, and then consent to, the courses of foreign policy?

There is a sentimental subjectivist scriptural fundamentalism. But this theory by definition has nothing to say about foreign policy. It is at best a theory of interpersonal relationships and therefore irrelevant to international relations, which are not interpersonal. There is also moral ambiguism. But this, in the final analysis, is not properly a moral theory. It is perhaps a technique of historical analysis, highly doctrinaire in style; but it is not an ethical philosophy. It is an interesting paradoxical structure of rhetorical categories; but it is not a normative doctrine that could base discriminating moral judgments. All norms vanish amid the multiplying paradoxes; and all discrimination is swallowed up in the cavernous interior of the constantly recurrent verdict: "This action is morally ambiguous."

The school of ambiguist thought has done some useful negative service by its corrosive critique of older types of moral simplism and political utopianism. But it has no positive constructive power to fashion purposeful public policies in an age of crisis. It can throw rocks after the event, but it can lay no cornerstones. It points out all the moral hazards, and takes none. The self-contradiction inherent in sin is indeed a massive fact of the human condition; but not for this reason, or any other, does ambiguity become a virtue in moral judgment. Ambiguism can judge no policies save those that history has already judged. It can direct no policies because it can specify no ends toward which policy should be directed. And it can correct no policies since all policies deserve by definition the same qualification, "ambiguous," and what use is it to correct one ambiguous course by substituting another? We can discard ambiguism as the moral premise of public policy.

What is there left? There is, of course, the pseudo-morality of secular liberalism, especially of the academic variety. Its basic premise is a curious version of the Socratic paradox, that knowledge is virtue. It asserts that, if only we really could get to understand everybody, our foreign policy would inevitably be good. The trouble is that the past failures of the political intelligence of secular liberalism, and its demonstrated capacities for misunderstanding, have already pretty much discredited it.

Finally, there is the ubiquitous pragmatist, whose concern is only with what will work. But he too wins no confidence, since most of us have already learned from the pragmatist source of truth, which is history, that whatever is not true will fail to work. We want to know the political truth that will base workable policies.

It would seem, therefore, that the moral footing has been eroded from beneath the political principle of consent, which has now come to designate nothing more than the technique of majority opinion as the guide of public action—a technique as apt to produce fatuity in policy and tyranny of rule as to produce wisdom and justice. It was not always so. In the constitutional theory of the West the principle of consent found its moral basis in the belief, which was presumed sufficiently to be the fact, that the people are the living repository of a moral tradition, possessed at least as a heritage of wisdom, that enables them to know what is reasonable in the action of the state—in its laws, its public policies, its uses of force. The people consent because it is reasonable to consent to what, with some evidence, appears as reasonable. Today no such moral tradition lives among the American people. As Professor Hartt suggests, the tradition of reason, which is known as the ethic of natural law, is dead. Those who seek the ironies of history should find one here, in the fact that the ethic which launched Western constitutionalism and endured long enough as a popular heritage to give essential form to the American system of government has now ceased to sustain the structure and direct the action of this constitutional commonwealth.

The situation is not such as to gladden the heart. But at least one knows the right question in the present matter. It is not how foreign policy is to be guided by the norms of moral doctrine. It is, rather, what is the moral doctrine by whose norms foreign policy is to be guided?

~

CHAPTER THIRTEEN

The Doctrine Lives:
The Eternal Return of Natural Law

The news reported in the last chapter—that the tradition of natural law is dead—calls for some verification, before it is accepted as true. For one thing, it may be a case of mistaken identity; perhaps it was for some contrefaçon of the doctrine that the funeral rites were held. This is possible. So many misunderstandings have conspired to obscure the true identity of the doctrine that it is often mistaken for what it is not. Some of the misunderstandings are naive; others are of the learned sort. Some are the product of ignorance; others result from polemic bias.

The doctrine is accused of abstractionism, as if it disregarded experience and undertook to pull all its moral precepts like so many magician's rabbits out of the metaphysical hat of an abstract human "essence." The doctrine is also interpreted as an intuitionism, as if it maintained that all natural-law precepts were somehow "self-evident." It is also derided as a legalism, as if it proclaimed a detailed code of particularized do's and don'ts, nicely drawn up with the aid of deductive logic alone, absolutely normative in all possible circumstances, ready for automatic application, whatever the factual situation may be. The theory is also rejected for its presumed immobilism, as if its concept of an immutable human nature and an unchanging structure of human ends required it to deny the historicity of human existence and forbade it to recognize the virtualities of human freedom. It should already be clear from the earlier chapter on the origins of the public consensus that these conceptions are caricatures of the doctrine of natural law.

There is also the biologist interpretation, which imputes to natural-law theory a confusion of the "primordial," in a biological sense, with the "natural." This is a particularly gross and gratuitous misinterpretation, since nothing is clearer in natural-law theory than its identification of the "natural" with the "rational," or perhaps better, the "human." Its whole effort is to incorporate the biological values in man, notably his sexual tendencies, into the fuller human order of reason, and to deny them the status of the primordial. The primordial in man—that which is first in or-der—is his rational soul, the form of humanity, which informs all that is biological in him. Natural-law argument against sexual aberrations (in-cluding artificial contraception) indicts them precisely because in them man succumbs to his own biological inclinations in violation of the pri-mordial inclinations of reason and real love.

There is also the objectivist-rationalist interpretation, which is the premise from which natural-law theory is criticized for its supposed neg-lect of the values of the human person and for its alleged deafness to the resonances of intersubjectivity. In point of fact, the theory never forgets that the "nature" with which it deals has no existence except in the per-son, who is a unique realization of the nature, situated in an order of other unique realizations, whose uniqueness, nevertheless, does not make them atomistic monads, since it is in each instance a form of participation and communication in the one common nature.

Finally, there is the charge that natural-law doctrine is not "Christian." If it be meant that the doctrine in structure and style is alien to the gen-eral Protestant moral system, in so far as there is such a thing, the charge is true enough. The last chapter will have made this clear. It would not, of course, be difficult to show that the doctrine is, in germinal fashion, scriptural. However, I shall be content here to make only four comments.

First, natural-law theory does not pretend to do more than it can, which is to give a philosophical account of the moral experience of hu-manity and to lay down a charter of essential humanism. It does not show the individual the way to sainthood, but only to manhood. It does not promise to transform society into the City of God on earth, but only to prescribe, for the purposes of law and social custom, that minimum of morality which must be observed by the members of a society, if the social environment is to be human and habitable. At that, for a man to be reasonably human, and for a society to be essentially civil—these are no mean achievements. The ideal of the reasonable man, who does his duty to God, to others, and to himself, is not an ignoble one. In fact, it puts such a challenge to the inertness and perversity which are part of the human stuff, that Christian doctrine from the day of St. Augustine has taught the necessity of divine grace for this integral fulfillment of the natural law.

Second, beyond the fulfillment of the ideal of the reasonable man there lies the perennial question of youth, whatever its age. It is asked in the Gospel: "What do I still lack?" (Matthew 19:21). And there remains the Gospel's austere answer, put in the form of an invitation, but not cast in the categories of ethics, which are good and evil and the obligation to choose between them. The invitation opens the perspectives of a higher choice, to "be a follower of mine." For the making of this choice there is no other motive, no other inner impulse, than the free desire to respond to the prior choice of Him whom one chooses because one has been first chosen.

Third, the mistake would be to imagine that the invitation, "Come, follow me," is a summons somehow to forsake the universe of human nature, somehow to vault above it, somehow to leave law and obligation behind, somehow to enter the half-world of an individualist subjectivist "freedom" which pretends to know no other norm save "love." In other words, the Gospel invitation, in so far as it is a summons to the moral life, is not a call to construct a "situation ethics" that knows no general principles of moral living but only particular instances of moral judgment, each one valid only for the instance; and that recognizes no order of moral law that is binding on freedom, but only a freedom that is free and moral singly in so far as it is sheer spontaneity.

Fourth, the law of nature, which prescribes humanity, still exists at the interior of the Gospel invitation, which summons to perfection. What the follower of Christ chooses to perfect is, and can only be, a humanity. And the lines of human perfection are already laid down in the structure of man's nature. Where else could they be found? The Christian call is to transcend nature, notably to transcend what is noblest in nature, the faculty of reason. But it is not a call to escape from nature, or to dismantle nature's own structure, and least of all to deny that man is intelligent, that nature is intelligible, and that nature's intelligibilities are laws for the mind that grasps them. In so far as they touch the moral life, the energies of grace, which are the action of the Holy Spirit, quicken to new and fuller life the dynamisms of nature, which are resident in reason. Were it otherwise, grace would not be supernatural but only miraculous.

I list these misunderstandings of natural law only to make the point that those who dislike the doctrine, for one reason or another, seem forever to be at work, as it were, burying the wrong corpse. For my part, I would not at all mind standing with them, tearless, at the grave of any of the shallow and distorted theories that they mistake for the doctrine of natural law. The same point will come clearer from a bit of history. At about the turn of the century it was rather generally believed in professional circles that the Scholastic idea of natural law, as an operative concept in the fields of ethics, political theory, and law and jurisprudence, was dead. In other words, it was generally assumed that the great nineteenth-century attack on natural law had been successful.

In this respect, of course, the nineteenth century exhibited those extensive powers of learned misunderstanding which it possessed to an astonishing degree. In its extraordinary ignorance of philosophical and legal history, it supposed that the "law of nature" of the Age of the Enlightenment was the *ius naturale* of an earlier and in many ways more enlightened age. It supposed therefore that in doing away with the former, it had likewise done away with the latter. This was by no means the case. The theory of the "law of nature" that was the creature of the Enlightenment was as fragile, time-conditioned, and transitory a phenomenon as the Enlightenment itself. But the ancient idea of the natural law is as inherently perennial as the *philosophia perennis* of which it is an integral part. Its reappearance after its widely attended funeral is one of the interesting intellectual phenomena of our generation.

Admittedly, the phenomenon is not yet as plain as the old hill of Houth; but it is discernible. In 1902, when Sir John Salmond published his well-known book, *Jurisprudence*, he wrote: "The idea of a law of nature or moral law (*lex naturalis, lex naturae*) . . . has played a notable part in the history of human thought in the realm of ethics, theology, politics and jurisprudence. It was long the accepted tradition of those sciences, but it has now fallen on evil days, and it can no longer be accepted as in harmony with modern thought on those matters." However, when Parker

edited the ninth edition in 1927 he was impelled to add the cautious footnote: "Sir John Salmond's view that the doctrine in all its forms is now
discredited cannot be considered correct." Today, thirty years later, when
modern thought has caught up a bit more with the past, one might perhaps transcend the timidity of this footnote. As a matter of fact, it would
seem that the ancient tradition of natural law is beginning to climb out
of the footnotes of the learned books into the very text of our time, as the
conviction dawns that there are resources in the idea that might possibly
make the next page of the text sound less like a tale told by an idiot.

Here then might be an approach to the whole subject of natural law. It
would be a historical approach, on the theme indicated by Heinrich Rommen in the title of his book, *Die ewige Wiederkehr des Naturrechts*. The idea
would be to describe, first, the origins and political significance of the Western tradition of natural law; secondly, the supplanting of this tradition by a
newly conceived "law of nature" that had its greatest intellectual popularity
in the Age of the Enlightenment and its highest political success in the Era
of Revolution; thirdly, the reaction against this law of nature, that resulted
in the victory of juridical positivism (the triumph of the idea that "law is
will" over the ancient idea that "law is reason"), behind whose success lay
all the forces that came to power in the nineteenth century—scientific empiricism, sociologism, psychologism, historical and philosophical materialism; fourthly, today's reaction against the positivist theory, as the ideas of justice and of human rights have had a rebirth in the face of the problems
raised by totalitarian government and by the multiple aspects of the social
conflict and the international conflict. It is this reaction, which is in fact a
progress, that has effected the latest *Wiederkehr* of the idea of natural law.

Another approach to the problem of natural law is possible—a more directly philosophical approach. The idea of natural law goes back to the
remotest origins, not only of political thought, but of ethical thought—to
the day when man first began to reflect on the problem, whether there be
something that intrinsically distinguishes right from wrong, whether what
is right ought to be, and (on the political plane) whether laws ought to be
just, and whether what is just ought to be law. These problems raise the
basic ethical question, whether there is a connection between "being" and
"oughtness," whether the moral order is a reflex and prolongation of a
metaphysical order. In consequence, they bring man to the heart of philosophy itself. In fact, every system of natural law, whether it be Aristotle's

or St. Thomas's or Locke's or Pufendorf's, has its premises; it supposes an epistemology, and therefore a metaphysic (or the absence of one). On the other hand, every system of natural law has its conclusions; it issues in a political philosophy—a concept of the nature of the state, its end, scope, and functions. Consequently, to inquire what natural law is, means to inquire, on the one hand, what the human mind is and what it can know, and on the other hand, what human society is and to what ends it should work. But, as is obvious, all this is to inquire what man himself is—what this human "nature" is of which one predicates a law "natural."

Both of these approaches to the problem of natural law are evidently much too ambitious for the present purpose; I mention them only to suggest the architecture of the problem. Here I shall offer simply a comment on a conclusion suggested to the mind as it contemplates, in the light of contemporary problems, the two interpretations of the natural law that have historically put themselves forward as the basis of political philosophy. I mean the "law of nature" of the Enlightenment and the "natural law" of the *philosophia perennis*, whose origins go back to Heraclitus and to the greatest of Greek philosophers and Roman jurists, and whose developed expression is found in St. Thomas Aquinas and the later Scholastics. My suggestion is that the eighteenth-century "law of nature" (so I shall consistently call it, to distinguish it from the older "natural law") was indeed a potently revolutionary force in its own day, because of the nature of the problems of that day; today, however, its dynamism has run out, and its impotence in the face of the different problems that confront us is demonstrable.

"Today," Mr. John Bowle has suggested, "the tremendous initiative, the sprawling enterprise, of the nineteenth century may well be changing to an age of order, of consolidation."[1] Today, as perverted social patterns are attempting to impose themselves on human life, to the destruction of human freedom, our problem in the West is ourselves to create a new social pattern—a pattern of freedom, that will be truly a pattern, but that will leave to freedom all its necessary energizing dynamism. Our problem is not simply to safeguard "human rights," in the sense of fortifying each discrete individual in the possession of a heterogeneous collection of social empowerments; it is rather to erect, and secure against all assault, an *ordo juris*, an order of law that will be in consequence an order of rights and hence by definition an order of freedom. If this is so, as I think it is, the new "age of order," of just law and true freedom, must look to natural law as its basic inspiration.

The Law of Nature

Everybody knows that in the eighteenth century the "law of nature" and the "law of reason" were phrases to conjure with. With his usual engaging cynicism, that in this case does not veil the truth, the late Carl L. Becker described the phenomenon and the climate of opinion, set by Cartesian philosophy and Newtonian physics, that made it possible. To justify what one considered desirable, socially or personally, one appealed in those days to the "law of nature," as today one appeals to "democracy," always with fervor, if not always with good sense. This was true not only in France of the *philosophes*, but to a lesser degree even in America. Mr. Carl Van Doren in *The Great Rehearsal* recounts how one disturbed New Englander objected to the two-year senatorial term proposed by the Constitutional Convention, on the ground that a one-year term was a "dictate of the law of nature"; spring comes once a year, and so should a batch of new Senators.

If it is difficult for us today to share this enthusiasm for the law of nature, it is still more difficult for us to grasp the pivotal concept on which the seventeenth- and eighteenth-century theory of the law of nature depended—the concept of the "state of nature." Yet this was a concept that had all the power of a myth. It found its literary immortalizations, familiar to us all, in Defoe's *Robinson Crusoe* (1719) and Rousseau's *Émile* (1762). And its prominence in the philosophical and political literature of the time is a well-known fact.

This "state of nature" was a purely imaginary construct possible only to the eighteenth-century reason; it was an imaginary state that was nevertheless supposed theoretically to have existed. It depicted what man was and how he lived antecedently to the formation of all human communities and to the establishment of all the laws and customs of social life. The value of the concept was functional. It was a methodological postulate, an abstraction posited as the starting point for a theory of the law of nature; for in the state of nature man was ruled only by the law of nature, and consequently in this state the law of nature could be discovered in all its abstract purity. The further function of the state of nature was to explain, in conjunction with the theory of the social contract, the genesis of political society, its form, and the relative rights of government and citizen.

The state of nature was, of course, a purely formal concept; one could fill it with whatever content one wished, make it pregnant of whatever political consequences one fancied. Here, however, we may confine ourselves simply to the theory of John Locke; it had the greatest fortune both in the Anglo-Saxon and in the French political world. In Locke's system, the state of nature had the initial essential function of establishing the inalienability of the rights of man, as Locke conceived them. In the state of nature, man appears with complete suddenness as a full-grown individual, a hard little atom in the midst of atoms equally hard, all solitary and self-enclosed, each a sociological monad. The idea of man, therefore, is that of an individual who is "absolute lord of his own person and possessions, equal to the greatest and subject to nobody," as he says in his *Second Essay*. In this absolute lordship, equality, and independence consists the Lockean idea of man's "freedom," a freedom that is natural and therefore inalienable save within the limits of his own free choice. On this free individual rests a single law—the law of nature—with a single precept, that of self-preservation, the preservation of his own life, liberty, and property. This law has only one limitation—the same law as obligatory also on other individuals, who in their equally sovereign independence are likewise bound to preserve themselves. Beyond this duty of self-preservation, but subject to its primal exigencies, the individual has one further duty: "Every one, as he is bound to preserve himself, and not to quit his station willfully, so by the like reason, when his own preservation comes not in competition, ought he as much as he can to preserve the rest of mankind."

This is the Lockean state of nature and law of nature. On it is based, by a process of pure postulation, the inalienability of the rights of the individual to life, liberty, and property, and the limitation of these rights solely by the equal rights of other individuals. The chief difficulty about this state of nature is, of course (as Locke naively admits), the obvious fact that it is "not to be endured." With the optimism characteristic of his age and the inconsistency characteristic of himself, Locke prattles a bit about the "innocent delights" attendant on the "liberty" of the state of nature. But it is difficult to see how a state could be delightful wherein every individual is a sort of little god almighty, whose power to preserve himself is checked only at the point where another little god almighty starts preserving *himself*. At this point, one is more sympathetic with the ruthless logic of Thomas Hobbes, who says forthrightly in his *Leviathan*

that the state of nature is a "condition which we call Warre," and that the
life of the omnipotent monads, among whom prevails the single law of
the right of all to all things, is "solitary, poore, nasty, brutish and short."
The first impulse of the law of nature, which is that of self-preservation,
is, says Hobbes, that of "getting themselves out of the miserable condition
of Warre." Locke puts it more politely: "Thus mankind, notwithstanding
all the privileges of the state of Nature, being but in an ill condition while
they remain in it, are quickly driven into society."

But how does one get these "absolute lords" into society, under government, subject to limitations on their natural omnipotence? Only by
their own free act: "Men being, as has been said, by nature all free, equal,
and independent, no one can be put out of this estate and subjected to
the political power of another without his own consent." Society is not
the product of nature but of artifice. It comes into being by the social
contract, by the act of men "agreeing together mutually to enter into one
community and make one body politic." Thus Locke establishes his second principle on the same grounds as the first: as the rights of man are
inalienable, because man is by nature an omnipotent sociological
monad, so for the same reason government must be by the consent of the
governed.

Moreover, the motive of the consent, as of the "drive" that gets men
into society, is self-interest, self-preservation, and particularly the preservation of what was very dear to Locke's middle-class heart, the preservation of property: "The great and chief end, therefore, of men uniting into
commonwealths and putting themselves under government, is the preservation of their property, to which in the state of nature there are many
things wanting." Society, paradoxically, is the product of egoism. It is an
artificial contrivance to rescue the ego by restraining somewhat its egoism. The essence of social man, as of individual man, is selfishness. Finally, pursuing the same line of thought, Locke comes to his third principle, the limitation of governmental power by the "common good." This
common good consists merely in the security of each individual in the
possession of his property. That is the end of social life as of individual
life; the social end differs from the individual end only quantitatively.

This, briefly, is Locke's theory of the law of nature, as embracing a theory of natural rights and their inalienability, of the origins of political society, and of the functions and limitations of governmental power—all

based, as is clear, on an idea of man. The three characteristics of the system are obvious—its rationalism, individualism, nominalism. The law of nature, the rights of man, and the origins of society are not derived from what is "real," from the concrete totality of man's nature as it really is. They are deduced from an abstraction, a fictitious state of nature, a disembodied idea of man that is put forward as "rational" and by that sole title real, whereas it was in effect but a reflex of the socio-philosophical individualism of a superficial age.

This individualism, this atomistic social outlook, is the predominant characteristic of Locke's system. His law of nature is solely a law of individual nature, conceived after the abstract fashion of the rationalist. The premise of Locke's state of nature is a denial that sociality is inherent in the very nature of man, and the assertion that the civil state is adventitious, that man is by nature only a solitary atom, who does not seek in society the necessary condition of his natural perfectibility as man, but only a utilitarian convenience for the fuller protection of his individual self in its individuality. Bentham's utilitarianism is, in fact, but the logical prolongation of Locke's thought. Locke's individualism completely deprives society of any organic character. Society is not organized in ascending forms of sociality that are made necessary by, and radicated in, nature itself, beginning with the family, through the occupational group, and culminating in the "perfect society," the political community as such, the *respublica*.

In Locke's theory all forms of sociality are purely contractual; they have no deeper basis in the nature of man than a shallow "reason" that judges them useful. (Even the church he will allow to be no more than a voluntary association of like-minded people—a concept congenial indeed to a certain wing of Protestantism, but one that an increasing number of Protestants today are finding it difficult to live with.) Against this evacuation of all reality from the notion of society and "social being" the Romantic movement, with its love of the "organic," was a reaction, that in time carried the world to the excesses of the totalitarianisms of race and class.

In England, of course, Locke's individualistic law of nature never had its logical social consequences. There were too many elements of the more human medieval tradition deposited in English institutions, and above all in the English common law, for the inherent consequence of Locke's theory to work itself out; I mean the dissolution of the organic character of the total political relationship and its reduction to the harsh antithesis, individual *versus* state, together with the connected idea of the juridical omnipotence of the state. However, the French enthusiasts who took up his ideas had none of the inhibitions imposed on him by his British common sense, caution, and feeling for tradition. In consequence, his law of nature, when it had passed through their politically irresponsible "reason," results in the complete social atomism of the Constitution of 1791 and the Declaration of the Rights of Man and Citizen. There it appears that there are only two "sovereignties": that of the individual over his private life and that of the state over all forms of social life. There are no autonomous social forms intermediate between the individual and the state. Not only are the traditional *états* dissolved, but it is decreed that: "There are no longer *iurandes*, nor corporations of professions, arts and crafts, nor any private humanitarian associations or private schools." (The famous *loi Chapelier* of 1793 carried this atomism to its ultimate absurdity, that produced a reaction; not even the conquering "reason" of the *philosophes* could convince a lot of sensible, provincial Frenchmen that they had only two loyalties—one to themselves as individuals and the other to the state.)

Finally, the individualism of Locke's law of nature results in a complete evacuation of the notion of the "rights" of man. It is quite evident that Locke's state of nature reveals no *ordo juris*, and no rights in any recognizably moral sense. There is simply a pattern of power relationships—the absolute lordship of one individual balanced against the equally absolute lordship of others. Significantly, Locke uses the word "power" more frequently than the word "right" in describing the state of nature. Moreover, what the social contract does, in effect, is simply to transfer this system of power relationships into the civil state, with the sole but significant difference that there is now added to it a "third power," the public power of government. In the naked essence of Locke's thought, government is the arbiter of "right," only in the sense that it is a power to check power. And its use is "right" when behind it is the consent of the community, that is, the consent of the majority, that is, again (in Locke's explanation of majority rule), "the greater force," in which is embodied "the power of the whole."

Again, Locke did not draw all the implications from his theory, but the French did. There was Montesquieu, for instance, with his doctrinaire theory that only power checks power, and that when the checks are adequate the mechanical resultant is freedom (unless, one is inclined to add, it be the situation in which the French to this day seem to delight—the paralysis of power and consequent chaos). Moreover, there was the fourth article of the Declaration of the Rights of Man, wherein the logic of Locke's theory runs out in the statement that the "limits" of individual rights "can be determined only by law," that is, by positive law. Here is the explicit denial of any *ordo juris* antecedent to the state; here is the seed of legal positivism, and the essence of Rousseau's omnipotent democracy, wherein there is complete identification of state and national community, and the consequent subjection of all forms of community life to total state control. The logical outcome of Locke's individualistic law of nature, in its French transcription, was the juridical monism of the successive French Republics. In consequence of the false antithesis, individual *versus* state, all self-governing intermediary social forms with particular ends are destroyed, in order to create "free and equal citizens," who are subject only to one law, the positive law of the state, the exclusively competent lawmaker. There is no longer any pluralism of social institutions existent and self-directing by natural or positive divine right (e.g., workers' unions or the Church), antecedent to, or above the state. There is only the monistic unity of the political order, under a legislative that is juridically omnipotent, the source and origin of all right. And to enforce this political unity, by destruction of all possibly competing allegiances, there was a state-fostered political mysticism—the "civil religion" of Rousseau, which was indeed no kind of religion but simply a means to homogeneity in the state. (I have already pointed out in a previous chapter that it was against this type of liberalist individualism—as positing a social and juridical monism and a concept of the juridical omnipotence of the state, both based on the concept of the absolute autonomy of the individual human reason—that the Catholic Church directed her uncompromising attacks during the nineteenth century, under appeal to the traditional natural law.)

The third characteristic of Locke's system of natural law is its nominalism. Since he was on the one hand an empiricist in epistemology (who denied the power of intelligence to reach anything beyond the individual singular thing), and since on the other hand he wished to talk as a philosopher (using the traditional terms—man, nature, law, right, authority, society, state, etc.), Locke could not be anything but that most decadent of all philosophical things, a nominalist. All these terms to him are mere *flatus vocis*, symbols to which corresponds no metaphysical reality. For instance, society as such, or man as *ens sociale*, signifies nothing real; the terms are symbols indicating a certain amount of material utility that the individual derives from contractual forms of association with other individuals. Similarly, the law of nature is but a nominalist symbol for a collection of particular empowerments considered desirable for the preservation of "property" in the wide Lockean sense. Or again, the "common good" is nothing real in itself, a social good qualitatively distinct from individual goods, but simply a symbol for the quantitative sum of individual goods. Finally, "right" is not a term relating to a moral order deriving from the essences of things; it is simply a symbol flourished to assure the free functioning of self-interest. In the rarefied mental climate of the *philosophes*, as well as in the muzzy mysticism of Rousseau, this purely symbolic value of the phrase, "the rights of man," as a potent form of political incantation, is still more marked.

The Law of Nature as a Political Instrument

What then does one say about this individualistic law of nature in Locke's statement, and the French restatement, of it? What one says depends on whether one regards it as a piece of philosophy or as a political weapon. As a piece of philosophy—that is, as ultimately resting on an idea of man and human society—it hardly needs refutation today. As a matter of fact, the refutation of the system was supplied before the system itself was born; Aristotle himself suggested its substance, even apart from the development of Aristotelian epistemology, ethics, and political philosophy in the Scholastic tradition. However, one need not appeal to thinkers antecedent to Locke; those subsequent to him will do. Darwin, Freud, and Marx are sufficiently his judges in what concerns the pillars of his system. The genuine and true insights that lie at the root of these three latterly proposed systems have destroyed completely the Lockean idea of man, of the state of nature, and of civil society; this, notwithstanding the fact that these true insights are so denatured by their incorporation into falsely monistic systems that in their own context they are themselves false.

Darwin and the principle of continuity in nature dealt a mortal blow to the atomism of post-Reformation anthropology, with its theory of discrete individuals who "happen" suddenly and live "unattached" save in so far as with sovereign freedom they attach themselves. In evolutionary theory, man is solidary, by all that is material in him, with all life. Purified of monistic connotations, the notion is compatible with a central thesis of Christian anthropology, that asserts the law of solidarity for both flesh and spirit; but it is not compatible with Lockean individualism. Again, when Freud fulfilled his promise, "Acheronta movebo," he shattered forever the "angel-mindedness" of the Cartesian man, and the brittle rationalistic optimism founded on it with the aid of eighteenth-century mechanism, which supposed that there were "laws of reason" in human affairs that needed only to be discovered to be acted upon, and likewise (with Rousseau) supposed that all men would, as has been said, cease to be evil, if only no one tried to compel them to be good. Finally, the Marxist intuition of the reality of the "collective" and its organic character, of the importance of material factors in society, and of the conditions of heteronomy and loss of freedom produced by the individualism of capitalist society, effectively disposed of the empty nominalism and false idealism of the "law of nature" concept of human community based solely on the social contract struck between "absolute lords."

In this day and age, therefore, one need not take with any philosophical seriousness Locke's account of human nature, or his individualistic law of nature, or his simplistic theory of the origins of society; these are all as "dated" as the clothes Locke himself wore. The same remark goes for Rousseau. How "dated" he, and the Declaration of the Rights of Man and Citizen inspired by him, actually are, may be seen, for instance, by a glance at the Italian Constitution of 1948, into whose making went the four currents of the contemporary world—the Christian Democratic, the Liberal (of the Mazzinian tradition), the Socialist, and the Communist. The Second Article will illustrate the difference of spirit: "The Republic recognizes and guarantees the inviolable rights of man, both as an individual and in the social formations in which his personality unfolds itself, and calls for the fulfillment of the duties of political, economic and social solidarity." Neither Locke nor Rousseau could have written that.

At all events, Locke's law of nature did not owe its undeniable success to its philosophical shallowness (though in a philosophically shallow age that was no disadvantage). Its philosophical weakness vanished before its strength as a political weapon in the performance of the political task that at the moment needed to be done. At bottom, the focus of Locke's thought was narrow and practical. He was not searching for a generalized theory that would make society right, but simply for a theory that would make it right for England to have resisted an autocratic king—to have cut off his head (Charles I) or at least dethroned him (James II). He wrote, as he admitted, to justify the "Glorious Revolution" of 1688, and to settle William of Orange on a throne to which his theoretical title was highly dubious. Besides this particular political aim, he had other preoccupations of a practical order that appealed to common sense. He wrote at a time when the common sense of England was weary of the socially sterile enthusiasms of the Civil Wars; when the business community of England stood looking into the long horizons of commercial prosperity opened by colonial expansion and the development of foreign trade; when mercantile influence on government in the interests of property and freedom for commercial enterprise was on the rise; when economic advantage rather than dynastic or religious rivalries was becoming the moving force in the international field. Consequently, Locke was interested in seeing government influenced by the propertied class through the principle of representation; he wanted government by the consent of the landowners and merchants (this, in effect, is what Locke's "consent of the governed" meant). He was further interested in advancing the concept that government's sole function is the guaranteeing of individual liberty (i.e., property, and the freedom to increase it). In a word, his problem was to devise a law of nature that would support a political theory that would in turn support a businessman's commonwealth, a society dominated by bourgeois political influence through the medium of the "watch dog" State whose functions would be reduced to a minimum, especially in the fields of business and trade.

As an instrument for these particular political and politico-economic aims, his theory of the individualistic law of nature was admirably adapted, whatever its philosophical shortcomings. With the last of the Stuarts gone, and a new world opening up, the time was ripe for a new kind of polity; and since Locke was not its prophet but its apologist, he had honor in his own country. Whether his law of nature made philosophical sense or not, the ordinary English property owner did not trouble to ask; it delivered the goods demanded at the moment, and that was enough. I should add, too, that Locke delivered the goods—helped to create a stable and vigorous political community—largely because he restated, and did not quite succeed in denaturing, the great political truths that were the medieval heritage, but that had been obscured in the era of absolutism and the divine right of kings (which, as Kern has pointed out, was not a development but a denial of medieval ideas).

Against the principle of absolutism—the assertion of the irresponsibility of the king and the unlimited scope of his power—Locke asserted (in debased form) the central medieval tradition of the supremacy of law over government, and of government by law which is reason, not will. Against the central point of divine-right theory—that the monarch's right to rule is inalienable and independent of human agency—he asserted (on philosophically indefensible grounds) the medieval principle that sovereignty is "translated" from the people to the ruler, who is responsible to the people in its exercise and holds title to it only as long as he serves their common good. Finally, against absolute centralization of power in the monarch, he asserted (again on false premises) the medieval doctrine of the right of the people to participate in government. In other words, though Locke knew only an artificial law of nature, he asserted in effect the fundamental positions of the natural-law philosophy of the state that had been the creation of greater minds than his, operating at the center of a tradition to whose periphery he himself had moved. These truths, that were not of Locke's own devising, furnished the essential dynamism of his system. Their truth stood up, in spite of Locke's failure to understand and demonstrate it; and this truth gave them their impact on the political conscience of the time. Not even Locke's narrow individualism, his thin rationalism, and his empty nominalism could quite veil their absolute validity as imperatives of a human reason that has a greater and more universal power than was dreamt of in Locke's philosophy.

Locke had great honor also in France. The success of his theory of the law of nature, put into more doctrinaire form by French theorists, might be explained on similar lines. It was congenial to the individualistic and rationalistic mentality of that extraordinarily small group of men whose ideas succeeded in turning France upside down. They were not concerned, as Locke was, with justifying a revolution, but with making one. And they made it in the name of the law of nature. The prime value of the idea lay in its power of destruction. What these men, for a variety of reasons, wanted to do was to destroy the rigid, clumsy, anachronistic, crippling absolutism of the *ancien régime*. What they needed to lay hands on in the first instance was a corrosive, not a constructive, force. And they found it in the theory of the "rights of man," based on the individualistic law of nature.

There is no need here to go into the history of the lengthy, complicated, very bloody revolution that strove to incorporate this theory into political institutions. What I want to note is that the revolution was professedly political. It has been remarked that the political essence of the revolution was in the decision of the Third Estate on June 17, 1789, to set about the making of a constitution quite by itself, apart from the nobles and clergy, and in the subsequent resolution of the Estates General into the National Assembly. This was a political decision—the assumption by "the people" of their right to govern themselves. The problem of the moment was essentially political. And the temper of the times was largely that voiced by Rousseau when he said in his *Confessions*, describing the inspiration of his *Social Contract*: "I had come to see that in the last resort everything depends on politics, and that whatever men may do, no nation will ever be anything but what the nature of its Government may make it." The principle, like most things at the time, is on its head; its reverse is more certainly correct. However, it was the revolutionary principle. And it was allied with the further principle that government will necessarily be good, if "the people" run it; for "the people," according to Rousseau, are themselves necessarily good; it is only bad government that makes them bad. If then the "general will" of the people makes the laws, the laws will be right, because the sovereign people is always right.

Thus spake the *Éclaircissement*—as usual, mixing truth with nonsense. And also as usual, the truth derives from the Western political tradition of natural law; the nonsense, from the eighteenth-century philosophoumenon, the law of nature. The agglomeration of both (obviously, along with other causes) made the Revolution. But it was powerful enough to do so (and this is my point) for the reason that the Revolution to be made was political. The determination that existed was that of bringing to an end an era and an order of political privilege (or, in America, that of preventing the rise of such an order). The principle embedded in the political philosophy of St. Thomas Aquinas was having a rebirth under the pressure of arbitrary power on the conscience of the people: "In regard of the good ordering of rulers in a city or nation . . . the first thing [to be observed] is that all should have some share in the government. . . ." And the validity of the reason he gives, on the authority of Aristotle, was again being confirmed: "for in this way the peace of the people is preserved, and all love and cherish such an order, as it is said in the Second Book of the *Politics*" (*Summa Theologia*, I-II, q. 105, a. 1). Locke and Rousseau, in whose angular rationalistic thought there was little room for experience and psychology as sources of political philosophy, were, in fact, carried to popularity by a psychological drive of discontent born of harsh experience. In such times of discontent with the fundamental structures of society, as Laski has pointed out, the gospel of human rights always has a resurgence.

The eighteenth-century gospel, based on the individualistic law of nature, could not at the time fail to be popular. For the primary drive then was toward destruction, and the law of nature concept of human rights was an appropriate dynamism of destruction, precisely because of the philosophical nonsense it enshrined. I mean that its individualistic rationalistic nominalism, precisely because it disregarded the organic character of society, and precisely because its concept of "progress" entailed a complete denial of the past and of the continuity of human effort, was an effective solvent of the corporate institutional structure of society as it then was. It could not (in France, at least) initiate simply a movement of reform; it could only operate as an engine of destruction. In the same way, its rationalistic secularism was effective against the usurping theory of divine right on which sovereignty at the time was based. And its mobilization of the "power of the people," under the nominalist slogan of the "rights of man," was an effective counterpoise to the unendurable centralization of power in king and nobles. This theory, therefore, could ride against the evils of the time with all the force, not only of truth but of error itself. Its theoretic dogmas were, as theories, false; but, as dogmas, powerful. Its exclusive attention to the problem of politics, and its attempt to solve it by violently creating an artificial "equality of citizens" (free, supposedly, as men, because equal as citizens), could end, as it did, only in dictatorship. But at least it could accomplish the social ruin that made dictatorship inevitable. And for the moment, a work of ruin was the immediate objective; for anger was abroad as well as reason, and it was not averse to using "reason" as its instrument.

On the other hand, the theory of natural rights, based on a law of nature, had also a measure of constructive dynamism—this time, not by reason of the philosophical nonsense involved in its theoretical scaffolding, but by reason of the intuition of truth that even the scaffolding could not wholly obscure. By nature all men are, as Bergbohm despairingly said, natural-law jurists. Intuitively they reach the essential imperatives of their own nature and know them to be unthwartably imperative—however much they may subsequently deform them, and destroy their proper bases, by uninformed or prejudiced reflective thought. And just as all men by nature—by the native power of moral intelligence—know that there is a difference between the *iustum naturale* and the *iustum legale* (the one based on natural law, the other on positive law), so, too, they naturally "see" the natural-law truth that "sovereignty is from the people," however much they may then go on falsely to conceptualize this truth. Usually the suffering of injustice is needed to bring the vision, just as immunity from suffering may obscure it. It is, as Pascal said, "the passions that make us think." And in those days the theory of divine right, together with the oppressive weight of the remnants of the feudal system, generated enough passion to make men think—furiously. In their fury, they thought of the truth anciently deposited in the *lex regia* of Justinian's *Institutes*, and elaborated by the Christian intelligence since the eleventh century.

Being men of the eighteenth century, whose intelligences were by this time very superficially Christian, they did not see this truth in its proper setting, the natural law. But they at least dimly glimpsed it: "Sovereignty is from the people; therefore they are not to be ruled save by their consent, and for their common good, by a power subject to law, whose end is justice, which is an order of right." They did not, I say, know that they were looking at natural law; for the law of nature had shut off natural law from their vision. But it was, for all that, natural law that swam before them; and this obscure intuition furnished whatever positive, constructive dynamism there was behind their revolutionary, destructive efforts. So they set about their work of political liberation—the work of incorporating the doctrine of consent into the structures of government, of creating channels of consent, of establishing political institutions whereby the natural-law right of popular participation in government might be made effective. In a word, they brought into almost exclusive focus the problems of representation and suffrage, as the necessary expression of the doctrine of popular sovereignty, which was at the heart of the "principles of '89." Their dominant concern was with the external form of government.

To make a long story short, let it be said that this movement for political liberty through political equality expressed in the equal right of franchise ultimately succeeded; by the last decade of the nineteenth century "the people" were furnished with their political weapon in all the major countries of Western Europe. This was a great fundamental success indeed, though it is highly improbable that much of it was due to the law-of-nature concept of natural rights that was the theoretical justification of the original political explosion. At all events, by the end of the nineteenth century Rousseau's man, the individual atom, who had been born free and was everywhere in chains, had supposedly struck off his chains with the hammer of natural rights, based on the law of nature. The only remaining difficulty was that the unfortunate fellow found himself still in chains. And by a curious paradox, the new chains were forged by the very doctrine that was supposed to free him. The doctrine of natural rights that in the eighteenth century was the dynamism destructive of political privilege became in the nineteenth century the dynamism constructive of economic privilege. It was the bulwark of Manchesterism and the *laissez-faire* state.

No one need have been surprised at this who understood the empty nominalism of the doctrine. Its inherent ambivalence and susceptibility of opposite consequences had already been manifested. In Locke the state of nature and the individualistic law of nature had been so interpreted as to yield moderately liberalist consequences. But with Hobbes its consequences had been rigorously statist; it had been the justification of the royal absolutism of the Stuarts. The "omnipotent democracy" which Rousseau drew from the doctrine became, with Hegel, a statism that Rousseau would have repudiated. And the individualistic law of nature as evolved by Pufendorf and Thomasius was used to justify the "enlightened despotism" of the Prussian Fredericks and of the Austrian Emperor Joseph II. The law of nature was, in effect, a veritable Pandora's box. There seemed to be a great hope at the bottom of it, but on its opening many winged evils took their flight across the face of Europe.

If one were, in fine, to sum up its political significance, one would have to say, I think, that it was able to destroy an order of political privilege and inaugurate an era of political equality; but it was not able to erect an order of social justice or inaugurate an order of human freedom. The testimony to the fact is the contemporary protest, in the name of "human rights," against the order (if one can call it an order) which is our heritage from the law of nature of the eighteenth and nineteenth centuries. The characteristics of the law of nature—its rationalism, individualism, and nominalism—made it an effective force for dissolution in its time; but today we are not looking for forces of dissolution, but for constructive forces. Similarly, its power as a solvent made it a force for liberty, in the thin and bloodless, individualist and negative nineteenth-century concept of liberty; but today we are looking for liberation and liberty in something better than this purely formal sense. We want liberty with a positive content within an order of liberty of rational design. Rousseau's "man everywhere in chains" is still too largely a fact. Our problem is still that of human freedom, or, in juridical terms, human rights. It is a problem of the definition of freedom, and then, more importantly, its institutionalization.

But the statement of the problem that we have in common with Locke and with the men of Paris and Philadelphia in 1789 has greatly changed. It is now seen to have a social dimension that no longer permits its statement in the old individualistic terms. Its multiple factors are now grasped with a realism that will not suffer its solution in the old nominalistic categories. And its background now has a new depth that the old one-dimensional, rationalistic thought never penetrated. The background is an idea of man in his nature, history, and psychology, that transcends the limited horizons of the rationalist mind. Finally, the growing conviction as to the ultimate impotence of the old attempts to solve the problem of human liberty and social order in purely secularistic, positivist terms had created a new openness to the world of metaphysical and religious values. If these alterations in the statement of the problem of freedom and human rights have in fact come about, as I think they have, they will explain the contemporary *Wiederkehr* of the ancient natural law of the Greek, Roman, and Christian traditions. Only the old idea is adequate in the face of the new problem. It alone affords the dynamic basis from which to attack the problem of freedom as posited in the "age of order" on whose threshold we stand. And it is such a basis because it is metaphysical in its foundations, because it is asserted within a religious framework, and because it is realist (not nominalist), societal (not individualist), and integrally human (not rationalist) in its outlook on man and society. In other words, the structure of the old idea of natural law follows exactly the structure of the new problem of human liberty.

Natural Law in the New Age

This is the point to which I have been coming. However, I have been so long in coming to it that there is now no time or space to develop it! I shall have to be content with some brief comments on the vital resources inherent in the idea of natural law, that indicate its new validity.

First in importance is its metaphysical character, its secure anchorage in the order of reality—the ultimate order of beings and purposes. As a metaphysical idea, the idea of natural law is timeless, and for that reason timely; for what is timeless is always timely. But it has an added timeliness. An age of order is by definition a time for metaphysical decisions. They are being made all round us. No one escapes making them; one merely escapes making this one rather than that one. Our decisions, unlike those of the eighteenth century, cannot be purely political, because our reflection on the bases of society and the problem of its freedom and its order must be much more profound. And this in turn is so because these problems stand revealed to us in their depths; one cannot any longer, like John Locke, be superficial about them. Our reflection, therefore, on the problem of freedom, human rights, and political order must inevitably carry us to a metaphysical decision in regard of the nature of man. Just as we now know that the written letter of a Bill of Rights is of little value unless there exist the institutional means whereby these rights may have, and be guaranteed, their expression in social action, so also we know—or ought to know—that it is not enough for us to be able to concoct the written letter unless we are likewise able to justify, in terms of ultimates in our own thinking about the nature of man, our assertion that the rights we list are indeed rights and therefore inviolable, and human rights and therefore inalienable. Otherwise we are writing on sand in a time of hurricanes and floods.

There are perhaps four such ultimate decisions open to our making, and each carries with it the acceptance of certain political consequences.

First, one could elect to abide by the old Liberal individualism. At bottom then one would be saying that "natural rights" are simply individual material interests (be they of individuals or social groups or nations), so furnished with an armature by positive law as to be enforceable by the power of government. In this view one would be consenting to a basically atomist concept of society, to its organization in terms of power relationships, to a concept of the state as simply an apparatus of compulsion without the moral function of realizing an order of justice; for in this view there is no order of justice antecedent to positive law or contractual agreements. In a word, one would be accepting yesterday's national and international status quo; for one would be accepting its principles.

Secondly, by an extreme reaction from individualistic Liberalism, wherein the individual as an individual is the sole bearer of rights, one could choose the Marxist concept of human rights as based solely on social function, economic productivity. One would then be saying that all rights are vested in the state, which is the sole determinant of social function. It is the state that is free, and the individual is called simply to share its freedom by pursuing its purposes, which are determined by the laws of dialectical materialism. In this view one would be consenting to the complete socialization of man (his mind and will, as well as his work), within the totalitarian state, all his energies being requisitioned for the realization of a pseudo-order of "justice," which is the triumph of collective man over nature in a classless society that will know no "exploitation of man by man." In this view, as in the foregoing one, one accepts as the ultimate reality the material fact of power—in one case the power of the individual, in the other the power of the collectivity. One bases society and the state on a metaphysic of force (if the phrase be not contradictory).

A third decision, that somehow attempts a mediation between these extreme views, is soliciting adherents today; I mean the theory that its protagonists call "modern evolutionary scientific humanism," but that I shall call "the new rationalism."

It is a rationalism, because its premise is the autonomy of man, who transcends the rest of nature and is transcended by nothing and nobody (at least nothing and nobody knowable). It is new, because (unlike the old rationalism) it maintains (with Spinoza, whom Bowle has pointed to as one of its earliest forerunners) that man is something more than reason. It identifies natural law (though the term is not frequent with it) with "the drive of the whole personality," the totality of the impulses whereby men strive to "live ever more fully." It is new, too, because it abandons the old rationalist passion for deductive argument and for the construction of total patterns, in favor of the new passion for scientific method and the casting up of provisional and partial hypotheses. Finally, it is new because it does not, like eighteenth-century rationalism, conceive nature and its laws, or the rights of man, as static, given once for all, needing only to be "discovered." It adds to the old rationalistic universe the category of time; it supplements the processes of reason with the processes of history and the consequent experience of change and evolution.

Nature, therefore, is an evolving concept, and its law is emergent. It is also wholly immanent; for the new rationalism, like the old, denies to man, his nature, or its law all transcendental reference. The new rationalistic universe, like the old, is anthropocentric; all human values (reason, justice, charity) are man-made, and in consequence all human "rights," which are the juridical expression of these values, look only to man for their creation, realization, and guarantee. Their ultimate metaphysical justification lies in the fact that they have been seen, by experience, to be the contemporaneously necessary "expression of life itself." And for "life itself" one does not seek a metaphysical justification; it is, when lived in its fullness, self-authenticating. In this system, therefore, the theological concept is "fullness of life." As this is the end for the individual (to be realized as best may be in his stage of the evolutionary process), so, too, it is the end for the state. The *ordo juris* is conceived, after the fashion of the modern schools of sociological jurisprudence or realistic jurisprudence, as a pure instrumentality whereby lawmakers and judges, recognizing the human desires that are seeking realization at a given moment in human society, endeavor to satisfy these desires with a minimum of social friction. The ideals of law or of human rights are "received" from the "wants" of the society of the time and place, and any particular *ordo juris* is throughout its whole texture experimental.

Much could be said further to explain, and then to criticize, this subtle and seductive system, so much a product of the contemporary secularist mentality (its basic premise is, of course, secularism, usually accepted from the surrounding climate, not reached as the term of a metaphysical journey—few secularists have ever purposefully journeyed to secularism). I shall say only two things.

First, the new rationalism is at bottom an ethical relativism pure and simple. Its immanentism, its allegiance to scientific method as the sole criterion of truth, its theory of values as emergent in an evolutionary process, alike forbid it the affirmation of any absolute values (that is, as long as its adherents stay within their own system, which, being men and therefore by intrinsic necessity of reason also natural-law jurists, they frequently do not, but rather go on to talk of right, justice, equity, liberty, rationality, etc., investing these concepts with an absoluteness they could not possibly have within the system). Second as an ethical relativism, the new rationalism is vulnerable to all the criticisms that historically have been advanced against that ancient mode of thought, since the time when Socrates first argued against the Sophists and their dissolution of a knowable objective world of truth and value.

Chiefly, there are two objections. The first is that the new rationalism, like all the old ones, is unreasonable—surely something of a serious objection to a philosophy. "You do not," said Socrates to the Sophists, "know yourselves—your own nature, the nature of your reason." The same ignorance, though in more learned form, recurs in the modern heirs of sophistry. Secondly, the new rationalism, like all the old ones, is ruinous of sound political philosophy. "You are," said Socrates to the Sophists, "the enemies of the *polis*, who undermine its *nomoi*, especially its supreme *nomos*, the idea of justice, for whose realization all laws exist."

This objection, of course, will be vehemently repudiated by the new rationalists. They are fond of putting their system forward as the proper ideological basis of democracy; conversely, they say that democracy is the political expression of their philosophy. Its separation of church and state is the expression of their secular humanism. Its freedom of thought and speech are the reflection of their philosophical and ethical relativism. Its respect for human rights creates the atmosphere in which science may further the evolution of man to higher dignities and fuller life. For my part, however, I should maintain that, by a curious but inevitable paradox, the relativism of the new rationalists must find its native political expression in a new and subtle form of state absolutism. The essential dialectic has already been displayed in history. The absolute autonomy of human reason, postulated by the old rationalism, had as its counterpart the juridical omnipotence of the state. And with accidental variations the dialectic will repeat itself: the autonomy of human reason (the denial of its subjection to a higher law not of its own creation) = relativism in regard of human values = absolution in regard of the value and functions of the state. Admittedly, the new Leviathan would not be on the Hobbesian model, but it would be for all that the "Mortal God." And the outwardly humble garments that it would wear—the forms of political democracy—would hardly hide the fact that it was in effect the *divina maiestas.* It would be a long business to explain the workings of this dialectic; let me state the substance in a brief paragraph.

I take it that the political substance of democracy consists in the admission of an order of rights antecedent to the state, the political form of society. These are the rights of the person, the family, the church, the associations men freely form for economic, cultural, social, and religious ends. In the admission of this prior order of rights—inviolable as well by democratic majorities as by absolute monarchs—consists the most distinctive assertion of the service-character of the democratic state. And this service-character is still further enforced by the affirmation, implicit in the admission of the order of human rights, of another order of right also antecedent to the state and regulative of its public action as a state; I mean the order of justice. In other words, the democratic state serves both the ends of the human person (in itself and in its natural forms of social life) and also the ends of justice. As the servant of these ends, it has only a relative value. Now it is precisely this service-character of the state, its relative value, that tends to be undermined by the theories of the new rationalism—by their inherent logic and by the psychology they generate.

Psychologically, it is not without significance that evolutionary scientific humanism should be the favorite creed of our contemporary social engineers, with their instrumental theories of education, law, and government. And it seems that their inevitable temptation is to hasten the process of evolution by use of the resources of government, just as it is to advance the cause of scientific humanism by a somewhat less than human application of science. The temptation is enhanced by the circumstance of the contemporary welfare state in the midst of an urbanized and industrialized mass civilization. The "sin" then takes the initial form of a desertion of their own premises. The "socially desirable objectives" are no longer "received" from society itself (as in the theory they should be); rather they are conceived in committee and imposed on society. The humanism ceases to evolve from below, and is directed from above; it remains scientific, and becomes inhuman. This is the psychological dynamism of the system: the state tends to lose its character of servant, and assume that of master. The psychological dynamism would be less destructive were it not in the service of the logic of the system. In the logic of the system is the destruction of all barriers to the expanding competence of the state. For one thing, the new rationalism is far too pale and bloodless a creed to stand against the flushed and full-blooded power of the modern state. For another, it hardly attempts to make a stand; in fact, its ethical relativism destroys the only ground on which a stand can be made—the absoluteness of the order of human rights that stands irremovably outside the sphere of state power, and the absoluteness of the order of justice that stands imperiously above the power of the state.

These then are three possible metaphysical decisions that one can make as a prelude to the construction of the new age. None of them, I think, carries a promise that the age will be one of true order.

There remains the fourth possible decision—the option of natural law in the old traditional sense. Here the decision is genuinely metaphysical; one does not opt for a rationalization of power, but for a metaphysic of right. I say "right" advisedly, not "rights." The natural law does not in the first instance furnish a philosophy of human rights in the sense of subjective immunities and powers to demand. This philosophy is consequent on the initial furnishing of a philosophy of right, justice, law, juridical order, and social order. The reason is that natural-law thinking does not set out, as Locke did, from the abstract, isolated individual, and ask what are his inalienable rights as an individual. Rather, it regards the community as "given" equally with the person. Man is regarded as a member of an order instituted by God, and subject to the laws that make the order an order— laws that derive from the nature of man, which is as essentially social as it is individual. In the natural-law climate of opinion (very different from that set by the "law of nature"), objective law has the primacy over subjective rights. Law is not simply the protection of rights but their source, because it is the foundation of duties.

The Premises of Natural Law

The whole metaphysic involved in the idea of natural law may seem alarmingly complicated; in a sense it is. Natural law supposes a realist epistemology, that asserts the real to be the measure of knowledge, and also asserts the possibility of intelligence reaching the real, i.e., the nature of things—in the case, the nature of man as a unitary and constant concept beneath all individual differences. Secondly, it supposes a metaphysic of nature, especially the idea that nature is a teleological concept, that the "form" of a thing is its "final cause," the goal of its becoming; in the case, that there is a natural inclination in man to become what in nature and destination he is—to achieve the fullness of his own being. Thirdly, it supposes a natural theology, asserting that there is a God, Who is eternal Reason, *Nous*, at the summit of the order of being, Who is the author of all nature, and Who wills that the order of nature be fulfilled in all its purposes, as these are inherent in the natures found in the order. Finally, it supposes a morality, especially the principle that for man, a rational being, the order of nature is not an order of necessity, to be fulfilled blindly, but an order of reason and therefore of freedom. The order of being that confronts his intelligence is an order of "oughtness" for his will; the moral order is a prolongation of the metaphysical order into the dimensions of human freedom.

This sounds frightfully abstract; but it is simply the elaboration by the reflective intelligence of a set of data that are at bottom empirical. Consider, for instance, the contents of the consciousness of a man who is protesting against injustice, let us say, in a case where his own interests are not touched and where the injustice is wrought by technically correct legislation. The contents of his consciously protesting mind would be something like these. He is asserting that there is an idea of justice; that this idea is transcendent to the actually expressed will of the legislator; that it is rooted somehow in the nature of things; that he really *knows* this idea; that it is not made by his judgment but is the measure of his judgment; that this idea is of the kind that ought to be realized in law and action; that its violation is injury, which his mind rejects as unreason; that this unreason is an offense not only against his own intelligence but against God, Who commands justice and forbids injustice.

Actually, this man, who may be no philosopher, is thinking in the categories of natural law and in the sequence of ideas that the natural-law mentality (which is the human mentality) follows. He has an objective idea of the "just" in contrast to the "legal." His theoretical reason perceives the idea as true; his practical reason accepts the truth as good, therefore as law; his will acknowledges the law as normative of action. Moreover, this man will doubtless seek to ally others in his protest, in the conviction that they will think the same as he does. In other words, this man, whether he be protesting against the Taft-Hartley Act or the Nazi genocidal laws, is making in his own way all the metaphysical affirmations that undergird the concept of natural law. In this matter philosophical reflection does not augment the data of common sense. It merely analyzes, penetrates, and organizes them in their full abstractness; this does not, however, remove them from vital contact with their primitive source in experience.

Law Immanent and Transcendent

From the metaphysical premises of natural law follow its two characteristics. It is a law immanent in the nature of man, but transcendent in its reference. It is rational, not rationalist. It is the work of reason, but not of an absolutely autonomous reason. It is immanent in nature in the sense that it consists in the dictates of human reason that are uttered as reason confronts the fundamental moral problems of human existence. These are the problems of what I, simply because I am a man and apart from all other considerations, ought to do or avoid in the basic situations in which I, again simply because I am a man, find myself. My situation is that of a creature before God; that of a "self" possessed of freedom to realize its "self"; that of a man living among other men, possessing what is mine as the other possesses what is his. In the face of these situations, certain imperatives "emerge" (if you like) from human nature. They are the product of its inclinations, as these are recognized by reason to be conformed to my rational nature. And they are formed by reason into dictates that present themselves as demanding obedience. Appearing, as they do, as dictates, these judgments of reason are law. Appearing, as they do, in consequence of an inclination that reason recognizes as authentically human, they are "natural" law.

However, these dictates are not simply emergent in the rationalist sense. Reason does not create its own laws, any more than man creates himself. Man has the laws of his nature given to him, as nature itself is given. By nature he is the image of God, eternal Reason; and so his reason reflects a higher reason; therein consists its rightness and its power to oblige. Above the natural law immanent in man stands the eternal law immanent in God transcendent; and the two laws are in intimate correspondence, as the image is to the exemplar. The eternal law is the Uncreated Reason of God; it appoints an order of nature—an order of beings, each of which carries in its very nature also its end and purposes; and it commands that this order of nature be preserved by the steady pursuit of their ends on the part of all the natures within the order. Every created nature has this eternal law, this transcendent order of reason, imprinted on it by the very fact that it is a nature, a purposeful dynamism striving for the fullness of its own being. In the irrational creation, the immanence of the eternal law is unconscious; the law itself is a law of necessity. But in the rational creature the immanent law is knowable and known; it is a moral law that authoritatively solicits the consent of freedom. St. Thomas, then, defines the natural law as the "rational creature's participation in the eternal law." The participation consists in man's possession of reason, the godlike faculty, whereby man knows himself—his own nature and end—and directs himself freely, in something of divine fashion but under God, to the plenitude of self-realization of his rational and social being.

Evidently, the immanent aspect of natural law relieves it of all taint of tyrannical heteronomy. It is not forcibly imposed as an alien pattern; it is discovered by reason itself as reason explores nature and its order. Moreover, it is well to note that in the discovery there is a necessary and large part reserved to experience, as St. Thomas insists: "What pertains to moral science is known mostly through experience" (*Eth.*, I, 3). The natural law, Rommen points out, "is not in the least some sort of rationalistically deduced, norm-abounding code of immediately evident or logically derived rules that fits every concrete historical situation." Like the whole of the *philosophia perennis*, the doctrine of natural law is orientated toward constant contact with reality and the data of experience. The point was illustrated above, in the chapter on public consensus.

The "man" that it knows is not the Lockean individual, leaping full grown into abstract existence in a "state of nature," but the real man who grows in history, amid changing conditions of social life, acquiring wisdom by the discipline of life itself, in many respects only gradually exploring the potentialities and demands and dignities of his own nature. He knows indeed that there is an order of reason fixed and unalterable in its outlines, that is not at the mercy of his caprice or passion. But he knows, too, that the order of reason is not constructed in geometric fashion, apart from consultation of experience, and the study of "the customs of human life and . . . all juridical and civil matters, such as are the laws and precepts of political life," as St. Thomas puts it. The natural-law philosopher does not indeed speak of a "natural law with a changing content," as do the Neo-Kantians, to whom natural law is a purely formal category, empty of material content until it be filled by positive law and its process of legalizing the realities of a given sociological situation. However, the natural-law philosopher does speak of a "natural law with changing and progressive applications," as the evolution of human life brings to light new necessities in human nature that are struggling for expression and form. Natural law is a force conservative of all acquired human values; it is also a dynamic of progress toward fuller human realization, personal and social. Because it is law, it touches human life with a firm grasp, to give it form; but because it is a living law, it lays upon life no "dead hand," to petrify it into formalism.

In virtue of its immanent aspect, therefore, the natural law constantly admits the possibility of "new orders," as human institutions dissolve to be replaced by others. But in virtue of its transcendent aspect, it always demands that the new orders conform to the order of reason, which is structured by absolute and unalterable first principles.

Natural Law and Politics

In the order of what is called *ius naturae* (natural law in the narrower sense, as regulative of social relationships), there are only two self-evident principles: the maxim, "*Suum cuique,*" and the wider principle, "Justice is to be done and injustice avoided." Reason particularizes them, with greater or less evidence, by determining what is "one's own" and what is "just" with the aid of the supreme norm of reference, the rational and social nature of man. The immediate particularizations are the precepts in the "Second Table" of the Decalogue. And the totality of such particularizations go to make up what is called the juridical order, the order of right and justice. This is the order (along with the orders of legal and distributive justice) whose guardianship and sanction is committed to the state. It is also the order that furnishes a moral basis for the positive legislation of the state, a critical norm of the justice of such legislation, and an ideal of justice for the legislator.

This carries us on to the function of natural law in political philosophy—its solution to the eternally crucial problem of the legitimacy of power, its value as a norm for, and its dictates in regard of, the structures and processes of society. The subject is much too immense. Let me say, first, that the initial claim of natural-law doctrine is to make political life part of the moral universe, instead of leaving it to wander as it too long has, like St. Augustine's sinner, *in regione dissimilitudinis*. There are doubtless a considerable number of people not of the Catholic Church who would incline to agree with Pius XII's round statement in *Summi Pontificatus* that the "prime and most profound root of all the evils with which the City is today beset" is a "heedlessness and forgetfulness of natural law." Secretary of State Marshall said practically the same thing, but in contemporary idiom, when he remarked that all our political troubles go back to a neglect or violation of human rights.

For the rest, I shall simply state the major contents of the political ideal as it emerges from natural law.

One set of principles is that which the Carlyles and others have pointed out as having ruled (amid whatever violations) the political life of the Middle Ages. First, there is the supremacy of law, and of law as reason, not will. With this is connected the idea of the ethical nature and function of the state (*regnum* or *imperium* in medieval terminology), and the educative character of its laws as directive of man to "the virtuous life" and not simply protective of particular interests. Secondly, there is the principle that the source of political authority is in the community. Political society as such is natural and necessary to man, but its form is the product of reason and free choice; no ruler has a right to govern that is inalienable and independent of human agency. Thirdly, there is the principle that the authority of the ruler is limited; its scope is only political, and the whole of human life is not absorbed in the polis. The power of the ruler is limited, as it were, from above by the law of justice, from below by systems of private right, and from the sides by the public right of the Church. Fourthly, there is the principle of the contractual nature of the relations between ruler and ruled. The latter are not simply material organized for rule by the *rex legibus solutus*, but human agents who agree to be ruled constitutionally, in accordance with law.

A second set of principles is of later development, as ideas and in their institutional form, although their roots are in the natural-law theories of the Middle Ages.

The first is the principle of subsidiarity. It asserts the organic character of the state—the right to existence and autonomous functioning of various sub-political groups, which unite in the organic unity of the state without losing their own identity or suffering infringement of their own ends or having their functions assumed by the state. These groups include the family, the local community, the professions, the occupational groups, the minority cultural or linguistic groups within the nation, etc. Here on the basis of natural law is the denial of the false French revolutionary antithesis, individual versus state, as the principle of political organization. Here too is the denial of all forms of state totalitarian monism, as well as of Liberalistic atomism that would remove all forms of social or economic life from any measure of political control. This principle is likewise the assertion of the fact that the freedom of the individual is secured at the interior of institutions intermediate between himself and the state (e.g., trade unions) or beyond the state (the church).

The second principle is that of popular sharing in the formation of the collective will, as expressed in legislation or in executive policy. It is a natural-law principle inasmuch as it asserts the dignity of the human person as an active co-participant in the political decisions that concern him, and in the pursuit of the end of the state, the common good. It is also related to all the natural-law principles cited in the first group above. For instance, the idea that law is reason is fortified in legislative assemblies that discuss the reasons for laws. So, too, the other principles are fortified, as is evident.

Conclusion

Here then in briefest compass are some of the resources resident in natural law, that would make it the dynamic of a new "age of order." It does not indeed furnish a detailed blueprint of the order; that is not its function. Nor does it pretend to settle the enormously complicated technical problems, especially in the economic order, that confront us today. It can claim to be only a "skeleton law," to which flesh and blood must be added by that heart of the political process, the rational activity of man, aided by experience and by high professional competence. But today it is perhaps the skeleton that we mostly need, since it is precisely the structural foundations of the political, social, and economic orders that are being most anxiously questioned. In this situation the doctrine of natural law can claim to offer all that is good and valid in competing systems, at the same time that it avoids all that is weak and false in them.

Its concern for the rights of the individual human person is no less than that shown in the school of individualist Liberalism with its "law of nature" theory of rights, at the same time that its sense of the organic character of the community, as the flowering in ascending forms of sociality of the social nature of man, is far greater and more realistic. It can match Marxism in its concern for man as worker and for the just organization of economic society, at the same time that it forbids the absorption of man in matter and its determinisms. Finally, it does not bow to the new rationalism in regard of a sense of history and progress, the emerging potentialities of human nature, the value of experience in settling the forms of social life, the relative primacy in certain respects of the empirical fact over the preconceived theory; at the same time it does not succumb to the doctrinaire relativism, or to the narrowing of the object of human intelligence, that cripple at their root the high aspirations of evolutionary scientific humanism. In a word, the doctrine of natural law offers a more profound metaphysic, a more integral humanism, a fuller rationality, a more complete philosophy of man in his nature and history.

I might say, too, that it furnishes the basis for a firmer faith and a more tranquil, because more reasoned, hope in the future. If there is a law immanent in man—a dynamic, constructive force for rationality in human affairs, that works itself out, because it is a natural law, in spite of contravention by passion and evil and all the corruptions of power—one may with sober reason believe in, and hope for, a future of rational progress. And this belief and hope is strengthened when one considers that this dynamic order of reason in man, that clamors for expression with all the imperiousness of law, has its origin and sanction in an eternal order of reason whose fulfillment is the object of God's majestic will.

Note

1. *Western Political Thought.* London: Oxford University Press, 1947.